X8/27
£11-95

John A. Turner.

1989.

From the Halifax Branch of
the Parkinson's Disease
Society

Secretary : Mrs Hilda Hitchen

Chairman : ~~~~~ Myself
1981 – 1989.

THE
FAITH WE
CONFESS

An Ecumenical Dogmatics

THE FAITH WE CONFESS

by JAN MILIČ LOCHMAN

Translated by DAVID LEWIS

T. & T. CLARK LTD,
59 GEORGE STREET, EDINBURGH.

British Library Cataloguing in Publication Data
Lochman, Jan Milič
The faith we confess: an ecumenical dogmatics.
1. Theology, Doctrinal
I. Title II. Das Glaubensbekenntnis. *English*
230   BT77.3
ISBN 0-567-09367-0

Printed in the U.K. by Billing & Sons Ltd, Worcester, England.

To President James I. McCord and the community
of the Princeton Theological Seminary in
fraternal gratitude

Contents

Contents

Contents

Contents

Preface

The ancient custom of "walking the bounds" is still observed in some Swiss communities. The people of the village gather together on "Boundary Day" each spring and walk around the village boundaries, checking to be sure that the boundary markers have not been moved or covered over. This ceremony is followed by a community meal celebrating the people's joy and gratitude for what has been handed down to them.

That ancient Swiss custom may serve to illustrate the purpose of this present book—to sketch an outline of Christian dogmatics in which we survey the "landmarks" of the Christian faith, check them against the "land register," and claim anew our Christian heritage. We do this with a deep sense of gratitude for that heritage and a resolve to defend it in the face of contemporary criticisms, including those from other communities quite close to our own.

The task here described is one of the main tasks of theology, of dogmatic theology in particular. It is of course not the only task. "Doing theology" embraces a wide variety of tasks. Theology cannot be content with outlines alone. Its tasks range from detailed work on difficult individual themes to the projection of large-scale doctrinal systems. In between, however, is the recurring task of providing a condensed account of the basics of the Christian faith. In periods of rapid and tumultuous change, and therefore of widespread perplexity, this task takes on added urgency, especially in situations where the church is exposed to serious external pressure or feels insecure within itself. Theological efforts are then needed to present the Christian faith in a concentrated form.

The importance of such efforts was brought home to me not only by personal experiences in theology and church work in both East and West but also by the heritage of the Czech Reformation, the tradition to which I owe most from my own childhood and educational background. In the ancestral Czech lands the notion of a theological

ix

concentrate was raised to the status of a reformation principle. Matthias (Matěj) of Janow (1393), one of the leaders of the Czech reform movement, strongly emphasized this point: "I am persuaded that, if unity and peace are to be restored to Christendom, the weeds must be uprooted (Matt. 15:13), the gospel stated in a concise and concentrated form on earth (Rom. 9:28), and the church of Jesus Christ led back to its basic source. For this it will suffice to retain just a few apostolic definitions."

This reform program must not be mistaken for doctrinal minimalism or religious primitivism. It was proposed by one of the best informed theologians of the time, one who took God's truth very seriously indeed. But this truth is certainly not to be equated with the sum total of church traditions. A good deal of what has grown up in the course of church history can only be described as "weeds." There is, as the Second Vatican Council in our own time has argued, a "hierarchy of truths." The task of theology, therefore, is not dutifully to stagger forward bearing the whole burden of all the collected works of Christendom, but within this tradition to weigh and adjust things so as to lay bare the prophetic and apostolic heart of the gospel—the sure center, the one thing needful.

The effort to produce a theological concentrate of this sort seems to me a worthwhile endeavor, particularly since I am persuaded of the importance of the emphases that accompanied it in the thinking of the Czech Reformers. Let me mention three of these emphases: First, these Czech theologians did their thinking within the open-ended framework of an (eschatologically) foreshortened time. If theology is to be realistic, it cannot be established as something timeless but can only be developed as a "pilgrim theology." Second, these theologians did their thinking not just in the groves of academia but in the context of the church. The fare they set before the people of God is not a menu of special dishes prepared in one or another of theology's gourmet restaurants. It is the bread of life (*Bethlehem*, the "house of bread," was one of their favorite preaching places). And third, their conscious aim—as can be clearly seen from Matthias's reference to the restoration of "unity and peace"—was to lay bare the common core of the Christian faith, to seek foundations for ecumenical accord amongst the members of the one Christian family. These three emphases all speak in favor of a program for arriving at a theological concentrate—and even today are indispensable for a realistic and relevant theology.

The first question confronting anyone who would offer such a sketch of basic Christian doctrine is the choice of a ground plan for the projected outline. What pattern can reduce to a minimum the very real danger of sectarian arbitrariness in the selection of themes? What reliable landmarks are available for our "walking the bounds"?

An examination of the available options will bring us sooner or later to that offered by the ancient church in its classic Christian creeds. This is the option I have gratefully chosen for this book. Not that I think it is the most obvious or necessarily even the most fruitful option open to us today. Indeed, the choice is itself fraught with problems that must be frankly faced and met, some of which we shall examine in the opening chapter.

But this choice of the creeds has one main advantage that in my view outweighs all its disadvantages, real or imagined. These creeds are foundation stones for the theological development of Christendom as a whole. They are "classic," not just historically but also doctrinally. In an exemplary way they establish the pattern of doctrinal statements that is still valid for us today. By this I mean that they faithfully combine two aims. They seek, with intellectual rigor and while keeping the whole faith clearly in view, to establish the binding "rule of faith," to formulate accurately and succinctly the key articles of the Christian faith. At the same time, they do so in a spirit of doxology, of liturgy and adoration. They are not satisfied merely with sharpened formulations and the interplay of concepts; their aim is rather the confession of a faith that is accepted by individuals and maintained by the community. I am convinced that dogmatic theology is possible today only if it approaches its task with this twofold concern. In this respect the ancient creeds continue to demonstrate their capacity to guide and instruct us today.

I have spoken of the classic Christian "creeds"—plural—for there are more than one. Which of them are we to choose as our guide? Two in particular claim our attention—the Nicene Creed and the Apostles' Creed. There are strong arguments for taking the former as our basic text. The sixteen-hundredth anniversary of the Nicene Creed was celebrated ecumenically in 1981; moreover, substantive considerations also argue in its favor, for it contains a number of important emphases. I have nevertheless chosen the Apostles' Creed as our guide, not only because of its greater historical influence throughout the history of Western Christendom but also because it is also better known here in the West by virtue of its widespread liturgical use. I personally regard this liturgical familiarity as an important point because my exposition is intended not only for professional theologians but also for theologically concerned lay people, both within and outside the congregations—in keeping with the effort toward a theological concentrate to which I have already referred. This does not mean that we shall ignore the Nicene Creed in our exposition. As is clear from the text of the two creeds, printed on the following pages, there is broad agreement between them. The distinctive emphases of the Nicene Creed will be noted in the course of the exposition.

Thus the purpose of this book is to set forth in succinct form an outline of Christian dogmatics based on the Apostles' Creed, an ecumenical sketch of the faith we confess as the people of God. The substance of the book was originally presented in the form of lectures to students in my dogmatics course at the University of Basel (and in abbreviated form also at the University of Berne). Selected portions of the material were also discussed by an interested group of pastors (and some nontheologians) during a week's conference in the Engadine in Switzerland. From the combined efforts of all these partners (and of my assistant, Erich Laubscher) in our common discussions and reflections on these themes I have received many valuable suggestions, some of which have led me to say things a bit differently; above all, though, I have been encouraged to see that the Creed still retains its strength and fruitfulness, and that even today it is well worth our while to examine its landmarks in the course of a theological "walking the bounds."

Basel, 13 October 1980

Text of the Creeds *

The Apostles' Creed

Credo
in deum patrem omnipotentem
creatorem coeli et terrae;
Et in Jesum Christum,
filium eius unicum,
dominum nostrum,
qui conceptus est
de Spiritu sancto,
natus ex Maria virgine,
passus sub Pontio Pilato,
crucifixus, mortuus et sepultus,
descendit ad inferna,
tertia die resurrexit a mortuis,

ascendit ad coelos,
sedet ad dexteram dei patris
omnipotentis,
inde venturus est iudicare
vivos et mortuos;
Credo in Spiritum sanctum,
sanctam ecclesiam catholicam,
sanctorum communionem,
remissionem peccatorum,
carnis resurrectionem,
et vitam aeternam.
Amen.

I believe
in God the Father almighty
Creator of heaven and earth;
And in Jesus Christ
His only Son
our Lord,
who was conceived
by the Holy Spirit,
born from the virgin Mary,
suffered under Pontius Pilate,
was crucified, dead and buried,
descended to hell,
on the third day rose again from the
  dead,
ascended to heaven,
sits at the right hand of
God the Father almighty,
thence he will come to judge
the living and the dead;
I believe in the Holy Spirit,
the holy catholic Church,
the communion of saints,
the remission of sins,
the resurrection of the flesh,
and eternal life.
Amen.

The Nicene Creed

We believe in one God the Father almighty,
Maker of heaven and earth, of all things visible and invisible;

xiii

And in one Lord Jesus Christ,
the only-begotten Son of God,
begotten of his Father before all ages,
light from light, true God from true God, begotten not made,
of one substance with the Father,
through whom all things came into existence,
who for us human beings and for our salvation
came down from heaven and was incarnate
from the Holy Spirit and the virgin Mary,
and became a human being,
and was crucified for us under Pontius Pilate,
and suffered and was buried,
and rose again on the third day according to the Scriptures,
and ascended to heaven and sits on the right hand of the Father
and will come again with glory to judge living and dead,
of whose kingdom there will be no end;
And in the Holy Spirit, the Lord and Life-Giver,
who proceeds from the Father,   *Filioque* ?
who with the Father and the Son is together worshipped and
together glorified,
who spoke through the prophets;
and in one holy catholic and apostolic Church.
We confess one baptism for the remission of sins;
we look forward to the resurrection of the dead
and the life of the world to come.
Amen.

*The Latin and English texts of the Apostles' Creed and the English text of the Nicene Creed are here taken from J. N. D. Kelly's *Early Christian Creeds*. New York and London: Longmans, Green, & Co., 1950. Pp. 369 and 297.

1

Introduction

A Misguided Venture?

The proposal to use the Creed as the basis for an outline of Christian doctrine raises many problems. If it is to be part of a living program of contemporary systematic theology, an outline of Christian doctrine must imply that we try to grapple with themes that are particularly relevant to our theological existence today and to deal with them in the light of two polar concerns—the biblical tradition on the one hand and contemporary requirements on the other hand. If we further qualify that outline by saying that it is based on the Creed (which in this exposition means the Apostles' Creed of the ancient church) we surely handicap the venture from the start. Does the Creed actually furnish such relevant themes? Does it not act instead as a barrier between the biblical experience and the experiences of our own time? Does it not tend to inhibit and even end all living commerce between systematic theology and these two poles of Bible and contemporary experience? Misgivings are legitimate here for at least three reasons.

1. The Apostles' Creed is not in itself the apostolic preaching; it is a doctrinal formulation of the ancient church. While this does not detract from the importance of the Creed, it nevertheless qualifies it, and this indeed in both the directions mentioned—in respect of the biblical message and in respect of the questions that confront us today. In the present context, I am thinking particularly of this second aspect. As a historical doctrinal text the Apostles' Creed bears unmistakable traces of its origin. It was the fruit of a long and in part confused process. It emerged from the doctrinal conflicts of the early church, from the questions and answers of that time. This is how a Christian confession of faith always has emerged and always will emerge, legitimately and necessarily so. But every Christian genera-

1

tion has to confess the faith within its own context, following but not slavishly imitating the example of the early church. We cannot accept the decisions and assumptions of our predecessors in the faith as absolutely binding on us, for their struggles and the challenges which confronted them are not identical with our own.

2. The text of the Apostles' Creed also poses problems. In the first place, there is its method, its doctrinal approach. It has an impressive unity and coherence: "I believe in God the Father . . . and in Jesus Christ, his only Son. . . . I believe in the Holy Spirit." The faith confessed here in an uncompromising and concentrated way is faith in the Triune God. The theme of "God," the majestic theme of Christian faith, dominates the Creed. The theme of "humanity"—one which is also reflected, and in a supremely dramatic way, in the biblical history, the history of the covenant between God and his people, his creation—is here overshadowed by the grandeur of the confession of faith in God. The theme of humanity has not simply disappeared, of course. The entire Creed has to do with the human beings who confess this faith in God. And even the Creed in all of its three main articles deals with the realities of our human world. How could it possibly be otherwise in the light of God the Father, Jesus Christ, and the Holy Spirit? But the focal point is clear: what is offered us here is a "theology from above." The pathway or method followed in this act of faith and understanding leads directly and continuously—undialectically as it were—"from heaven above" (to use the phraseology of Luther's famous Christmas hymn). And here the question inevitably arises: Is this the only way of doing theology, or, in more concrete terms, is it the most obvious way for us to do theology? Would not a theology from below or a dialectical theology be more sensible? Is not this appeal to the Apostles' Creed in actuality a detour that is difficult to justify in the present theological and intellectual climate?

3. Critical misgivings increase when we consider not just the method but also the contents of the Creed. Do its statements really cover the ground sufficiently for an outline of Christian doctrine? When we compare it with the heritage of biblical doctrine, does not this credal confession of faith reveal serious gaps? This is a question that no expositor can evade, as Leonhard Ragaz for example has sharply and polemically suggested in his popular exposition of the Apostles' Creed:

2

Introduction

The Creed speaks of God, of Christ, of the Bible, of the creation, of redemption, of the beyond, of individual salvation, but not of the living God and his kingdom of justice for the earth. . . . The true confession of faith is simply the always present and direct testimony to the kingdom of God. The *church* confesses the Creed; the Christian *community* confesses the *kingdom*.[1]

And Wolfgang Trillhaas, repeating criticism already aired in various forms at the time of the Reformation, lists a whole catalogue of themes that are missing from the Creed:

The Word of God, Holy Scripture, as well as the sacraments of baptism and the Lord's Supper. Central concepts of Christian doctrine are missing: justification, reconciliation, and redemption; even terms such as repentance and the kingdom of God, which are central in the preaching of Jesus. . . . Moreover, everything relating to the Christian life—the divine commandments and prayer—is missing.[2]

We must be careful not to exaggerate, of course. We really cannot expect a brief creed to mention everything. Yet it is impossible to deny that certain themes of doctrinal reflection are absent from the Apostles' Creed. These substantial doctrinal lacunas give a radical edge, therefore, to the skeptic's question as to whether our proposed reference to the Creed in this exposition of the Christian faith does not represent a priori a liability against the fruitfulness of any attempt in this direction? Is not the whole effort misguided from the very outset?

Dialogue with the Tradition

These are all honest objections, valid questions that are not easy to answer. Our venture is indeed fraught with difficulties and dangers, and it is good to be aware of them from the outset. If I nevertheless stick to my plan, I have two main reasons for doing so.

In the first place, the Apostles' Creed is not just one ancient church document among many; it is the classic rule and guide for faith that has had an exceptional and even unique influence far beyond its immediate historical origin and purpose. Jan Amos Comenius (1592–1670) speaks for many when, looking back on a long life of theological endeavor, he testifies: "When I am asked what I believe, I simply reply with the Apostles' Creed. For no other creed is as brief,

3

as simple, and as pithy as this. No other summarizes the essentials so effectively."[3]

This witness to the special place of the Apostles' Creed is true not only as regards the history of ideas but also with respect to the liturgical context. The Creed has a prominent role in the worship (and instruction) of most of the Christian churches. True, it cannot be said to enjoy an ecumenical monopoly. The Eastern Orthodox churches give pride of place to the Nicene Creed—which is of course related to the Apostles' Creed—and we shall have occasion to refer to that creed more than once in this exposition. In the worship and instruction of the Western churches, however, particularly in the Roman Catholic Church, the Apostles' Creed has a unique place. Eloquent testimony to the importance attached to it is the almost self-evident way in which the word "creed" itself (*credo* means "I believe") has come to be inseparably identified with this specific document. In other words, in this Apostles' Creed we have a very lively bit of history whose vitality is far from exhausted even today. In it throbs something not only of the classic but also of the contemporary ecumenical faith of Christendom, even if we are under no illusions about the degree to which its doctrinal contents are rightly understood and livingly appropriated by ordinary parishioners. To build our outline of Christian doctrine on this text, therefore, is certainly not to build on a merely historical, archaic, or exotic foundation.

The second main reason for persisting with the venture is that a dogmatics based on the Creed does not necessarily involve an approach subservient to the Creed. To put it in positive terms: Historical theology (like systematic theology) can only mean a dialogue with the tradition, and that means a personal existential engagement involving both address and response.

To take our doctrinal hearings from basic statements of our predecessors in the faith does not mean letting them dictate to us their themes, their positions, their answers. From the moment the dialogue begins we are ourselves present with our own themes, positions, and tentative answers, listening attentively but also joining in the discussion. We inquire into the views of our predecessors but are not engulfed by them. We search testimonies of the tradition because a theology that slips its moorings in the history of doctrine soon becomes superficial; sooner or later it loses its staying power and becomes sterile even in its witness to its own time. But we do not succumb to the views of our predecessors because a credally conformist theology, while carefully "straining out gnats" will still "swallow a camel"; it will fail to recognize what is really worth imitating in the witness of our predecessors, what is really essential in their act of confession. Because we want to avoid such blindness, we take these three critical questions very seriously from the outset. Our grounding of this outline of Christian doctrine on the Creed, therefore, is understood and tested in open and critical discussion. Only in this relative sense does our undertaking, despite all misgivings, make sense.

2

The Apostles' Creed: Its Origin and Earliest Context

The Poetry and Truth of a Legend

What exactly is the "Apostles' Creed"? We use this title to designate that ancient church document which, in a letter addressed to Pope Siricius by the Synod of Milan (390), was first referred to as the "Symbol of the Apostles." The best indication of what the title meant is found in an account given a few years later by Tyrannius Rufinus. He tries to explain the apostolic origin of the Creed by appealing to what was obviously an old and familiar tradition: When the twelve apostles resolved, shortly after Pentecost, to go as missionaries into all the world, they first agreed on a common rule of faith to serve as the doctrinal standard for their preaching. Under the guidance of the Holy Spirit this rule of faith was produced in a quite miraculous fashion. Each of the twelve apostles contributed his main concern in a succinct formula. These twelve formulations were then welded into a unity and the result was the Apostles' Creed.

According to Rufinus, what happened was this:

Peter said: "I believe in God the Father Almighty, Maker of heaven and earth" . . . Andrew said: "And in Jesus Christ His Son . . . our only Lord" . . . James said: "Who was conceived by the Holy Spirit . . . born from the virgin Mary" . . . John said: "Suffered under Pontius Pilate, was crucified, dead and buried" . . . Thomas said: "Descended to hell . . . on the third day rose again from the dead" . . . James said: "Ascended to heaven, sits on the right hand of God the Father Almighty" . . . Philip said: "Thence he will come to judge the living and the dead" . . . Bartholomew said: "I believe in the Holy Spirit" . . . Matthew said: "the holy catholic church . . . the communion of

7

saints" . . . Simon said: "the remission of sins" . . . Thaddaeus said: "the resurrection of the flesh" . . . Matthias said: "eternal life."[1]

This narrative has many interesting features. It is a heroic attempt to demonstrate the apostolicity of the Creed by showing it to be an authentic document actually composed by the apostles. With this in view, it was necessary to divide the text—in some cases with considerable violence—into twelve parts in order to include the whole group of the apostles.

The distribution of the twelve parts among the individual speakers is not completely arbitrary. Indeed it is based on ideas suggested by the New Testament itself or the primitive church tradition. This is particularly obvious in the case of the most sharply delineated "confessors." As might have been expected, for example, Peter is called upon to speak first, as in the Gospels. John bears witness to the message of the cross. The resurrection, clearly with the Johannine Easter narrative in mind, is assigned to Thomas.

What we have here in this Rufinus account is obviously a legend—a legend, however, that reflects the enormous prestige that this Creed enjoyed, not only in the ancient church but also subsequently throughout the whole medieval period, the lone exception of course being the Eastern church that did not share the Western view on this point. At the Council of Florence (1438–45), when attempts were made to reunite the churches and Western delegates proposed the Apostles' Creed as an ecumenically viable basis for unity, the Metropolitan of Ephesus roundly rejected the proposal on behalf of the Eastern churches: "We do not have, nor have we ever seen, this creed of the apostles. Had it ever existed, the Book of Acts would have mentioned it in its account of the first apostolic synod in Jerusalem to which you appeal."[2] Critical views were soon being expressed in the West too, most trenchantly by the humanist Laurentius Valla (who vigorously attacked other legends as well) and then by many other critics, despite the countermeasures taken by the official church.

The question of the apostolicity of the Creed, in the formal sense of direct apostolic authorship, has finally been laid to rest today. More pertinent and theologically productive is the question of the indirect but substantial apostolicity of its affirmations, that is, its substantive agreement with the apostolic preaching. Here a much more positive answer is possible and indeed inescapable today. It cannot be a categorical answer, of course, for there is great variation in the degrees to which the individual credal clauses correspond to the New Testament message. On the whole, however, there is a basic continuity between the Creed and the "faith of the apostles." This, at any rate, was the almost axiomatic opinion not only of the ancient and the medieval church but also of the Reformation. The Apostles' Creed is praised by Luther, for example, as "an excellent brief and accurate summary of the articles of faith," and Calvin describes it as "the summary and, as it were, epitome of the faith."[3]

More critical views have also been expressed, surprisingly enough by post-Reformation Protestant orthodoxy, which took exception to the omission from the Apostles' Creed of "many articles of faith that are of great importance for the Reformation position, such as original sin, the merits of Christ, justification."[4] But it was mainly in liberal Protestantism, in the light of historical criticism, that the apostolic status of the Creed was challenged and declared to be untenable. In these circles it was usually assumed that there had been a clean break between the New Testament period and that of the ancient church. This particular theory of the beginnings of Christianity, positing a "sharp antithesis . . . between the Spirit-guided, spontaneous New Testament phase and the second-century epoch of incipient formalism and institutionalism,"[5] has now been completely revised and corrected by recent scholarship. "Nothing could be more artificial or more improbable" than this theory, says Kelly.[6] There never was any such clear-cut divide.

This is true of all aspects of the life of the ancient church, of course, but it applies especially to the Creeds. Certainly the Apostles' Creed is not a New Testament text, and many of its clauses cannot be derived directly from the New Testament in so many words. But neither is there any sharp contrast between some era of the "Spirit" on the one hand and that of "doctrine" on the other. Recent scholarship has demonstrated not only a substantive continuity in the contents of the credal affirmations but also—and this perhaps even more important for our inquiry—a formal continuity as well. Already in the New Testament we find an astonishing number and variety of rudimentary confessions of faith, credal formulas. In the central christological sections of his study of the earliest Christian confessions, Oscar Cullman, for example, demonstrates a clear connection between the New Testament and the Creed.[7] And this is the conclusion reached by Kelly in

9

his *Early Christian Creeds*, on the basis of thorough and extensive research:

> The story that the Twelve, meeting in solemn conclave, composed an "Apostles' Creed" is no doubt a pious fiction. But the second-century conviction that the "rule of faith" believed and taught in the Catholic Church had been inherited from the Apostles contains more than a germ of truth.[8]

The road which led eventually to the settled text of the Apostles' Creed and to its recognition in the Western church as a whole was certainly a long and sometimes complicated one. It will be helpful to bear in mind some of the most important steps along this way.

Faith, Confession, Baptism

The original context of the Apostles' Creed is probably to be sought in primitive Christian baptismal practice. The warrant for this baptismal practice was derived from the risen Christ's command to baptize, recorded in Matthew's Gospel: "Go therefore and make disciples of all nations, baptizing them in the name of the Father and of the Son and of the Holy Spirit" (Matt. 28:19). From the beginning this command set the course for a trinitarian confession of faith in the context of baptism. It is in this context that, at the end of the second century and the beginning of the third, accounts of baptism appear in which the core of the later Creed is included. One such account, for example, describes the baptismal context as follows:

> Thus, when the baptizand has stepped down into the water, the baptizer would place his hand upon him and say, "Dost thou believe in God the Father almighty?" and the baptizand should reply, "I believe." At once let him be baptized for the first time. Then the priest should say, "Dost thou believe also in Christ Jesus the Son of God, Who came from the Father, Who is with the Father from the beginning, Who was born from the Virgin Mary through the Holy Spirit, Who was crucified under Pontius Pilate, died, rose again on the third day reanimated from the dead, ascended into heaven, sits at the right hand of the Father, and will come to judge the living and the dead?" And when he answers "I believe," let him baptize him a second time. Then he should say, "Dost thou believe also in the Holy Spirit, in the holy Church?" And the man who is being baptized should say, "I believe." Then let him baptize him a third time.[9]

10

In this account the core of the Apostles' Creed is already present in very clear outline if not in every detail—though not, be it noted, in the form of a continuous declaratory text. The person being baptized does not recite the Creed; it is put to him or her in question form, and the threefold "I believe" comes as the baptized person's response to these questions and as the condition required for the thrice-repeated act of baptism. This would change later on. There is, however, another significant point to be noted which is most important for the understanding of the Apostles' Creed right down to our own time, namely the intimate connection between confession, faith, and baptism. The Apostles' Creed is the verbal correlative to the binding decision of faith, solemnly entered into for life, as set forth in the act of baptism.

During the course of the third century such baptismal questions developed into the Creed in its continuous declaratory form. Since the various Christian communities formulated their baptismal affirmations somewhat differently, this Creed soon existed in a whole series of variant forms, all with the same basic content. The credal form used in the Roman Church—the *Symbolum Romanum* (usually referred to by the specialists as R)—soon became the most influential of all of them. The relatively stable form of this text was as follows:

Credo in deum patrem omnipotentem
et in Christum Jesum filium eius unicum, dominum nostrum,
qui natus est de Spiritu sancto et Maria virgine,
qui sub Pontio Pilato crucifixus est et sepultus,
tertia die resurrexit a mortuis,
ascendit in caelos,
sedet ad dexteram patris,
unde venturus est iudicare vivos et mortuos;
et in Spiritum sanctum,
sanctam ecclesiam,
remissionem peccatorum,
carnis resurrectionem.
I believe in God the Father almighty
and in Christ Jesus His only Son, our Lord,
Who was born from the Holy Spirit and the virgin Mary,
Who under Pontius Pilate was crucified and buried,
on the third day rose again from the dead,
ascended to heaven,
sits at the right hand of the Father,

11

whence He will come to judge the living and the dead;
and in the Holy Spirit,
the holy Church,
the remission of sins,
the resurrection of the flesh.[10]

The history of the development of the apostolic Creed did not end with the emergence of this Roman Creed. In the fourth century a whole series of slight variations and additions is to be noted. The most important of these are as follows. In the First Article the words "Creator of heaven and earth" were soon added. In the Second Article the rather clumsy "born from the Holy Spirit and the Virgin Mary" was replaced by the more precise "conceived by the Holy Spirit, born from the Virgin Mary." In the account of Christ's ministry, the new clause "descended to hell" was inserted. In the Third Article, "catholic" was added to the description of the church and a new clause "the communion of saints" placed after it. The Creed was also given a new ending by the addition of the clause "and eternal life."

In this way a version of the Creed emerged which could be called the Textus Receptus (T). Surprisingly enough, this form was developed not in Rome but in the Spain and Gaul of the West Goths in the late sixth century. It was still far from being the "canonized" text of the Western church. This "canonization" finally took place in the West only as the result of political developments connected with the imperial church policy of Charlemagne, The emperor worked patiently to achieve maximum uniformity not only at the political level but also in church affairs. Obligatory liturgical uniformity seemed to him of supreme importance in this connection. An obligatory standard form of the Creed was a step in this direction. The choice fell on the Textus Receptus, which already enjoyed considerable authority in the West though not in Rome itself. Charlemagne and Otto I successfully urged the adoption of the Textus Receptus in Rome and so the Apostles' Creed became an integral part of the Roman liturgy, thereby attaining its status as the main Creed in Western Christendom.

As is so often the case in the history of the church and its doctrine, we are confronted here with an ironical—or providential?—turn of events: "In persuading Rome to accept the new baptismal confession, the church beyond the Alps was merely handing back to her, enriched and improved, that same venerable rule of faith which she herself had compiled in the second century as an epitome of the everlasting gospel."[11]

Faced with such a turn of events, the question arises: Is this a case of human confusion or of divine providence? My own answer would be that both are involved. Undoubtedly, the "confusion" caused by human beings was a factor, together with the vigorous pursuit of political interests and power by secular rulers from Constantine down to the Carolingians. But also, in the midst of this human confusion a development took place that in some of its features undeniably had a certain providential character. In spite of everything, the confused church discovered a way and acquired a Creed in which essential elements of the apostolic foundation can be recognized. It was not for nothing that this Creed was called the *Apostles'* Creed. Not—we repeat—in the sense that it is a written document handed down to us directly from the apostles, but because of its undoubted spiritual kinship with the New Testament origins.

3

The Credal Frame—
"I Believe . . . Amen"

Nature and Limit of the Creed

We turn first of all to the two words that open and close the Creed and constitute, as it were, its "frame": the words *Credo* and *Amen*. The frame is not the picture, of course, but in the case of the Creed the frame goes with the picture and is inseparable from it. To remove the picture from the frame, to detach the content of the Creed from the opening key signature "I believe" and the closing doxological signature of adherence "Amen—so be it!" would be to negate the possibility of understanding the Creed at all.

These two framing words announce both the nature and the limit of the document. They define it unmistakably as a confession of faith. Two points are emphasized in this definition: from beginning to end this Creed is an act of faith; and its ultimate purpose (as indicated by the little word "Amen") is doxology, thanksgiving, praise, the response of faith—that is, confession.

In the first place, then, the Creed must be characterized as a confession of faith; this is its very nature. What is offered here is no theory or panorama of the divine mysteries, no impartial information, but a witness that can really be understood only as one participates in, shares in, is drawn into and affected by it. As has already been pointed out, the original setting of the Creed is baptism. In other words, what we have here is a formula that derives from a situation calling for decision, a decisive turnabout in a person's whole existence—away from the powers of the past and toward the coming kingdom of Christ. We recall, too, that the primary context of the Creed right down to our own day is typically the liturgy of the Christian church, and that in the Creed we are therefore confronted not with individual or even collective speculations but with the doxology

15

of the Christian community. The statements here affirmed do not describe metaphysical realities; they take a past salvation and make it contemporary in its eschatological relevance to our own lives. If we are to understand the Apostles' Creed at all, then, this is how we must approach it from the very outset, as a confession of faith. For that is its nature.

This very nature of the Creed, however, is also its limit. The opening and closing words of the Creed are what mark this limit. They do not allow the formulated text to stand on its own; they situate it, rather, within the orbit of faith and doxological existence. In other words, the credal text makes no sense in isolation as a self-contained or even sacrosanct document. The Creed is a rule of faith, not a "paper pope." It has no magical power. It is not an automatic guarantee of salvation. Its words are not holy words, but the "words of saints" in the biblical sense, namely, confessions of faith that attain their true meaning and goal only in actual confession. As Christians, we are not bound to a literalistic acceptance of the Apostles' Creed; neither are we confronted with the disabling demand to "take it or leave it!" The Apostles' Creed is accepted, and can only be accepted, as part of the gospel. It is good news that we are privileged to share, not something externally imposed on us. It is an invitation, an encouragement to the adventure common to all Christians, namely, to join in this *Credo* and this *Amen.* In the absence of this voluntary "I believe" and without this personal and voluntary affirmation "Amen," the Creed fails to attain its path-breaking, limit-transcending, and self-transcending goal; it remains no more than a document, very ancient and very respectable to be sure, but nonetheless a mere document that in the end is quite lifeless.

This then is the nature and the limit of the document to which the two modest "framing" words point. The Creed is a confession of faith. We shall be wise to keep that constantly in mind.

Faith in Dispute

What does the opening word of the Apostles' Creed mean, and how are we to define it more precisely? Faith is undoubtedly a constitutive element of the Christian life, even its quintessence. We speak of the Christian faith and often mean by this the Christian religion as a whole. But we must certainly not deceive ourselves here: in the present cultural and historical climate, it is precisely this central concept of *faith* that causes us the greatest difficulty. It is a striking fact that, of the three classic concepts of the Christian life, namely, faith, hope, and love—the three "cardinal virtues," as they were called in the medieval period—it is precisely the first of the three, faith, that is the most disputed or the least vivid. The second of the three, hope, has enjoyed an astonishing renaissance, even a "boom," in recent times, not just in theological circles but above all in philosophy (think of Ernst Bloch, for example) and in art. Love too enjoys a high credit rating among young and old, and even theologians find that it still gives them a foothold amidst the rising tides of skepticism within and without, whether doctrinally (e.g., in their attempts to communicate the biblical concept of God) or ethically (in the question of the central commandment).

Faith presents a much more difficult problem than either hope or love. It has had a decidedly less favorable press in our contemporary culture. From the standpoint not only of people outside the church but even of some theologians within, all that is dubious, questionable, and off-putting in the religious attitude seems to be connected with this dimension of faith.

This comes out very clearly in the brief exposition of the Apostles' Creed by Leonhard Ragaz. He distinguishes two kinds of faith and takes a dim view of the first, which he labels "credal faith":

> Credal or doctrinal faith merely enlightens the mind while leaving the heart cold. It begets arrogance and a condemnatory spirit. It makes people indolent and reactionary. It is an obstacle to truth, freedom, and humanity. It builds prisons and lights funeral pyres, literally as well as spiritually. It turns the gospel into dogma. It substitutes religion for the Kingdom and orthodoxy for discipleship.[1]

That sounds like a blanket condemnation. Yet Ragaz confronts this distorted concept of faith with the other positive concept on which he lavishes praise:

> True faith, faith in the sense of confidence and trust, is the begetter of everything good and great, of all truth and freedom, all courage and heroism. It is the creative power that summons the seen from the unseen, and makes the possible real and the impossible possible. It is the worker of miracles. It is the eternal revolutionary of the world, from God and towards God.[2]

17

This polemical distinction between two kinds of faith is certainly an oversimplification. Yet it has some justification and should therefore be taken seriously, both in its negative protest and in its passionate plea for "true faith." What Ragaz is protesting against, obviously, is any equation of *faith* with *knowing*—against any narrow intellectualistic view of faith. This "cerebral faith" leaves the heart cold. Worse still, it leads to the arrogance of those who "know," "possess," and "control" divine truth. It is the source of ecclesiastical fanaticism in its various forms, including the notorious "rage of the theologians" with their penchant for merciless condemnation. According to Ragaz, it is the doctrinally orthodox who are especially prone to this kind of perversion. They imagine they can substitute their "orthodoxy" for truly evangelical "orthopraxy"; as a result they inevitably corrupt the joyful news of Jesus by a new "Christian" pharisaism—a strategy that profoundly discredits the cause of Jesus, faith in his kingdom, and Christian discipleship.

According to Ragaz, the chief concern of faith, in the biblical view, is precisely this discipleship, this orthopraxy of the kingdom. True faith accordingly consists not in knowledge, but in trust. Faith (trust) is not calculating but venturesome. More specifically, it sees things from God and towards God. It looks at the world as in the presence of God—which for Ragaz always means with sights set on the coming kingdom of God and his righteousness. Faith in this God and this kingdom makes us unaccepting of the world as it is. Faith will not let us leave the world to stew in its own juice. It prevents us from capitulating to a counterfeit reality and constrains us, rather, to make the possible real and the impossible possible. This faith makes miracles both possible and real, not as prodigies and marvels but as new opportunities of life. Faith demonstrates its reality by again and again venturing in such ways.

Both these aspects and emphases, however weak or imprecise the brief Ragaz description of them, are relevant in our contemporary situation. I referred earlier to the contemporary crisis in the understanding of faith, both in the church and in society generally. This crisis is certainly in large measure connected with the misunderstandings in theology and church to which Ragaz has pointed. The bad press reserved for faith (in contrast to love and hope) is surely to be explained, in part at least, against the background of this distorted intellectualistic view of faith, and above all in the light of the attendant proprietary claim on the part of dogma to have dominion over the whole of reality—to know all the answers, even to scientific questions. There is a certain logic to the way in which an arrogant intellectualized conception of faith has been first pilloried but then in certain currents of thought also supplanted by an equally arrogant intellectualistic conception of science.

I am thinking here particularly of the positivist philosophy of history and of the concept of truth and knowledge on which it rests. According to the positivist view, human progress is regarded as achieved in three stages: humanity advances inexorably from the mythological stage through a metaphysical stage to the stage of positive science. Since today we have already entered the scientific era, religion and faith are regarded as behavior patterns that in principle have now been outmoded and superseded. But even where faith has not been so negatively regarded, where it has even been paid certain compliments (as in Hegel's philosophy of religion), the assessment of faith from the standpoint of scientific knowledge has still had one point in common with the positivist denigration of faith: in comparison with scientific conceptuality, religious imagination is still a primitive, underdeveloped way to knowledge. Religion and faith are the "philosophy of the common person." Even today, there are still many people—and not only positivists and Hegelians—who think of religion and faith in this way.

If Christian theology and the church are in some measure responsible for this understanding, indeed this misunderstanding of faith, it is high time for them to get back to something better, that is, as Ragaz rightly emphasized, to return to the prophetic and apostolic foundation. The biblical understanding of faith certainly cannot be accused of intellectualistic reductionism.

The Biblical Concept of Truth

The biblical view of faith can be defined in the light of two important passages, one from the Old Testament and the other from the New. First, the trailblazing and influential statement of Isaiah: "Have firm faith or you will not stand firm!" (Isa. 7:9, NEB). The original Hebrew contains a pregnant play on words that, to me, seems very important. This play on words depends on the Hebrew root *'mn* (amen!)—a bridge linking the opening and closing words of the

Creed. This root has a rich variety of connotations: "to be enduring," "to last," "to be trustworthy," "to be faithful and true." All these connotations are important for the biblical concept of faith. Faith has its place not in the "see clearly and understand" dialectic but in the dialectic of "trust and stand firm." Certainly faith also involves understanding, and being related to the truth; it is not a blind irrational act. Faith aims at understanding, at seeing and knowing. Augustine and Anselm both had it right: "I believe in order to understand." The truth of faith, however, is not a "knowing" in the sense of a descriptive knowledge, but a recognizing in the sense of a loving and trusting personal experience.

There are two different concepts of truth here. We could label them *alētheia* (the Greek term) and *'emeth* (the Hebrew term)—the two main words for "truth" in the Western tradition. The focus of the Greek term is on the unveiling of the mysteries of being, on *theoria* as insight into the ontological structures. The Hebrew word, on the contrary, appeals not so much to the transparency of the cosmic laws as to the fidelity of the living God. Its focus, therefore, is on the steadfastness of life, on lives lived in constant faithfulness, persisting in faith despite all trials and temptations. Not that these two concepts of truth are mutually exclusive; both are part of human life in its full range, having to do with two distinct but inseparable dimensions. In any event faith is anchored in the realm of *'emeth*, in the covenant of fidelity. Its basis is constancy—not in the sense of a sure possession, something that puts life beyond risk, but in the sense of trust, confidence, concentration on the guiding goal. In the terminology of traditional dogmatics, this constancy is not the *securitas* of one who knows, but the *certitudo* of one who trusts. It is in this direction that the prophetic message of faith points: "Have firm faith or you will not stand firm."

This understanding of faith is made even clearer in the New Testament. I am thinking, in particular, of Hebrews 11, one of the key passages on faith in the New Testament. This chapter opens with one of the rare "definitions" of faith: "Faith is the assurance of things hoped for, the conviction of things not seen." Notice that faith here means venturing to transcend existing reality, refusing to be content with what is visible but considering rather the invisible. That sounds rather idealistic and makes some of us rather skeptical. Is Christianity after all only "platonism for the people"? We must be careful here

20

and not jump to conclusions! When Platonism insists that there is more to reality and human life than what meets the eye, it deserves a hearing. But faith looks in yet a different direction. Here too Ragaz rightly grasped the focus of "true faith." When he speaks of "the seen and the unseen," what he has in mind is not a metaphysical dualism but a life lived on the basis of the kingdom of God and in the light of God's promises.

This interpretation receives strong support from Hebrews 11. In that chapter the opening definition of faith does not stand alone but is buttressed and illustrated by a whole series of examples culled from Old Testament narratives. We are reminded not only of Abel, Enoch, Noah, Abraham, and Moses but also of the harlot Rahab, of Gideon, Barak, Samson, Jephthah, David, Samuel, and the prophets "who through faith conquered kingdoms, enforced justice, received promises, stopped the mouths of lions, quenched raging fire, escaped the edge of the sword, won strength out of weakness" (Heb. 11:33ff.). It is a long and varied list of situations and actions, all of which have one feature in common: they all refer to men or women who refused to capitulate to the pressure of circumstances, and who in the name of "God's new world" challenged the "old world" and set it moving. Jesus takes a similar view of faith, seeing it—together with repentance and conversion—as the primary, proper, and due human response to the coming kingdom of God and investing it in this sense with the power "to move mountains" (Mark 11:22f.). The situation is much the same in the Johannine writings, albeit in a somewhat spiritualized context and with a different concept of world: "This is the victory that overcomes the world, our faith" (1 John 5:4).

This cannot be dismissed as triumphalism or mere fanaticism. Hebrews 11 certainly does not disguise the fact that this story of the overcoming of the world is no victory parade but a history full of blood and tears: "Others suffered mocking and scourging, and even chains and imprisonment; they were stoned, they were sawn in two, they were killed with the sword" (Heb. 11:36f.). As the New Testament sees it, faith always knows of its exposure to danger and temptation; faith is always aware of the "not yet," of "having as if it had not" (1 Cor. 7:29f.). Nor is this merely accidental; there is a basic reason for it: At the center of New Testament faith stands the cross as its very foundation. "As long as the world turns, the cross stands." Standing as it does under the cross, faith necessarily means not "seeing" but living by the promise. But no more nor less than that! Faith means breaking out from "things as they are now," an exodus, a departure, not arbitrarily, not at random, not "into the blue," but in the direction indicated and laid upon us by the promise that has already appeared in Christ and been lived out and fulfilled by him in his own life and work. This is the vision of human and cosmic reality which the *credo* of the Christian Creed confesses, to which it says its "Amen," its practical and doxological "so be it!" What is at stake in our faith is this vision of the world, or, more precisely, this ground of life and attitude toward it.

Faith as Deliverance from a One-Dimensional World View

The rediscovery and development of the biblical view of faith, I am convinced, is an important responsibility and opportunity for theology and the church today, a top priority if we are to be of service to contemporary society and culture. The fact is that we are confronted in our society and culture with powerful currents in the direction of a one-dimensional (and therefore impoverished and truncated) view of life, and with the kind of practical behavior that accompanies such a reductionist view. We are increasingly in danger of losing our humanity in a world of predetermined, prefabricated, and manipulable (and therefore to a large extent actually manipulated) things. We see this in the endless routines of daily life, whether lived feverishly or indolently, and in the preprogrammed rhythm of production and consumption, of making, achieving, and enjoying. Although it may assume different forms, the temptation is the same in the East as in the West. In the East it arises from the insistence on total planning, the tendency to shape not only economic and political affairs but cultural and intellectual life as well from one politically established center. In the West we see it in the tendency of a technocratically oriented society to try to take control of the human being either crudely by economic pressure or subtly and cunningly by the manipulation of people's needs, whether as workers or as consumers. This is the situation of our time which Herbert Marcuse in a different context accurately described with his phrase "The One-dimensional Man"—a wholesale reduction of the *humanum* to a dimension that can be shaped and manipulated.

22

In the face of this situation, Cardinal Joseph Ratzinger of Munich, in his "Introduction to Christianity," a series of lectures on the Apostles' Creed, prefaces his effort to define the place of faith in the context of the modern scientific view of reality with an interesting excursus on the history of thought. His starting point is the transformation that has taken place in the modern view of knowledge and science:

> A characteristic feature of our basic contemporary outlook as determined by science, an outlook which whether we like it or not fashions the attitude to life of every one of us and assigns us our place in the world, is its restriction to the "phenomena"—that which can be seen and controlled. We have abandoned the search for the hidden reality of things in themselves, the exploration of the nature of being itself. We deem such efforts to be useless because we consider the depth of being as ultimately beyond our reach.[3]

Post-Kantian world.

In antiquity and the medieval period, on the contrary, the presupposition of all thought was the metaphysical premise: "being is truth"; the Being which is supreme over us all is the basis of truth. Whether in the general ontological sense, as in antiquity, or in the ontological sense of theology, as in the medieval period, the conclusion is the same: to the extent that our thinking is true, it is a derivative, secondary thinking.

The movement of the history of thought, as also the subsequent movement of modern pragmatic technology, leads away from that premise. The development takes place in two stages. Two more short phrases can capture the characteristics of these two stages: "true because done" and "true because *to be* done." The first phrase describes the attitude of historicism, according to which humanity recognizes as true primarily, but then very soon also exclusively, what it has itself achieved in its history. "The dominance of the fact (the thing done) begins, that is, humanity's radical concentration on its own work as the only thing it can be certain of."[4] The second phrase describes the stage of technocracy: from the mid-nineteenth century onwards the dominance of the fact is increasingly replaced by the dominance of the thing *to be* done, the thing that is doable, and so the dominance of history is replaced by that of technology.[5] In the first of these stages what predominates are positivist and rationalist currents, the demolition of myths and a passionate desire to understand things as they really are; in the second stage, the technocratic solution of problems takes priority. To take an example from the area of human biology, whereas the main preoccupation in the nineteenth century was to understand the origin of species and the history of human origins, the real challenge today is already "cybernetics, the capacity to shape the human being who is to be created anew by his own planning."[6] The two stages are, of course, interconnected: "The reduction of the human being to a 'thing done' is the presupposition that makes it possible to understand the human being as a 'thing *to be* done,' a shapeable object that is to be led from what it now is into a new future."[7]

I do not accept these arguments of Ratzinger in every detail. For one thing, his three stages can all too easily look like stages in a "rake's progress," as one more variation in the traditional Catholic reading of history, with its excessive tendency to regard the modern period as a destructive and self-destructive decline from and dissolution of the medieval synthesis; that is a much too one-sided presentation of history. Modern historicism and the technocratic spirit were not the only factors involved in the achievement of a critical distance vis-à-vis classical metaphysics; the renaissance of biblical thought also played its part. In any theological analysis of modern times, account has to be taken of the distinctions between "secularization" and "secularism" that have been developed in Protestant thought. A second hesitation about Ratzinger's analysis derives from my unwillingness to locate the "place of faith" (which is ultimately what his "Introduction" is all about) too one-sidedly in the neighborhood of a metaphysical openness to being, as he seems to do. Ratzinger undoubtedly puts his finger on one important aspect, but there is another aspect that needs to be mentioned immediately alongside it, namely, that faith is certainly also to be understood—as I suggested earlier in connection with Ragaz and his concept of faith—as "true because to be done" (though not, of course, in any absolutized sense!), that is, as obedient action. The two aspects are inseparable and must be kept together. To quote an important insight of Bonhoeffer: "Only faith is obedient and only the obedient person believes."[8]

But, with this reservation, I would strongly endorse Ratzinger's central concern to define faith's "place" and inalienable significance in the contemporary context. By way of summary, therefore, and in complete accord, I quote him once again:

In the sense intended in the Creed, faith is not an immature form of knowledge, not merely an opinion that could or should be translated into the kind of knowledge we can achieve on our own. On the contrary, it is essentially a different kind of mental behavior, standing as something independent and distinctive alongside (and incapable of being reduced to or derived from) the knowledge we can achieve for ourselves. . . . It is the way we grasp our human status in the whole universe, the meaning without which the human being would remain in every respect homeless, the meaning which takes priority over human calculation and action, and without which we are in the last analysis incapable of calculation and action since these are possible only where there is a meaning that upholds us. For, in fact, we do not live by the "bread" of self-achievement alone; we live as human beings our distinctively human life by the Word, by love, by meaning. The meaning is the bread by which we exist and live our distinctive humanity.[9]

This is how the life of faith is oriented, that which is inaugurated by the little word *Credo* and has its goal in the little word "Amen."

Who Is the Subject of This Confession of Faith?

By way of conclusion, a brief comment on the question as to who is the subject of this confession of faith. Who does the confessing? Is it the individual or is it the church, the "communion of saints"? The question arises when we compare the ancient versions of the Creed (in Denzinger's Enchiridion Symbolorum, for example). We discover as a general if not inflexible rule that the Latin texts clearly prefer the singular whereas the Greek texts incline to the plural "We believe." This is particularly evident in the Nicene Creed, preferred in the Eastern church. The two tendencies can hardly be deemed accidental or explained linguistically; in all probability, theological factors also play a part. In his exposition of the Nicene Creed, Heinrich Vogel offers the following explanation of the plural form:

The "we" of the Christian East could indeed . . . be connected with the East's preference for the christological formula, which states that, in the incarnate Son of God, God "assumed" our "humanity." The use of the first-person singular of the Western Creed could be interpreted in the light of the Western emphasis on the affirmation of the divine incarnation in the birth of this Jesus of Nazareth as a concrete individual human being.[10]

25

In other words, behind the slight difference of grammatical form there may be a subtle difference in christological emphasis. It might also be legitimate to think here—as Vogel too ventures to do with considerable caution and with contemporary references—of the corresponding "collectivist" and "individualist" tendencies that have continued in various ways to characterize the picture in East and West down to our own day.

Are we confronted here with a straight choice between clear-cut alternatives? Certainly not. The examples given by Vogel himself provide ample warning against thinking in terms of such an "either-or." To be sure, important differences of emphasis were at stake in the early christological controversies between East and West, but it was certainly not a stark choice between true and false. The same can be said—even by those of us who are committed to our own Western heritage—for the cultural problem today between East and West. Even more important here, however, is the background of biblical anthropology. Biblical faith, both anthropologically and soteriologically, is quite innocent of any dichotomy between "individualism" and "collectivism." In the biblical view there is no such thing as an abstract individual; cohumanity is the very structure of humanity. The human being who exists apart from all other human beings is a phantom. But conversely, too: the human being is a first-person singular, a responsible self, a named and personal subject, an "I" who is not lost in the mass, in some amorphous "world of human beings." And what is true with respect to anthropology is even more true with respect to faith. Heinrich Vogel is right, therefore, when he argues in favor of both the Latin singular "I believe" and the Greek plural "We believe":

> This I and this We, this We and this I, are to be heard and spoken together as a unity. Anyone who is privileged to say here "I believe" is already incorporated in the church's We. Anyone who is privileged here to say with the whole of Christendom: "*We* all believe in one God . . . " is already the individual human being that he or she really is in God's sight, already summoned to the decision entailed in the "I believe."[11]

Once again, misunderstandings can be avoided if we keep in mind the concrete lifesetting of the Apostles' Creed, which is a baptismal confession of faith. Particularly in the pre-Constantinian church, where its roots lie, the Creed rested on a personal decision as demanding as any an existentialist could imagine: a decision to break with one's past, indeed with one's whole world, and enter upon a new way, a new beginning, a "narrow path" involving a personal hope and responsibility all one's own. The direct personal question "Do you?" put to the individual and the equally direct personal response "I believe" gave expression to this existential engagement. But the secret and the comfort of this now highly personalized faith was the promise, and undoubtedly too the joyous realization, that the individual is not alone is this faith, not left to his or her own devices, even sociologically. The individual now becomes a member of the body of Christ and enters for the first time and in the full sense into a close-knit fellowship of brothers and sisters. Like all genuine creeds, so the Apostles' Creed is the documentary record of this transaction. We recite its words on our own, with a sense of responsibility that no one can take from us. At the same time, each solo voice blends with the great choir of believers and confessors who stand both near to us and far from us in space and in time. Both the "I believe" and the "We believe," therefore, are entirely in place.

4

I Believe in God

The Objective Focus of Faith

In the *credo* of the Apostles' Creed, in the act of faith as the Creed understands it, the human being does not remain alone. This is where we came out in our discussion of the Christian understanding of faith. This means, in the first place sociologically, that as we confess our faith we are not left on our own as isolated individuals but enter the encompassing fellowship of our brothers and sisters in the faith. But there is still another dimension to this basic affirmation that we are "not alone," a dimension that must likewise be spelled out if we are to remain faithful to the Apostles' Creed. We are to understand it not only "horizontally" (sociologically) but also "vertically" (theologically, in the strict sense of this word). The opening and closing words of the Creed do not stand alone, divorced from what follows and what precedes. The Creed is recited all in one breath. The opening key signature, the "I believe," is not to be separated from the content of the Creed, the immediately succeeding words "in God, the Father . . . and in Jesus Christ . . . and in the Holy Spirit." The "form," or frame, of the Creed and the "substance" of the Creed go hand in hand.

To point this out is not to belabor the obvious. The old dogmaticians introduced a distinction between the *fides quae creditur*, the objective aspect of faith, and the *fides qua creditur*, the subjective aspect; the two sides together constitute the Christian "I believe." The distinction is a useful one provided it does not imply separation. But how often these two aspects of faith have been not only distinguished in theology but also divorced! Indeed, the whole history of doctrine, especially in modern times, could be sketched in terms of this distinction, showing how the pendulum has swung repeatedly from one aspect to the other. On the one hand, attention has often been so concentrated on the objective *fides quae*—

29

especially in the various kinds of "orthodoxy"—that the need for a subjective element in the life of faith, for personal commitment in the practice of faith, was neglected! On the other hand, in reaction against the cold "objectivism" of the orthodox, the "warm" subjectivity of the *fides qua* and concern for the personal authenticity of the individual believer have often been so exclusively stressed that the material contents of the Creed, its traditional biblical and doctrinal substance, was reduced to something optional and unessential. By either route the *credo* of the Apostles' Creed—faith in the sense in which the Creed understands it—is narrowed and diminished.

The point to be emphasized in the present context—as an essential complement to what was said about faith in the previous chapter—is that apostolic faith in not an empty container to be filled with whatever contents we choose. The apostolic concept of faith is not something abstract ("faith as such") but is focused on and dynamically related to its distinctive contents, and this indeed in respect to both its origin and its focus of intention. Far from being a mighty achievement of the creative consciousness, faith originates in the encounter with the prophetic and apostolic message, with the person of Jesus, with the Christ event. Faith is not self-contained; self-understanding does not bring it to its goal. On the contrary, faith is a response that leads on to discipleship; it points beyond itself to its object.

I appeal here to a witness whom no one could justly accuse of an "objectivistic" orthodoxy. Rudolf Bultmann hits the nail on the head when he asserts categorically:

> When theology has abandoned its particular object, the "faith which is believed," it *can* then no longer understand the "faith by which one believes." It assumes that faith to be a human attitude which can be seen without seeing the object of faith. It misjudges the *intentionality of faith*. For the "faith by which one believes" is what it is only in relation to its object, the "faith which is believed" . . . Faith which is conceived as a human attitude, as a spiritual function, as a pious frame of mind, as a sense of the numinous, and the like, is *not* faith at all. Faith exists only as faith *in*, that is as faith in its object, in God known in revelation.[1]

The last words of this Bultmann passage specify concretely the focal point of faith, the contents of the *credo*. In substantive agreement with the Apostles' Creed, Bultmann defines this focus and content in the single all-important word *God*: "I believe in God." Apostolic faith always understands itself decidedly and unmistakably, as faith in God.

Reference to God No Longer Axiomatic

But is this as obvious as it sounds? It seemed so for centuries and not least at the time when the Creed took shape. Some scholars consider the classic "Shema Israel"—"Hear, O Israel, the Lord our God is *one* Lord" (Deut. 6:4)—as a definite model for the Christian creeds. This Jewish confession of faith indeed approximates closely the opening words of the Apostles' Creed, though here there is less emphasis on the singularity of God; unlike the Nicene Creed, the Textus Receptus has no emphatic "one," probably because this Old Testament emphasis was practically unchallenged. To confess the faith undoubtedly meant to confess faith in God. For centuries the association of faith with God, the affirmation "I believe in God," remained axiomatic in the church and even in Christian society. Wolfhart Pannenberg justly remarks in his commentary on the Creed:

> Not very long ago, the idea that there was a God and Father in heaven was a matter of course for most Christians. This first article of faith was not even felt to be exclusively Christian; Christians assumed that here they were at one with the majority of civilized people. The difficulties with the creed as it has been passed down to us only began with the statements about Jesus Christ as Son of God and with the miracles of his birth and resurrection from the dead. Belief in Christ seemed to many people a troublesome addition to the simple faith in God which Jesus himself had taught.

I share this view and would illustrate it from personal experience. Looking back to my high school and early university days and recalling my own attempts to get my Christian bearings, I well remember that during World War II and in the early postwar period theistic affirmations were on the whole still valid and convincing for most of us, whereas many of us had problems with a straightforward confession of faith in Jesus Christ in the terms used in the traditional christological doctrine. Expressing this in the traditional terminology of the "Three Articles"—belief in Father, Son, and Holy Spirit—we

31

did not find it difficult to accept "a theology of the First Article." On the one hand, such a theology was impressively exemplified in certain very influential currents of contemporary culture and in some of the leading personalities of the time (in my own case, for example, in the religious philosophy of T. G. Masaryk), and it was quite respectable and acceptable in academic quarters. On the other hand, to accept the Second Article and believe in Christ called for a much more strenuous intellectual and personal effort. There was greater opposition here and you had to struggle hard, for here you were on territory that was culturally alien and could be conquered only by a "leap of faith" or by a long and laborious effort to clarify the faith, or both.

Is it not precisely in this respect that our present situation has completely changed—both for budding theologians and for theology generally? Looking back at the recent history of Protestant and even ecumenical theology, the trend seems to have been in exactly the opposite direction. First, there has undeniably been a certain concentration on christology, or at least a very marked emphasis on Jesus, and this among thinkers of very diverse schools. Second, and above all, however, for many of our contemporaries, has not the First Article in particular, and especially the idea of God in general, been relegated to the status of a remote, strange, and most unlikely possibility? The emergence of "atheistic theologians"—even if they are no longer as prominent as they were—is only the tip of a cultural iceberg. There is talk today of a "crisis in the notion of God," of "transformations of God," "the eclipse of God" and, even more universally, of "the death of God." Much of this talk is simply a fad, not to be taken seriously. Yet slogans like these are certainly symptoms of a complex and deep-seated current that cannot be dismissed as irrelevant to faith and its confession today. The idea of God has lost its ideologically self-evident character. It is no longer axiomatic.

With singular insight and prescience Dietrich Bonhoeffer was one of the first to draw attention to these profound changes. From his Berlin cell on 8 June 1944 he wrote to his friend Eberhard Bethge:

Humanity has learned to deal with itself in all questions of importance without recourse to the "working hypothesis" called "God." In questions of science, art, and ethics, this has become an understood thing at which one now hardly dares to tilt. But for the last hundred years or so it has also become increasingly true of religious questions; it is becoming evident that everything gets along without "God"—and, in fact, just as well as before. As in the scientific field, so in human affairs generally, "God is being pushed more and more out of life, losing more and more ground."[3]

These words are part of those "prophetic fragments" by which their author exercised a lasting influence on the course of postwar theology. They were sometimes misunderstood; they were interpreted, for example, as paving the way for an abandonment of *faith* in God, as a blueprint for an "atheistic theology," or even as encouraging a complete break with theology and as a prelude to the atheism of the future. This was how some thinkers tried to understand and "develop" Bonhoeffer: in one direction by certain theologians such as Herbert Braun, Dorothee Sölle, and the American "God is dead" school; in another direction by a few Marxist thinkers such as Milan Machovec. Bonhoeffer himself, however, was looking in yet a different direction. His statements were formulated quite consciously "in God's presence": "God Himself compels us to recognize it [this truth]. . . . [He compels us] to a true acknowledgement of our situation in his presence."[4] Moreover, even in his Berlin cell and, as attested by the last eyewitnesses, even on his way to execution, Bonhoeffer lived out his faith in a deeply personal relationship to God, as his prayers also eloquently attest. Bonhoeffer's arguments had nothing whatever to do with the elimination of God, either as a theme or as a reality. But they do reflect the radically changed context in which we and our contemporaries confront the question of God. Concretely, Bonhoeffer's arguments reflect awareness of the nonaxiomatic character of our discourse about God and our life in his presence.

For thousands of years the theme of God was part and parcel of Western thought; not only in the "Christian era" but already in antiquity, "God" was part of the stock in trade of the dominant world view. The sophisticated version of this axiom was the metaphysical theistic concept of God—the great achievement of Western civilization in the philosophical and theological realm! In the hierarchical order of being and thought, God is the First Principle and the Final Goal, the Guarantor of meaning and the ultimate Arbiter of our human life. "In theistic metaphysics, the Deity was the necessary basis for the continued existence and concept of reality as a whole and in all its details, a basis which is inescapable for human thought and on which in the last analysis everything finite and incapable of autonomous existence rests and is sustained in being; and all this is so in the best and most beneficial sense for the whole universe."[5] The interests of philosophical theory, practical morality, and organized religion (not to mention politics and culture) coalesced to produce the logical conclusion: God exists. Even in the case of theology and the church, the almost axiomatic presupposition of thought and action was to a large extent the theistic metaphysical world view inspired by that overall vision.

The shaking and even the possible collapse of this theistic world view, and particularly the consequent loss of the quasi-axiomatic character of the theme of God, is reflected in Bonhoeffer. He points to the historical and sociological developments in modern culture that are usually described and analyzed in terms of "secularization," those developments to which we referred in the last chapter in our discussion of Ratzinger. Bonhoeffer ventures a prognosis which, after more than three decades, now stands in need of certain modifications, of course, particularly his two key terms—a "religionless world" and a "world come of age." As descriptions of our world, both terms probably go too far. Religion (I am not thinking especially of Christianity but of religion generally) has certainly not been eliminated and at times can even boast of making some kind of a "comeback"—public as well as private—within our secularized world. Neither is "old lady" metaphysics yet dead—with all the attendant themes and questions. Far from it! Nor is it really possible, despite all the strides made in the direction of emancipation, to speak seriously and without qualification of the "maturity" of the "secularized" inhabitants of our technocratic world. Again and again developments within the culture reveal at the same time depressing symptoms of incapacity and incompetence, of having not "come of age." Nevertheless, corrections and qualifications of this sort do not by any means disqualify Bonhoeffer in the present context. In our culture, the axiomatic character of "God" has disappeared, on human reckoning and despite all countervailing tendencies, probably forever.

Increased Difficulty of Communication

What is the effect of these developments in general on the theological enterprise, and in particular on our approach to the credal affirmation "I believe in God"? Have theology and faith been made more difficult, or even impossible? Difficult yes, impossible no; although both parts of this sentence need to be borne in mind, I would particularly emphasize the second part, and will do so in the next section.

But first: communicating the theme of God has undoubtedly become more difficult in our time. As theologians, we find ourselves—along with our theology—relegated to a "cultural ghetto." There was a time when we were undisputed masters in the house of Western scholarship and culture. The acclimation of theology to culture, its accepted place in the life of society, even its status in the world of scholarship were unchallenged, indeed evident and convincing to all (or at least to the vast majority). The situation today is quite different. Even in the universities, the home of the scholars, ours is a suspect and more or less contested discipline. In culture and society too, for the most part, the relevance of theology is far from evident and often seriously doubted. In saying this, I am not speaking nostalgically or longing secretly for the restoration of theology's cultural prestige. My reason for mentioning this change is because it has to do with what has happened to the theme of "God." It is not that the prestige of theology is to be equated with the prestige of the theme of God. That is not the case, thank God! There is, however, a connection between them. The position that theology once occupied in culture and society was not won by violence; neither was it accorded to theology by chance but by inner necessity. Within the cultural framework of metaphysical theism the object of theological endeavor was the highest conceivable theme—the fundamental presupposition and the final goal of every scholarly pursuit and every order of being. In this sense it was true that "philosophy (and really every scholarly discipline) is the handmaid of theology." In this frame of reference the effort to deal with the affirmation "I believe in God" was the highest, most urgent and hence most self-evident of human activities.

The quandary in which theology finds itself in our contemporary culture is an indication of the far deeper quandary over the theme of God itself. The inner necessity of the whole theistic argument has collapsed. The theological enterprise—together with its object—is no longer located within the realm of urgent necessity but has been moved to the fringe, to the sphere of the contingent; it has become "marginalized." Recalling what we learned from Ratzinger in the previous chapter, we may describe the situation as follows: Because of the predominance of the positivist "thing done" and the technocratic "thing *to be* done," the "truth" of theology was turned into an anachronism, a vestige of times past, a foreign body. And this happened irrespective of the economic and political systems which divide our world. This view, this assessment of the role of theology and the destiny of its theme, is frankly and sharply expressed in the ideological tendencies of Eastern Europe. On the one hand, in a society of "real socialism," theology and the church, and above all God as a theme for reflection, have no place at all. They are a reactionary diversion, the "opium of the people." In the new society conceived totally in terms of things to be done, they are troublemakers. In the climate of an ideologically "neutral" West with its pluralistic technocracy, on the other hand, theology and its theme are not banished for ideological purposes. What happens here is that the de facto predominance of "production" and the "producible" ends up by evoking in economy and society an estrangement from the theme of theology. In such a context it is not easy to see the relevance of the question of God. This is why I conclude that the possibility of communicating the theme of God has become more difficult. The context in which we live makes access to an understanding of the apostolic affirmation "I believe in God," much more difficult, both inwardly and outwardly.

But not impossible. This brings me to the second aspect of the question.

A Liberating Alternative

The fact that the theme of God is increasingly difficult does not necessarily mean that it is completely impossible. Why not? In answering this question I want to begin from my own personal experiences, in Eastern Europe especially. Eastern Europe is particularly important in this connection, for during its Marxist socialist period East European culture and society has for decades witnessed a variety of aggressive organized attempts "to solve the religious question" in a radically atheistic way by completely erasing the theme of God from the annals of human history. After thousands of years of religious alienation throughout all of previous history in all its forms, the socialist-communist society was at last to offer something quite new, nothing less than a full-orbed atheism. The ways of achieving this new society differed in the different countries and at particular periods. The strategies, and above all the tactics, varied. They ranged from the brutal suppression of religion (in Albania, for example, which described itself already in 1967 as the world's "first atheist state") and the use of various administrative measures to intimidate Christians, through education based on atheistic ideology and a corresponding propaganda pursued vigorously in all spheres, to more guarded repressive policies with respect to culture and the church (as in Poland). But the goal was always the same—the achievement of a Marxist socialist culture and society based on the scientific atheistic world view. Religion was to die out; its presence—that is, its specific themes, especially its central theme "God"—was to be banished, in the first instance from official cultural and social life but also, in the end, from the "hearts" of the individual citizens.

I would not describe this attempt as a failure. For one thing, it would be premature to do so after the relatively short time so far allotted to it, the thirty to sixty years of Marxist-socialist experimentation in Eastern Europe. For another thing, there is no denying the real achievements of this consistent policy toward culture and the church. In official cultural life at least, with the exception of Poland, religion really has been repressed in the countries of Eastern Europe. Religion and "God" play a very minor role in the whole region; they have been ruthlessly "silenced"—almost completely so far as contemporary culture is concerned, but also to a large extent so far as transmission of the cultural heritage is concerned. Here too, that is, retrospectively, every effort has been made to reinterpret, minimize, and if possible eliminate all reference to the role of religion, the presence of the theme of God. The "silence of God"—a phenomenon that is certainly discernible also in Western culture—is in Eastern Europe deeply imprinted on the visible face of culture and society.

This, however, is only one side of the coin. The situation has another dimension, an invisible or just barely visible side that is nonetheless very real. While it is possible in this connection to speak of the "silence of God," there can certainly be no talk of the "death of God," not even in the context of the officially atheistic society. One of my deepest theological and human experiences in Czechoslovakia was the discovery that the process just described, determining what happens to the question of God in this atheistically conceived culture

37

and society, far from being linear and one-dimensional was in fact an intensely dialectical and two-sided process. The officially "silenced" theme, far from disappearing from the spectrum of vital human interests, became for many people, at the very moment when its suppression was being planned, for the first time in their lives a really *questionable* question (in both senses of the word, that is, both questionable and worth asking), a vibrant and therefore eminently contemporary theme. In fact, at the very moment when the question of God was being shorn of all direct and indirect protection by official society, at the very time when this theme was becoming culturally "homeless" because its axiomatic metaphysical and theistic character had been internally and externally shattered, it suddenly acquired a new "questionability," fresh legitimacy, and—still more important— a new credibility.

This fresh opportunity was of course closely connected with the radical nonconformity of the theme, given the circumstances we have just described. At the same time, however, it cannot be attributed simply to the attractions of nonconformity. What happened was rather the discovery that the fundamental question of the irreplaceable, particular, personal identity of human life in mind and conscience, in life and in death, is very intimately bound up with the question of God. The official ideology tried to persuade citizens, and in particular party members that the question of the meaning of individual existence is best left to the leaders of socialist society, whose party could safely be trusted in this matter. "Trust the Party, comrades!" The word to the masses went out more vociferously, the more problematic this trust inevitably became for so many thinking people, as for example during the political "show trials" in the 1950s.

In such a setting the question of God came to seem a possible option. Not, of course, an overtly political option; not as a banner or cloak for anti-socialist currents, though attempts were certainly sometimes made in this direction. As Josef L. Hromadka stressed so often, such attempts did not really help, least of all with respect to the theme of God; on the contrary, political misuse of the idea of God only reduces and hampers its real relevance and radical thrust. What should concern the church in its witness to God is precisely this genuine relevance of its theme. Hence the importance of not abandoning that witness to those either on the right or on the left, who wished merely to misuse it, of not allowing its potential for enhancing humanity to be squandered for short-term "gains." In the situation of a Marxist socialist society, the theme of God provided an option not *against* society but *within* it. It was relevant to the basic question citizens were asking in their search for the meaning of life: Is it possible for an ideology or a political party simply to erase the question of the meaning of my individual destiny, the question of my mind and conscience, of my life and my death? Does not this question arise in a context that is wholly impervious to determination, manipulation, or control by other human beings? Is there not in my life a point of reference, a dimension that can never be accounted for in terms of culture and society, human ways of organizing and relating? Important as these social and cultural systems and relationships undoubtedly are, does the human being—even the socialist human being—really merge without remainder into the horizontal dimension, into what Marx called "the nexus of human relationships"? Is there not also a vertical dimension, a dimension that is not opposed to the horizontal but complements it and intersects it, a dimension in which each of us is both required and permitted individually to live out our particular human destiny without any conceivable surrogate or replacement, and so in our unique individual identity?

It is possible to raise this question in philosophy, in the context of existentialist thought, for example, or as part of a literary or artistic quest. But the theological answer offers a particularly radical option. Two aspects of it may be mentioned here.

First, in the context of the Christian message about God, the question of our final human destiny is formulated very clearly as the question of death and resurrection. Theologically, the term "God" points not just to the depth dimension of our earthly human existence but also to our "eternal destiny." In this sense especially, there is the closest possible connection between the opening and closing words of the Creed: "I believe in God . . . and a life everlasting." "In the Bible, God is . . . centrally identified with a promise of life, with an incursion of life into the world of death."[6] This sharpens the question of personal identity. My being who I am is not subject to cancellation; it is not simply for a long or short stretch of earthly existence. I stand under the promise of—and responsibility to—eternity. I live "in the light of eternity"—to use a phrase that was often on the lips of T. G. Masaryk; for him those words had concrete implications for everyday life and conduct and for the ordering of society. It was no accident that in the East European context people felt the relevance of the theme of God most powerfully and liberatingly in face of the question of death. I am thinking here particularly of funeral services, which offer the church its only opportunity to speak directly to the unchurched on off-church premises about its message. Funeral services became a highly effective opportunity for witness; they were followed eagerly, with deep interest and emotion, even by the outsiders. For many people, including practicing atheists, what was offered here was an alternative, a questionable option that was at the same time also a credible option.

This brings me to the second aspect of the thoroughly radical character of the option offered by the theological answer. The term "option" can be used not only in connection with the question of individual identity but also in connection with the question of the social destiny of the human being, for both—according to Christian understanding—are involved where there is faith in God. In the Bible, "God" is both a personal theme and a communal—indeed a social—theme. Expressed in biblical terms, there is an indissoluble connection between God and his kingdom. When in the biblical revelation the divine name is uttered, it expresses not only a longing for the final fulfillment of personal identity but also a longing for the new "kingdom of peace and justice," the new "city of God"—and hence for new connections and interrelationships in our common human destiny. This is true also in the socialist society, again not in opposition to it but on its behalf, for its good, to the extent that it represents an effort to achieve greater justice in human relationships. At the same time, however, the biblical reference to the "coming kingdom" rules out any premature equation of present social achievements with the ultimate eschatological reality; it serves as a safeguard against all attempts to sanctify and absolutize present conditions—and not only socialist conditions!—against all forms of political messianism and fetishism. To put it positively: where the kingdom of God is our horizon there always emerges a restive quest for an extra measure of common humanity, for seeing things as they are in light of the promises of what is to be, for taking new steps in the direction of a more human political order.

Not surprisingly, this potential and actual relevance and vibrancy of the theme of God did not go unnoticed in the Christian-Marxist dialogue initiated in connection with our efforts at "humanizing socialist society" and achieving a "socialism with a human face"; it actually acquired fresh significance for many of those involved—not just the Christian participants. As our starting point in this dialogue we quite deliberately chose the anthropological problem—the question of the meaning of human life. The idea was to avoid the theme of "God," considered as being too much a matter of controversy between Christians and Marxists. It soon became clear, however, that the two themes—humanity and God—could not be divorced. Even for Marxists, the question about God was a clear signal that certain realities simply demanded further study. This was evident as regards both the contexts mentioned earlier—the search for a solid basis for personal identity, and the question of opening up the established social system with its dogmatic fetishes, opening it up to a "transcendence" that could allow new possibilities to emerge for socialist society and culture today. The inexhaustible relevance of the theme of God both for the individual and for society had been demonstrated on the crusty exterior of Stalinism! "God is not quite dead!" Vitezslav Gardavsky's famous slogan, which originated in this Christian-Marxist, was more than just a whimsical joke. It had its real-life setting in the extremely serious discussion of questions of Christian—and human—existence in a socialist society. Gardavsky's formula fits exactly the real experience that I would propose for reflection as a basis for the thesis that the theme of God is still an open possibility even in the conditions of a secularized society. Even here, God is not quite dead!

Lessons for the West from the East

These experiences in an East European context have important implications for what is also happening with the theme of God in Western culture and society. Certainly the situation in the West is different. There is not the same massive atheistic pressure. There are no official restrictions on the church and its message; indeed they sometimes have special advantages. Indirectly, however, there are within a technocratically ordered industrialized capitalist society certain cultural and social tendencies that despite all the differences— think of the Bonhoeffer quotation and of our reflections on one-dimensionality—operate in essentially the same direction, namely, toward the marginalizing of the theme of God.

For this very reason the lessons learned from experience in Eastern

Europe could conceivably have a wider ecumenical relevance. They could offer guidance for our situation in the West, not just negatively but even in a positive sense. The statement that "God is not quite dead" is no less true in the West than in the East. With its clearly defined features, the East European experience could bring home to us in the West a fact that does not make such a vivid impression when garbed in the milder forms of technocratic temptation, namely, that at inescapable points of the human quest, in the life of both individuals and of society, the question of God is always a potentially explosive question. In the complex pluralism and relativism of the Western market economy, the scene is everywhere dominated by "supplies" of a bewildering variety, an incredible "supermarket of possibilities." Simply in virtue of all that they see around them, many people find it impossible to regard theology as an obvious option; they regard it as an "also ran," a "discontinued line." Worse still, theology sometimes becomes unsure of itself and engages in feverish efforts to make itself more attractive by dressing itself up in finery borrowed from its rivals in the marketplace—from psychology, sociology, and allied disciplines. The experience in Eastern Europe can again be of help. While remaining receptive to other views and possibilities, theology need not leave unexploited the rich potential of the promise expressed in the credal "I believe in God"; it can rather develop that potential and, despite the undeniably diminished possibilities of communicating the promise, nonetheless persevere in its specific task and communicate its distinctive message—not only for its own sake but also for the benefit of its contemporaries.

Difficult as our here and now may be, we Christians and theologians are offered certain distinct opportunities today; of that I am convinced. Once again, the experience of the East has something to teach us. When fundamental human questions arise—on the one hand the longing for an individual human life that is personal and marked by an identity that is not socially or culturally derived, and on the other hand the question of an open and caring human society—the biblical theme of God once more becomes relevant. What it offers is no slick answer but a distinctive and radical perspective. Its relevance remains undiminished by unidimensional tendencies, whether ideological or pragmatic. Indeed, the very opposite is the case. That basic human longing in both its forms can in the long run only be intensified by a stubborn one-dimensionalism, a rigid horizontalism. We do not live "by bread alone," and still less by the "thing done" or the "thing to be done"—indispensable though these may be. On the contrary, it is precisely the one-sidedly technocratic culture that poses with renewed urgency and directness the question of an "alternative." In such a setting, the first affirmation of the Apostles' Creed—"I believe in God"—which seems at first sight to have been truly filed and forgotten, acquires among us in the West as in the East a new dimension of reality and relevance. This being the case, we should not shed too many tears over the fact that the theme of God has lost its axiomatic and self-evident character or the fact that the communication of this theme has become increasingly difficult in a secularized society, as if we had been saddled here with an unbearable burden. Rather must this situation be seen and grasped as an opportunity to claim for this theme of God a renewed right both to be heard and to be believed.

5

The Father Almighty

The Unobvious God

We noted that the unaxiomatic, unobvious character of the theme of God in contemporary culture is not merely a handicap for theology but at the same time an opportunity. I tried to show in what sense this is the case by demonstrating the "think-ability" and "credibility" of the theme of God in the context of certain specific contemporary challenges. We turn now to another aspect of this opportunity, one that is no less important theologically. The fact that the idea of God has ceased to be axiomatic and self-evident gives theology the opportunity to understand more precisely and more "originally" (more radically!) the brief affirmation of the Apostles' Creed: "I believe in God." The One to whom this statement refers is not some "self-evident God" who can be taken for granted as already there, generally accessible and intelligible.

Throughout the centuries of Christian civilization, people have often been mistaken on this score. The Gibraltar of the theological tradition, namely, the "fortress" of Christian metaphysics, has sometimes become the "confining prison" of the distinctively Christian belief in God. Reference has already been made to the logic of the metaphysical concept of God. Its ultimate intention was to "prove" God's nature and being: God is inevitably to be thought of as necessary; it is of his very essence to be rationally and ontologically necessary. The underlying purpose here was undoubtedly a respectable one, and it was often achieved in a most impressive manner. Undoubtedly, too, these arguments were for the most part the fruit of genuine faith: "I believe in order to understand; I understand in order to believe." This much can be positively affirmed about the metaphysical tradition in Christian theology and the way it develops the theme of God.

Yet this development of Christian thought in the direction of a

45

theistic metaphysics undoubtedly had its dangers too. The biblical name of God was turned into something alien and unrecognizable. To confine ourselves to what has already been said, the biblical God is not a God of logical necessity, a "rigidly necessary" God. He is, on the contrary, the God of his own free history, the God of grace, that grace which cannot be accounted for by any chain of necessary steps. There is no denying that the main exponents of the metaphysical tradition never lost sight of the majesty and transcendence of God. Even in their attempts to prove the existence and nature of God, there was one maxim they never forgot: "God is always greater." From the standpoint of biblical faith, however, the program of a theistic metaphysics is still open to question. The biblical God cannot be grasped through intellectual efforts any more than through the devices of cult or magic. His first words of command impress on believers his absolute inaccessibility: no other gods, indeed, no images even, are to be connected with his name. He "is who he is"— or, keeping closer to the original Hebrew, he "will be who he will be"—the Coming One. His essence is not that of a necessary concept but his own free revelation—in biblical terms, his covenant, his salvation, his history. But all this means that he is the God who is not self-evident, the God who is "more than necessary."[1]

It was not easy to do justice to the distinctive biblical understanding of faith in God when the attempt was made to fit it into this picture of a self-evident and necessary idea of God as propounded in the theistic world view. "Brothers, there must be a loving Father beyond the starry skies"—the "must" in this well-intended statement is typical: "God" comes as no surprise; he is—he must be—part of our system; he is its guarantor—but often its prisoner too. Now, this is *not* the God that the Creed has in mind. The God presented to us in the Creed is no universal necessary idea of God but a distinctive God who is not self-evident. Precisely, here, therefore, lies the opportunity for us who live in a culture characterized by shattered concepts of God. We have an opportunity to listen carefully and to discern what the Creed actually means when it affirms "I believe in God"—instead of simply collating its affirmations with arbitrary truisms. In other words, we have an opportunity to gain more direct access to the apostolic witness.

In whom then does the Creed confess its faith? The first concrete answers to this question are given in the three definitions of God with which we shall be concerned in this chapter and the next: God is the Father, the Almighty, the Creator of heaven and earth. Before turning to these definitions, however, a preliminary remark is in order that applies to the entire Creed: The God of whom the whole Creed speaks is the Father, Son, and Holy Spirit, the Triune God. All the creeds of the ancient church are in agreement on this point. They think not in general theistic terms but specifically in terms of the Holy Trinity. What was gained by this more precise designation? What was at stake in this trinitarian concept of God, to which Christians obviously attached such great importance?

It is not possible, in the present context to deal in greater detail with the problem of the Trinity, nor would I want to overemphasize the problem. Above all, I would not wish to ignore the special intellectual difficulties that confront anyone who tries to understand the full-blown doctrine of the Trinity. For us the language in which the doctrine is couched is no longer easily accessible; indeed it is almost an esoteric speculative language: Father, Son, Holy Spirit; three in one, one in three. But we should not allow ourselves to be put off by the strange terminology in which the doctrine is couched. The speculative aspects of its form do not get to the heart of its substantive concern. As I understand it, this trinitarian doctrine of God is rooted not in the speculative needs of theological experts but in the concern to deal seriously with the actual experience of salvation in Jesus Christ, in particular with Easter and Pentecost, and all that they imply for the Christian understanding of God. For the Christian communities, these were eschatological events. The only interpretation of them that made sense was that they represented unparalleled initiatives by God himself. But the converse was also true: as far as Christian faith was concerned, in the ministry of Jesus it was God himself who "came to expression." It became impossible for the church to think of God without Jesus, and without the Spirit who is at work in and among Christians, or, conversely, to think of Jesus and the Spirit without God. What was at stake here for the church was nothing less than its own foundation, namely, the true interpretation of the history of salvation and liberation in Jesus Christ. The Creed is the confession of faith in the God of this history, who is not self-evident, this God who is not to be confused with but is inseparably bound up with the name of Jesus. This is the God whom the church confesses in the First, Second, and Third Articles of the Creed.

No Authoritarian Patriarch

It is against this background that the first three credal definitions of God are to be understood. This is particularly true in the case of the "I believe in God, the Father . . ."

The name "Father" has always been a well-known appellation for God in the world's religions. To confine ourselves here just to the ancient world, Zeus is described in Homer as the "father of humanity and of the gods." Here the reference is not only to an "origin" in the sense of the divine "begetting," but also to the paramount authority of the supreme God in the whole cosmos. The concept of "father" was even used by the great philosophers, as when Plato, speaking in the *Timaeus* of the creation myth, calls the idea of the Good the "father" of all things. Through the intermediary of the Stoics, "father" became the usual term to describe God in Hellenistic philosophy and Greek religion.

By adopting this terminology, is the Creed referring us to the general history of religion, attaching itself to the riches of this history? Is it staking out for itself a background against which it will only subsequently deploy its own distinctive ideas, to be specified in detail only in the Second Article? The opening words of the Apostles' Creed have often been interpreted this way, especially in the modern period. They have been regarded as an affirmation of what is true generally, universally, and for all human beings, and precisely for this reason there was a definite preference for the First Article. One has to respect some of the reasons that led people to adopt this interpretation. I am thinking, for example, of the Deists and rationalists and of their profound dislike of orthodox hairsplitting and the dogmatic niceties over which so much blood was spilled in the era of the religious wars. But justice cannot be done to the Apostles' Creed by proceeding in this way. The three articles of the Creed cannot be divorced from each other, still less treated as rivals to be played off one against the other. All three refer to the one common foundation, to the eschatological history of redemption in Jesus Christ.

If we are to understand the definition of God as "Father," this common point of reference is quite indispensable. The decisive background for faith in God as "Father" is not general history and the philosophy of religion, rather it is specifically biblical history, above all the history of Jesus of Nazareth. We may be able to see more clearly here if we bear in mind the baptismal context, that is, the original life setting of the Creed. Baptism with its confession of faith certainly did not signify even a momentary lingering on the terrain of religion in general. On the contrary, it was a determined and clearcut departure from the realm of the "gods" into the realm of the God of Jesus Christ. And it is to this realm that the name "Father" points.

This is true not just in principle, as regards the trinitarian form, or structure, of the Creed, but also concretely, as regards the substantive contents of this history. For the "father motif" plays an important part in this history, both in Jesus' understanding of God and in the apostolic interpretation of the christological "history of God." We turn briefly to each of these aspects.

The use of the term "father" by Jesus of Nazareth pointed to a fundamental dimension of Jesus' faith in God. New Testament scholars are in no doubt on that score. As has already been pointed out, the father motif was certainly no novelty in the vocabulary of the history of religion or in Jesus' own times. To the examples already given can be added others from the Old Testament and the Jewish tradition. But Jesus gives the name "father" a unique and characteristic thrust, or, more precisely, application. When the term "father" is used in the Gospels, the dimensions it brings emphatically to the fore are those of a distinctive and almost tender intimacy, love, and trust, whereas the authoritarian patriarchal dimensions usually associated with the term take a back seat.

In this connection the original Aramaic spoken by Jesus is pertinent: the word he actually used was "Abba." This was the diminutive form of address used by children within the inner circle of the family. Its equivalent in the Greek is *pappa* rather than *pater*, in English "daddy" rather than "father." How are we to interpret this? Certainly not as a sort of theological infantilism, a casual "buddy-ness" in the conception of God as if it were a matter of being pals with the deity. The same Jesus of Nazareth also spoke of God the father in a way that leaves no room for doubt as to that Father's majesty and sovereignty; and the Apostles' Creed is clearly thinking along the same lines when it combines the name "father" with what is clearly an attribute—"almighty." But this is certainly consonant with other characteristic sayings of Jesus that emphasize the intimate connection between children and the kingdom of God (Mark 10:15), specifically in the notion of covenant—the fidelity and trust which, on Jesus' testimony,

49

bind this father and his children together in spite of everything, un-conditionally.

On the basis of exhaustive studies of the word "Abba" in the teaching of Jesus, Joachim Jeremias reached the conclusion, which I personally find convincing, that the distinctive message of Jesus comes out particularly clearly in this mode of address:

> There are no analogies to the message of Jesus. . . . There are no parallels for the authority with which he ventured to address God as "Abba." Simply to recognize the fact that in the word "Abba" we hear the *ipsissima vox* of Jesus himself is to find ourselves confronted—provided we do not make light of this term—with the sublime claim of Jesus. To read the parable of the lost son, which is part of the original strata of the tradition, and to notice as we do so that in this parable, in which Jesus describes the inconceivable pardoning kindness of God, he is justifying his own table-fellowship with tax-collectors and sinners, is once again to be confronted with the claim of Jesus to be God's representative and plenipotentiary.[2]

At this point the apostolic Christology—which is the other aspect of the New Testament use of "father" as a name for God—takes up the story. In the light of the events of Easter, the central motif of Jesus' message about God is now fleshed out—it literally acquires "flesh and blood"—from the whole history and destiny of Jesus of Nazareth. The unconditional character of the sacrificial love of the father for his children is now understood not just verbally but fac-tually; his sacrifice was even unto death, indeed through and beyond death. The cross and resurrection became the "bearings" by which God's location—indeed God's very being—was defined. *Ecce Pater*—"Behold the Father!"—means, in New Testament terminology, "Behold the God of the cross—the God of the resurrection!" It is to this God that the apostolic message bears witness; it is to this Father—the "father of Jesus Christ" as the New Testament repeatedly declares—that the Apostles' Creed bears witness.

This simple name of "Father" thus signals a complete revolution in the concept of God, accomplished in the message and, above all, in the destiny of Jesus Christ. Jesus Christ is "Immanuel"—God with us, the God who is really close, but now in the profoundest, most binding, and really unconditional sense—that of his incarnation, his identification with sons and daughters in life and in death, for all eternity. Here is God not only in the majesty and height of his heavenly life but also in the depths of his earthly life and destiny. This God is the Father confessed in the Apostles' Creed.

We have every reason in our theological work to follow the implications of this revolution in the concept of God. Loyal adherence to the distinctively New Testament concept of the fatherhood of God is theologically more important than ever today. Without it, theologians lean toward authoritarian and patriarchalist views of God. The history of Christian doctrine shows how often such tendencies prevail when the concept of the divine fatherhood is not christologically informed and controlled. History so far has largely been dominated by the patriarchal tradition, by a social order ruled by the "fathers." In that tradition the supreme gods had correspondingly authoritarian features. They were heavenly authorities, rulers, cosmic policemen. Not even the history of Christian theology remained untainted by this conception.

The patriarchal view of the divine fatherhood was from the outset a serious misunderstanding, but in our present culture it is a fatal one. For in government and in society today—one hopes!—the age of authoritarian patriarchalism and paternalism is long gone. A paternalistic concept of God in theology and church today would be all the more incredible.

Accordingly it becomes all the more necessary today to concentrate attention on the christological basis of the apostolic appellation of God as "father." The father of Jesus Christ is an utterly unpaternalistic father. We have already pointed out—in our quotation from Jeremias—the importance of the parable of the lost son in this connection. Consider the figure of the father in that parable. Contrary to all the laws and customs of the time, he does not stand in his sons' way but lets them have their freedom, even in the extremely risky and misunderstood form chosen by his younger son. And when the dropout shamefacedly returns, the father, instead of first reading the riot act, laying down conditions and demanding restitution, hurries out to meet his returning son: "While he was yet at a distance, his father saw him and had compassion, and *ran* and embraced him and kissed him." Such behavior was quite unheard of in the patriarchal code. The apostolic concept of the divine fatherhood is stamped precisely with this note of unexpectedness in the conduct of the father. It runs quite counter to all pagan and pseudo-Christian ideas

51

of God. Far from being just an extension of the authoritarian patriarchalist mentality and system, this apostolic concept of the father who comes forth to meet us is a challenge to it in all its forms.

The Omnipotence of Nonviolent Love

Alongside the basic theological affirmation of the Apostles' Creed, "I believe in God the Father," stands the forthright qualification "the Almighty." How is this to be explained? As a sort of theological hiccup, a reckless leap into the dark, a retreat from the realm of freedom into the realm of necessity? As an abandonment of the warm title "father" for the clinical coldness of strictly theological concepts? That is the impression many of us quite understandably have of it. We are put off by omnipotence. It is a cold concept. We are quite right to be critical of all undefined power—and doubly critical of all undifferentiated omnipotence. What I have in mind here are not only the dehumanizing aspects of political power as it has sometimes been uncritically conceived and exercised historically, though it is easy to understand Jacob Burckhardt when with recent European history in mind he describes power as evil in and of itself—and he did not live to see the worst forms of the totalitarian abuse of power! I am also thinking, however, of the disturbing historical effects of the preaching of omnipotence in Christian theology and in the life of the church. How easily and how frequently has the problem of the divine omnipotence been misunderstood and even abused as if it were a general philosophical problem, a question of the limits—or the absence of limits—to the divine power.

Take, for example, the discussions of omnipotence in scholastic theology. The scholastics were much troubled by this question and indeed from two points of view, each characteristic of one polar position in this controversy. In the first place, they were concerned for the rational character and the natural order of the world. The divine omnipotence has its limit in the created order: "Things which are inherently contradictory do not come within the divine omnipotence because they lack any basis for their possibility."[3] God has no power, for example, to make a triangle the sum of whose three angles does not equal two right angles. Or, to take another example frequently discussed, while God can certainly destroy the city of Rome, he cannot have it blotted out of history, as if it had never existed.

Another group of scholastics took a different view and argued that from the side of nature no limits could be set to the sovereign omnipotence of God. This view was incisively presented by Peter Damian (1007–1072) in his work on the Divine Omnipotence: "He who gave nature its origin can easily cancel its necessity if he so wills." Even that pillar of Western logic, the principle of contradiction (in any given circumstance nothing can at one and the same time both exist and not exist), did not apply to God. Even God can turn something that has happened into something that has not happened. The divine omnipotence is the supreme authority bar none.

I am not suggesting that the scholastics—or those in other ages who argued along similar lines—were simply mistaken in their speculations. The concerns behind their cogitations certainly have to be taken seriously. First, there was a legitimate concern that the divine omnipotence should not be misinterpreted in an irrational way as a charter for arbitrariness in heaven or on earth. Second, there was a concern, especially important for theology, not to fit the freedom of God too smoothly into the natural orders and in this way to "domesticate" the sovereign God in accordance with our own human criteria. But both these scholastic efforts have one feature in common: their approach to the problem of the divine omnipotence is logical and ontological rather than concretely theological. They do not approach the problem in the context of Christology and soteriology. Not surprisingly, therefore, they often landed themselves in speculative blind alleys.

What the Apostles' Creed is affirming here has a quite different focus. It may be helpful at this point to note a difference of emphasis between the Latin and Greek texts of the Creed. Where the Latin uses the adjective *omnipotens* (almighty), the Greek has the more pregnant term *pantokrator* (ruler of all things). Heinrich Vogel gives the following explanation of this difference: "*Pantocrator* has a personal dimension, whereas *omnipotens* is an adjective. But omnipotence is not a divine attribute; it denotes God Himself."[4] In other words, what concerns the Apostles' Creed is not the general problem of omnipotence but the omnipotence of *God*. "Almighty," therefore, is not an empty concept but filled with content from the history of salvation. Specifically, the term directs us to the history of the prophetic and apostolic faith of the Bible, not to the rarefied heights of philosophical speculation.

The prophetic and apostolic faith! Both aspects must be stressed. First, the prophetic Old Testament faith: the term *pantocrator* echoes the Old Testament definition of God as *Yahweh Zeba'oth*, "Lord of hosts," "Lord of the powers." This brings out the connection with the history of Israel and, above all, with the experiences of the people of God within this eventful history. The key event in this history was undoubtedly the Exodus, the joyful departure of former slaves into a newfound freedom, that inner and outer freedom which, though repeatedly imperilled, is also constantly being renewed.

This exodus event was the focus of the prophetic faith and the key to its proclamation of God's power and omnipotence: "Thou didst bring Thy people Israel out of the land of Egypt with signs and wonders, with a strong hand and outstretched arm, and with great terror" (Jer. 32:31). At the same time, Israel looked back to this event as the foundation of the covenant between God and his people, the ground of his liberating and faithful, judging and renewing presence amid all the dangers to which this people individually and collectively were exposed in the course of their lives. To grasp the Old Testament idea of God's omnipotence it is essential to keep in mind the Exodus as its origin and the Covenant as its setting. The basis of Israel's faith in the divine omnipotence is not some notion about unbounded caprice but a coherent and connected event of liberation. It is always to be understood and attested, therefore, not as the unlimited and unpredictable arbitrariness of some hidden divinity but as the revealed faithfulness of the God who delivers his people.

The apostolic preaching takes up this prophetic heritage and enriches and deepens it by particularizing it in a wholly new way. God's omnipotence is experienced in cross and resurrection and proclaimed by reference to these Easter events. One of the credal formulas—one of the definitions of God—most frequently used in the New Testament is the confession of faith in "him that raised from the dead Jesus our Lord" (Rom. 4:24; cf. 8:11; 10:9; Acts 3:15; 4:10; 1 Cor. 6:14; 15:15). As Vogel puts it: "The resurrection of the One who in final weakness was delivered up for us all is the Pantocrator's central act of sovereignty."[5] This has decisive implications for the New Testament view of omnipotence. "The divine omnipotence (unlike abstract concepts of power) is essentially its power to take the form of the man on the cross and, in all the weakness and helplessness of that form, nevertheless to conquer."[6]

I referred earlier to the revolution in the concept of God implicit in the distinctive use of "father" for the divine name in the teaching of Jesus. We could equally well speak of a revolution in the concept of power taking place in the New Testament in connection with the history of Jesus Christ. First, in the life of Jesus himself, it is characterized not by the love of power but by the power of love. Second, from the standpoint of the apostolic Easter message, the divine omnipotence takes concrete form in the fate of Jesus of Nazareth and this means in the form not of an arbitrary and willful despotism but of a love that is free, free even to make the final sacrifice. As the New Testament witnesses interpret it, here is the supreme demonstration of the Spirit and of power—the preeminence, the "omnipotence," of nonviolent love.

The distinctively biblical view of God's omnipotence has consequences not only in doctrine but also in ethics. It impels us toward a "transvaluation of all values," especially those of power and of the marketplace. It does not go as far as Jacob Burckhardt and describe power as essentially evil. That would be oversimplification. In the ordering of our personal life and above all in our social life, it is impossible to ignore the reality of power and, above all, its positive potential. But the history of Christ confronts us in our understanding and exercise of power with radically critical questions. It enquires into the conditions and aims of power. If power is not essentially evil, neither is it essentially good.

Karl Barth, by insisting on the christological dimension of the divine omnipotence, helped more than most theologians to clarify, specify, and reevaluate this concept. In his *Dogmatics in Outline*, with special reference to the Nazis' totalitarian worship of power, he warns against every unqualified and irrational positivism or even fetishism of power:

> This intoxicating thought of power is the chaos, the *tohu wabohu* on which God in his creation turned his back, which he rejected when he created heaven and earth. It is the *opposite* of God. . . . Where "power in itself" is honored and worshipped, where "power in itself" wants to be the authority and to impose its law, we are confronted with the "revolution of Nihilism." . . . From the very beginning, God's power is the power of justice. . . . This power of God is the power of his free love in Jesus Christ.[7]

Justice and love are the two coordinates that not only determine the direction of the critical questions to be put to all totalitarian and authoritarian exercise of power but also stake out the perspectives of a legitimate view of power. A moment ago I used the phrase "the power of nonviolent love." That expression points the direction we must take when we confess our faith in "God the Father Almighty." It indicates this direction not in the sense of a foolproof prescription, an ever-ready model, but in the sense of an impetus and signpost inviting us to the unwearying search for new possibilities of demolishing individual and structural lovelessness of every kind and of strengthening and developing nonviolent relationships in church and society, each of us beginning at the point where we actually live and work. Only in the practice of nonviolent love do we set the seal of a genuine "Amen" to the confession of faith in God the almighty Father.

Lest there be any misunderstanding, however, be it noted again that in this clause too the standpoint of the Creed from start to finish is that not of "law" but of "good news." What is at stake in all of this is God's omnipotence—which we cannot establish but can only witness to in faith. Yet precisely as "gospel" this article of faith is supremely relevant for today, not least of all in the political realm. Faith in the divine omnipotence demythologizes all other powers, and by doing so removes the element of fatalism from our human world, including the world of politics. In this respect it performs a singular service today. We are all aware that the world in which we live is perishing because of its lack of practical solidarity, because of its violent lovelessness in individual and international relationships. This microcosmic and macrocosmic deficiency is threatening us all with destruction. The more alert among us are alarmed and frightened by it. But it also depresses and inhibits us. Faced with seemingly insoluble problems, it is easy for us to become cynical and apathetic. We have only to consider the current political scene: Some try to muddle through, others try to shoot their way out. Politically, both approaches represent a "sickness unto death."

In this situation it helps if we remember the apostolic faith. To take the risk of nonviolent love, to seek ways of living in solidarity with all other human beings—these are not an oppressive imperative imposed upon us, to be achieved or enforced by desperate efforts on our part, cost what it may. On the contrary, even in failure, even in powerlessness of all kinds, this way is the one that carries the seeds of the future, the way that can influence the shape of things to come. We have God the Almighty behind us, or rather before us, when we are called to say No to violence and Yes to love. We have no reason, therefore, to become fatalistic or to succumb to political immobility. To discover and seize the opportunities of nonviolent love is something we are not condemned to do but something we are encouraged, indeed authorized and enabled to do. Believing in God the Father Almighty, it is never futile to commit ourselves in this direction, and to do so with no illusions, but soberly, persistently, and resolutely. For in God's sight this world of ours, while it may be a fallen world, is never an abandoned world. It remains what it has always been—a world upheld and sustained by the almighty Father, and therefore a world that we too are to uphold in hope.

This brings us then, to the final affirmation of the First Article: God, the Father, the Almighty, is the Creator of heaven and earth.

6

Maker of
Heaven and Earth

A Distinctively Biblical Dimension

In comparing the texts of the three creeds of the ancient church—
the Roman Creed, the Nicene Creed, and the Apostles' Creed—we
notice at once that the only clause in the First Article in which there
is a striking variation is here, in the description of God the Father
Almighty as "Maker of heaven and earth." This clause is absent
altogether from the Roman Creed, whereas in the Nicene Creed it is
expanded by the addition of the words: "and of all things visible and
invisible."

What significance do these variations have? Do they indicate a
relative uncertainty at this point on the part of the ancient church?
Probably not. There is no evidence of any conflict of opinion about
faith in the Creator in the circles actually responsible for the three
credal texts. To be sure, in the turbulent early period of doctrinal
history there were currents of thought that openly or covertly
registered their doubts in this respect. The Gnostics, for example, in
their view of the cosmos would not allow a visible creation to be part
of God-given reality. The Docetists for similar reasons had serious
problems with the idea of a real incarnation of the divine Logos. In
their doctrine of God and redemption the followers of Marcion
posited a deep gulf, indeed a radical conflict, between the beneficent
Father of Jesus Christ and the malignant demiurge of creation. In
these circles, which were very influential in some respects, the clause
"Maker of heaven and earth" was challenged wherever it was construed as a reference to the "Father of Jesus Christ."

But our three texts originated in none of these currents of thought.
On the contrary, they were united in resisting the dangers of
Gnosticism and Docetism. They had their roots in the common faith

59

of the apostolic church—for which the Old Testament view of creation was an indispensable part of its prophetic foundation. Faced with the specific challenges of their diverse situations, they did of course have their different emphases—the Nicene Creed its stronger emphases, the earlier Roman Creed its weaker ones (probably because it assumed that the appellation "Father Almighty" already included God's being as Creator). All three creeds, however, are in agreement that the being of God as Creator is to be confessed as an integral part of the Christian faith in God. For, from the very beginning, it was the creation motif that clearly set the biblical faith apart from the other contemporary faiths and philosophies that surrounded it. In the intellectual environment of Hellenistic culture and its oriental religions, Christians and Jews stood for a distinctive view of God's world, a view that most other people found offensive. What was this view? I shall try to describe its essential aspects under three headings: the theological (in the narrower meaning of that term), the cosmological, and the anthropological.

Undisputed Authorship

The theological aspect is undoubtedly primary in the Apostles' Creed. The clause "Maker of heaven and earth" is primarily a statement about "God the Father Almighty." It is intended as a supplement, a rider, to what precedes it. God's being as Creator is regarded in the Creed as the consequence rather than as the basis and justification of its trinitarian faith in God. We have already seen that in the Creed God's fatherhood is understood not in any general patriarchal sense but first and foremost with reference to the history of Jesus Christ. And knowledge of the Almighty—of *Yahweh Zeba'oth*, of the God who raised Jesus from the dead—is rooted, according to the Bible, not in the universal processes of the world of nature but in the covenant history of Israel and in the events of Easter.

This "status" assigned to belief in creation corresponds, moreover, to the view of the Old Testament. Old Testament scholars point out that the Old Testament account of creation is a relatively late formulation. The prophetic faith does not root in creation and then move on to the Exodus as its consequence. Its course is precisely the reverse: Meditation on the mighty acts of Yahweh in establishing his covenant in history is what gave rise to Israel's faith in creation. Karl Barth sums this up in a succinct formula that rightly plays an important role in his doctrine of creation: the covenant is the "inner basis of the creation," and the creation is the "external basis of the covenant."[1]

If the first statement is clearly affirmed, the second—faith in the creation as the logical consequence—must also be taken seriously. In the present context this means that the "supplementary" clause—"Maker of heaven and earth"—is no arbitrary and optional rider but a necessary and solidly grounded addition. For the God of Israel, the father of Jesus Christ—or, in the concrete context of the baptismal creed, the God confessed by the recipient of baptism—is no local tribal deity, no sectarian chieftain or private savior. He is the one God, the Almighty, who is related to—and in faith to be related to—the whole of reality; he is in other words the "Maker of heaven and earth."

According to the biblical witness in contrast to most mythologies and religions, there is no doubt concerning the origin of all things; there is no hesitation as to the paternity (or maternity), the authorship of the created universe. The father is known! He is the Father Almighty, the God of Israel: "In the beginning God made the heaven and the earth." The classic Old Testament term for "make," or "create," used here in Gen. 1:1 is instructive in this respect. As *bara* is used in the Old Testament, God—more specifically the God of Israel and never some alien divinity—is always the subject of the statement (cf. Ezek. 28:13, 15); and since in the Old Testament this verb is always reserved for God alone this kind of creation is quite without parallel.[2] Neither nature nor history, neither mind nor matter has any world-creating powers that could compete with God in his sovereign action as Creator. He who creates "in the beginning" is the *One*. Here in the very idea of creation is to be found one of the earliest roots of the classic formulation "to God alone be the glory" (*soli deo gloria*).

In the Old Testament this emphasis on the incomparable sovereignty of the Creator permeates the whole of piety and life. In an essay on "Aspects of the Old Testament View of the World," Gerhard von Rad has pointed out, for example, the vital significance of the prohibition of images for the biblical view of creation. In the various "image religions" it encountered Israel came upon views of God and the world in which the sacred and the profane were combined and merged. All such "nature religions" were intolerable to

61

the faith of Israel. They tied the Creator to circumstances of the created world and thereby trespassed on his sovereignty and glory. "In the prohibition of images, the boundary between God and the world was defined differently and very much more sharply for Israel than was the case with the image religions. Yahweh was not one of the basic world forces, nor even the sum total of them all, but their Creator."[3] The Apostles' Creed with its "I believe in . . . the Maker of heaven and earth" follows precisely the same line as the First Commandment of the Decalogue: "You shall have no other gods before Me" (Exod. 20:3).

A Positive and Critical View of the World

Although the primary focus of the faith expressed in this credal clause is on God the Creator, this is not to be taken as a flight from the world or even as a desecularization of the faith along acosmist lines, that is, denying the existence of a universe distinct from God. Such a tendency is certainly present in the history of religion generally and even in part of the church's history. That religious folk usually withdraw from the world is almost an axiom of the religious world view. For many religious people whatever their reasons—mythological, mystical, or existentialist—the logical consequence of this is separation from the world, or even denial of the world.

The Creed can hardly be accused of such an attitude. To be sure, its attention is unmistakably concentrated on God. Its confession is focused on the triune God. It knows no other name to confess. But this God is not a "world-forsaking" but a "world-seeking" God. This orientation, this character of the triune God is attested already in the two preceding definitions, "Father" and "the Almighty"; the present clause only serves to reinforce this witness. In the presence of this God it would be a mistake to say with the mystics: "If I may only have Thee, I ask not for heaven and earth." In the context of biblical piety we should say instead: "If I may only have Thee, I ask *all the more* for heaven and earth!"

This, at any rate, is the language of the Apostles' Creed: "Maker of heaven and earth." In his being as Creator, God reveals his resolve not to remain alone but to follow his "propensity to communion" (traced by dogmatics in its concept of the Trinity) and establish a new reality, namely, heaven and earth as the sum total of all created being. So the world actually *exists*. It is rooted and grounded in the loving decision of God the Father Almighty. And because this divine love purposes genuine relationship, genuine encounter, the world is not a sham and a fraud, not a basically suspect and illusory reality, but the real and unambiguously good creation of God. The creation story in Genesis, speaking from the standpoint of God himself, clearly confirms this: "And God saw everything that he had made, and behold, it was very good" (Gen. 1:31).

It would be a mistake to conclude that we could turn the implications of this approach into a complete ontology. This is hardly what the Apostles' Creed has in mind. What is legitimate, however, is that we should look for a "cosmological dimension" of this credal affirmation. It is at this point in the Creed that the cosmic reality enters its field of vision and is explicitly referred to. It may be wise, therefore, to inquire into this cosmological aspect. Two points need to be made.

1. Faith in God the Creator determines the basic structure of a theological view of the world. It does this in the sense that "the creation is established in contingency; it persists in constancy."[4] Both these aspects, the contingency and the constancy must be emphasized together, in their incessant interaction.

First, with respect to contingency: The world is not an absolute, self-established and, in this sense, self-sufficient reality. From the biblical standpoint, the world is not the cosmos of antiquity, the "visible God," the "completed" being, perfect in itself and eternally at rest. This is why the world can never be "deified." In this connection, too, the prohibition of images acquires a critical role: faith in the divine act of creation demythologizes the world and prevents any absolutizing of its values and conditions. Since it is a contingent reality—since, in more specifically theological terms, it has been created by a free decision—the world must be regarded and ordered as an open reality. Since it is not at rest in itself, we are not to leave it undisturbed and "at rest." The creation is the beginning but not the end; it points beyond itself to a "new heaven and a new earth" (Rev. 21:1). Ludwig Köhler states the point as follows: "In Old Testament theology, creation is an eschatological concept. To say that God is Creator of the world is to say that he embraces the whole of time, all times, ruling and ordering, setting the goal and fulfilling it."[5]

At the same time, by affirming that God is the Creator, the Creed

63

also points to the constancy of the creation. The contingent world is not a creature abandoned to chaos and meaninglessness. It owes its existence not to some wildly arbitrary freedom but to God's free "decree" and stands therefore in the light of God's primordial *and* eschatological Yes. This divine Yes does not remain unchallenged and uncontradicted. The first two chapters of Genesis are followed by a third. The biblical faith in creation is under no illusions but knows that the world's being is at risk and its meaning assailed. Both in the Old and New Testaments we find prophetic laments at the state of the world. We need only recall Job and Ecclesiastes! Yet precisely in a book such as Job it finally becomes clear that, however radically imperiled and alienated the world may be, it is nevertheless not an abandoned world. It continues to be upheld and preserved, not by the constancy of "healthy elements" in nature or history, church or society, but by the constancy or, in more specifically biblical terms, by the faithfulness of God. It is basically because of this faithfulness of the Creator, emphatically corroborated in God's covenant with Noah and "every living creature" (Gen. 9:9), that the biblical witnesses (the psalmists for example), despite all they have concretely to lament, again and again burst into praise of God in view of his creation and, in view of God, into praise of his creation.

By this dialectical combination of the two elements of constancy and contingency in its basic structure, the biblical faith in creation has the leavening effect of an ontology that is positive (though not positivist), soberly realistic, and dynamic. Without this faith in creation, which helped to shape it, the notion of a "Christian civilization"—whatever its attendant risks—would have been inconceivable.

2. The second cosmological point concerns the formula "heaven and earth." Firmly anchored in the Bible, this two-term formula denotes in the first place simply the whole of created reality. The meaning of the two separate terms is suggested by the Nicene Creed, which adds the words "all things visible and invisible." "Earth," then means not simply the geographical planet but the entire realm of visible reality accessible to humanity, and "heaven" means the invisible world of God—what the Creed has chiefly in mind are the angels and spirits that comprise the invisible creation. What are we to make of this? Does it not represent a hopelessly antiquated picture of reality?

It does indeed. Yet behind the outdated images there are

cosmological insights that we ignore at our peril. First, the clear-cut "and": The creation includes not only the earth but also heaven. This little conjunction brings all of reality into common alignment as a single creation related to God, yet distinct from God. There is no "divine reality" alongside God; even in its highest reaches, the creation remains creation—a creature and not the Creator.

> What is opposed here is not merely all the astral idols of the ancient world but also the divinization of the "world of spirit," the world of ideas and ideals whose property is to be "invisible," so frequently encountered in the philosophy of religion. Even the ideas of the good, the true, and the beautiful in Plato's view of the divine—to name just one example—are creatures![6]

The liberating promise of this vision is voiced, and given christological depth, by Paul, "For I am sure that neither death, nor life, nor angels, nor principalities, nor things present, nor things to come, nor powers, nor height, nor depth, nor anything else in all creation, will be able to separate us from the love of God in Christ Jesus our Lord" (Rom. 8:38f.).

The little word "and," however, is not only conjunctive but also disjunctive: It affirms not only the unity of all creation, of heaven and earth, but also the distinction between these two realms within the one created reality. Heaven is not earth, and earth is not heaven. Creation consists not only of visible things but also of invisible things. This view of the world may strike some people as odd, especially when we consider the images associated with the so-called invisible world at the time the Creed came into being—and for a long time thereafter—such things as angels, spirits, supernatural forces and powers. But the intended meaning of a statement is not completely dependent on the dated imagery connected with its formulation. Even if the illustrative material has changed, the statement still has something of permanent importance to affirm. Paradoxical as it may seem at first sight, this distinction between heaven and earth is a profoundly realistic one, still relevant today. It requires us to exercise restraint and discrimination with respect to the world we regard as the "object" of our knowledge and action. God's creation is not limited to its "visible" aspects, that is, its "objective" accessibility. It has dimensions to which we simply have no access. "The reality of the world created by

God has other dimensions besides those that are ontologically accessible to us. We would be wise not to imprison ourselves within the immanence posited by our particular world view."[7]

We must all begin to take more seriously once again this realistic and critical aspect of the old concept of heaven. Reference has already been made to the positive, realistic, and dynamic elements introduced into Western thinking by the biblical faith in creation. But how often has this "positive" view of the world been turned into a "positivist" view, this "realistic" view into a "materialist" view, this "dynamic" view into an "aggressive" view!

The need today is for a more critical approach at this point. We would be wise, therefore, to take more seriously today this other dimension of faith in God the Creator, namely, the distinction between earth and heaven, between a reality that is accessible to human knowledge and action and a reality that is not. In modern times impatient rationalists have often consigned this distinction to the scrapheap as so much mythological junk. In view of the mythological components of traditional ontology, they had some justification for doing so. It is surely going too far, however, to lose sight altogether of the "heaven" dimension of creation by abandoning all respect for that portion of reality which is inaccessible to us and cannot be manipulated by us, while at the same time regarding the "earth" of the technocrats as the sole relevant reality. We do not wish to disparage the enormous positive and revolutionary achievements realized through this extreme concentration on the earth. In the long run, however, the enormous progress registered by this way of life has had its price. Think of the dangerous one-sidedness that threatens the life of humanity and even the existence of the world. God's world, the natural world, yes the whole creation in its depth and richness, has been put at risk. Indeed to a perilous degree it has already been destroyed by being reduced to a single dimension. Witness the ecological crisis and the superficiality of life in the supposedly developed nations.

Success or failure in correcting this lopsidedness in our relationship to the world will be of vital importance for the future of humankind, indeed, for the future of the whole creation. There are no easy answers to this problem. What is needed is a multiple strategy to revolutionize both our thinking and our behavior. Relevant contributions could here be suggested and stimulated by the cosmological aspects of the biblical concept of creation and of faith in God as the Maker of heaven and earth.

Human Right and Divine Grace

I turn in conclusion to the personal and anthropological dimension of this credal clause. In the matter of faith in God the Creator, Protestant theology and piety have largely been guided by Luther's answer to the question as to the meaning of the First Article, offered in his Small Catechism of 1529:

> I believe that God has created me and all that exists; that he has given me and still sustains my body and soul, all my limbs and senses, my reason and all the faculties of my mind, together with food and clothing, house and home, family and property; that he provides me daily and abundantly with all the necessities of life, protects me from all danger and preserves me from all evil.[8]

Between the credal text and Luther's interpretation, there is a marked shift of emphasis: the affirmation of the Creator of heaven and earth becomes focused on the first-person singular of the confessing subject. This shift of emphasis was not without its dangers. By transferring the main weight of the confession from faith in the Creator to the vital interests of the confessing Christian, characteristic tendencies in Protestantism were reinforced that led in the direction of a privatization of the faith in creation. It also lent credence to the assumption that the world had been created exclusively for humanity's sake, as our object, our domain. The biblical awareness that not just humanity but also the whole of creation is directly related to the Creator and must therefore be regarded and treated as our fellow creature, having a relative right to life independently of us, was weakened precisely in an age that had a fatal tendency anyway to regard nature, including the animal world, as the "world of objects" and to measure its worth solely in terms of its usefulness to people and its value. The dangerous consequences of this lopsided treatment of the world are becoming manifest in the distorted relationship between ourselves and nature, the so-called environmental crisis. What is needed is a critical—self-critical—examination of Luther's shift of emphasis.

In at least two respects, however, this presumed flaw in Luther's catechetical answer has its ongoing validity. First, by personalizing and updating the view of creation, Luther is faithful to an important interest of the biblical faith. Faith in the Creator is not a retrospective causal theory about the world; it is a present-oriented existential confession that affects and transforms our being in the world today—and not just our being in the world in the sense of a philosophical or religious self-understanding, important as this aspect of the faith in creation undoubtedly is, but our being in the world in *all* its dimensions. This is Luther's legitimate concern, and in this respect he is faithful to the direction indicated by the Apostles' Creed, particularly in its original character as a baptismal confession of faith.

Also of theological significance here is the language used by Luther. In a manner that seems almost naive, he evokes a richly colorful blend of the most ordinary relationships and conditions of our normal daily life. Faith in the creation has a "positive" aspect—a dogged bias in favor of created life, created things, and against any vilification of and contempt for one or another area of reality, spiritual or material, natural or historical, objective or nonobjective, heaven or earth.

It is in this direction that I look for the anthropological significance of this credal affirmation. Faith in the "Maker of heaven and earth" involves the disclosure of a promise. In this faith, we are assured that neither as a race nor as individuals have we been thrown into this world by some blind fate. We are not prisoners of the cosmic forces. In Genesis I even the stars, even sun and moon—the classic divine powers—are spoken of as created bodies, and hence dedivinized.

Moreover, as has already been pointed out, faith in the Creator also paves the way for a similar dedivinization in the realm of political history, whereby all fatalism is banished from the sphere of public affairs. Significantly enough, it was precisely when things looked hopeless for the people of ancient Israel that this faith in the Creator played a preeminent part as, for example, in Second Isaiah, unquestionably the most impressive Old Testament witness to faith in God the Creator. This is no accident but wholly consistent with the central thrust of faith. Since God is the sole Creator, nowhere in the whole world of his creation is there any power that could legitimately claim final authority over the nations. There is no earthly (or heavenly) power into whose hands God's people could be completely delivered.

This is why Isaiah, with this horizon of faith, can summon his afflicted people: "Fear not, for I am with you!" (Isa. 41:10 *passim*).

As in political affairs, so also in the personal realm, we human beings are creatures. We are limited and confined. None of us is, in spirit or in body, an absolutely sovereign being, wholly independent of our counterparts, that is, of God and other human beings. The subjectivity we are to cultivate as beings made in the divine image is undoubtedly part and parcel of our humanity, but it is and remains the subjectivity of finite creatures, creatures who are dependent on others and who are stricken and afflicted by sin and death. Biblically, there is no such thing as an "anthropology of glory," no aseity or independent existence of the human world. At the same time, however, it is necessary—and indeed a privilege—to remember the other side of the picture: From the biblical standpoint, to be a creature means not only to have the general characteristics of contingency, dependence, finitude, and mortality, but also, at the same time, to be adopted into the divine covenant, to be related to the Creator at all times—at the beginning and end of life and at all points in between. From the biblical standpoint, the decisive affirmation about our human condition in the light of faith in the Creator is this: the mandate to be *human* and the right to be human is rooted and grounded in God himself; human existence has unconditional validity. The contingency of our existence is indisputable, but it is not an arbitrary contingency. It represents the free decision of the Creator in favor of our existence—the contingency of grace. Here, in the witness of God's free grace focused directly on the creature, and in the resulting establishment of this unconditional human right, is the liberating significance of the apostolic (and prophetic) statement: "I believe in God . . . Maker of heaven and earth."

7

And in Jesus Christ

The Heart of the Apostolic Faith

"The starting point and dogmatic center of Christian faith is faith in Jesus Christ." Thus does Oscar Cullmann succinctly summarize the results of his study of the earliest Christian confessions.[1] The statement is first of all a historical statement, one that Cullmann seeks to verify by a careful analysis of ancient Christian credal formulas, especially from the New Testament period. The credal statements of the earliest Christians consistently focus on the name and destiny of Jesus Christ. The formula *Kyrios Christos* (Christ is Lord) is certainly the prototype and core of all subsequent confessions of faith.

But there is an even more important aspect to this undoubted historical fact. The "starting point" of the Christian movement is at the same time its "center"; its historical basis is its doctrinal foundation. Sounding in and through the confession of Christ is the heartbeat of the apostolic faith. This is undoubtedly true of the Apostles' Creed too, as indeed of the Roman Creed before it and of the Nicene Creed as well. Even from a purely formal standpoint—and the outward form here corresponds to the inner reality—all these creeds devote much more space in their trinitarian structure to this middle christological section than to the other two articles. Any exposition of the Creed must also respect these diverse proportions as recent commentators have frequently stressed, above all Karl Barth:

> The Second Article does not just follow the First, nor does it just precede the Third; it is the fountain of light by which the other two are lit. . . . Tell me how it stands with your christology and I'll tell you who you are.[2]

This focus on Christology in all Christian Creeds is not something to be taken for granted as routine. Especially from the standpoint of the general history of religions, it represents an offense and an incongruity, a stumbling block and folly, to use the language of the apostle Paul (1 Cor. 1:23). Even from a formal standpoint it was an unheard-of scandal when the Christian missionaries concentrated so uncompromisingly on Jesus Christ. They refused to compete in the marketplace of the Hellenistic religion with its rich and colorful array of tempting possibilities. They refused to go along with the prevailing business practices regarding trade or mutual exchange of offers of salvation and saviors. Instead they called unambiguously for clear-cut decision: "There is no other name under heaven granted to human beings by which we may receive salvation" (Acts 4:12).

Not only formally but also from the material standpoint the Christian missionaries were offensive. It seemed utter folly on the part of those who proclaimed the Christian faith in God (and it is primarily with faith in God that the Creed is concerned) to connect the idea of God so radically with a particular set of events—and such provincial events at that! Did this not make eternal truth completely dependent on transient happenings? To adopt this procedure was surely to revert to primitive religious ideas long ago abandoned by the most advanced contemporary thought, both Jewish and Greek. It is not difficult to understand why the earliest Christians drew sharp criticism on this score already from their contemporaries. The critical questions continue even today: "From a Celsus to a Radhakrishnan, countless voices have been raised in vehement protest at this point—and on specifically religious grounds, above all in defense of a direct mystical relationship to the divine."[3]

From the standpoint of the history of religions, and even more so the history of philosophy, this is a plausible and even logical objection which the church and Christian theologians must heed and deal with in their confession of faith. As regards the Apostles' Creed, however, taking this objection seriously can never mean capitulating to it in such a way as to raise doubts about this christological focus or to diminish its force. The emphasis actually placed on this Second Article, the understanding of it as both historical starting point and dogmatic base and center of the Christian faith, rules out any possibility of flight from its foolishness or disavowal of its scandal. I say this not merely out of respect for the letter of the Apostles' Creed but above all out of respect for its spirit. What is at stake here is the integrity and identity of *Christian* faith as understood by the Creed, that is, nothing less than the distinctively Christian dimension of the faith.

Scandal and Foolishness

Let me mention three basic facets of this emphasis on the person and work of Jesus Christ, in each case with reference to both the philosophical and the strictly theological context.

1. The christological starting point and center of the Creed seems scandalous and foolish, in the first place, in relation to the classic problem of contingency and particularity. In the intellectual world of ancient and particularly in Hellenistic philosophy there was a pronounced tendency to subordinate the particular to the universal, the contingent to the necessary. Metaphysically, the more one thought in universal terms, the closer one came to true being. In the realm of religion the divine mystery was disclosed above all in the renunciation of being in asceticism and mysticism, as one shrugged off the concrete physical and mental realities and turned away from the "many" to concentrate on the "one." Liberation was possible only by detachment; salvation was apart from the body, the world, and the self.

The Christian Creed sets itself in opposition to this tendency. It cleaves to a particular person and to a unique set of historical events. In its view of the world and of God it resists separation from this person and this history.

This has theoretical consequences—for the way we understand things. The mystery of being is disclosed and the salvation of the world takes place, not in some universal and abstract realm, but in what from a conceptual standpoint is contingent and specifically historical reality. "For humans the necessary is the accidental and external; their inward being opens up only as it is approached from the outside. The incognito of God as a human being in history is indispensable—and with it the necessity of freedom."[4] In other words, truth is concrete. Salvation is salvation with a human face. This also has practical consequences—for the way we act. It is precisely *in* the body, the world, and the self that faith, love, and hope are really demonstrated. Far from being realized only in detachment, liberation means redeeming God's promises in and for the creation. It means, on the basis of these promises, commitment and service in the very midst of the real world. The faith that is based on the work and suffering of Jesus would betray its starting point and center—Jesus Christ himself—if on idealistic or religious grounds it were to underestimate or even denigrate the contingent, particular, and personal character of the world.

In both practice and theory, therefore, the Christian faith champions the dignity and importance of every contingent, particular, "accidental" human being. There really is no reason whatever for Christians to be ashamed of this foolishness, which before God and even in the sight of our human world is sheer wisdom—right down to its detailed social implications (cf. 1 Cor. 1:18–29).

2. The scandal and foolishness of the Second Article have another aspect, intimately connected with what has just been said. This aspect concerns God's relation to history or, in more abstract terms, the question of time and eternity. In the Pauline passage just referred to, the apostle uses the two distinct terms "scandal" and "foolishness" in order to distinguish between the respective Jewish and Greek responses to the message of the cross and the history on which it rests. His distinction is a sound one, because these responses differed above all on the relation of God to history and of time to eternity.

In the classic idealist tradition and the tradition of Hellenistic Gnosticism, time and eternity were almost antithetical. As true being, God was understood to be outside of time. Logically, therefore, salvation was also understood as deliverance *from* history, not *in* history. When Christians proclaimed God's presence in the midst of time, in the midst of concrete secular history, this was felt a priori to be foolishness and nonsense. What could the eternal God possibly have to do with the mere semblance which is history?

In the case of the Jews, the situation was different. They not only did not deny but emphatically insisted that God is the Lord of history. This had been Israel's historical experience and this was how the people had been led to interpret that experience. Yahweh had revealed himself in historical events, and with clarity in the event of the Exodus. History, therefore, is not a sphere that has in principle been abandoned by God. Quite the contrary: even in the most dark and distressing times in the life of the individual and of the community, history and the future are still full of promise and hope. The hope for the future is none other than the salvation of Israel, the final salvation of the nation. Indeed this eschatological salvation *is* the coming

74

Lord. In itself, therefore, a historical and eschatological hope—the dimension, indeed the presence of God in history—was not foolishness for the Jews. Yet the unprecedented identification of this presence with a historical figure, and above all with this *particular* historical person—with Jesus of Nazareth and his death on the cross—was an offence and a scandal. To speak of the "Son of God," and to do so with specific reference to this man from Nazareth, seemed like sheer blasphemy.

The Apostles' Creed acknowledges this foolishness and this scandal. It purports to finds the face of God in the face of the crucified; in this scandalous history it claims to behold God's presence in history. The apostles were well aware that, given the Greek and Jewish concepts of the divine, their own identification of God with this person and with his life and death amounted in fact to a revolution in the concept of God. Yet they stood by this revolution and in doing so championed the distinctively Christian dimension of their faith. The God of the Creed is the God who is "with us" here in our human history where we live and suffer. He is not indifferent or without feeling, a God who achieves his victories offstage, outside the struggle. On the contrary, he is the God who shares our struggle and our suffering, the God of solidarity who identifies with us right to the very depths.

The ethical consequence of this is that our historical existence is not bereft either of meaning or of God. It is not a blind fate or hopeless disaster to be silently endured—or better, jettisoned—if we are to attain our "real" destiny. To be sure, the kingdom of God is not a mere prolongation of history (any more than eternity is just infinitely protracted time); but neither is the kingdom of God an antithesis to history or a counterblast to it. In Christ, the coming kingdom of God is already in the midst of us (Luke 17:21). In the light of this kingdom that is within history it is worthwhile to struggle *for* history—for greater justice and more sense and wisdom within its confusions and complexities. Worthwhile not in the superficial sense that it is possible to count on or even to guarantee success. No one is promised that—least of all in the light of the crucifixion of Jesus. Whoever gets involved in historical events is likely to get burnt fingers. Contemporary history provides many illustrations of this, witness the events of 1968, for example—and I refer here not only to my homeland Czechoslovakia. Complete withdrawal from history might be the wiser course. Involvement in such a dangerous and uncertain area might seem foolish from the standpoint of an all too-human wisdom. Paradoxically, involvement in history is worthwhile not from a temporal perspective but precisely in the light of eternity, as T. G. Masaryk, himself a model of the alert and involved contemporary, was fond of saying—and on the basis of his religious faith. To put it in more specifically Christian terms, involvement in history is worthwhile because of God's presence in the history of Jesus Christ, that is, as an act of discipleship.

3. That brings me to the third aspect of the christological scandal, which concerns the *name* to which Christian faith in God is inseparably attached here in the Second Article of the Creed. This connection with this particular name also runs counter to the general trend in the history of religion and in philosophy.

It is true, of course, that the names of the founders of religions are often known—for example, Buddha, Mohammed—as are the names of those regarded by various religions as saviors or gods—for example, Isis, Serapis, and Mithra. But those who are thus named are generally regarded as either starting point *or* center of the particular religious movement, as ways and passages along the way to the divinity. Never is there an absolutely essential connection between faith itself and those who are named. Never is there talk of a unique presence of God, or of the personal incarnation of God in those who bear these names.

In the case of philosophy, any such identification is quite unthinkable. The great philosophers of antiquity certainly use specific divine names. They take part in the religious life of their communities. But in their philosophical reflections they ignore these particular embodiments of divinity. The ultimate mystery of being, the God of metaphysical reflection far transcends all nomenclature—and all the personal dimensions that accompany it. At most, names are extrinsic symbols for the mystery of being, the mystery of God that lies behind them. That mystery shines forth in the most universal concept or in the mythical union. The connection with the name takes on, therefore, the character of a provisional, tentative, and intellectually immature attitude.

Not so in the case of biblical thought. Already in the Old Testament we find an unparalleled respect for and devotion to the one distinct and irreplaceable divine name—Yahweh. It is certainly no accident that the opening words of the Decalogue—which stress the absolute incomparable sovereignty of the God of Israel—are immediately followed by the Commandment: "You shall not take the name of the Lord your God in vain." And the same line is followed throughout the whole of the New Testament where again it is certainly no accident that the first petition of the Lord's Prayer points in the same direction, this time in a positive form: "Hallowed be thy Name." But it is also in the New Testament that this name is given its most radical specificity: Where Israel speaks of the name of God, of Yahweh, the New Testament ventures to speak of "the Lord Jesus Christ." Thus, in one of the first (conventionalized) sermons in the Acts of the Apostles we hear the ringing affirmation already cited: "There is salvation in no one else; for there is no other name under heaven given among men by which we must be saved" (Acts 4:12).

The Significance of the Name "Christ"

What is the real significance of this foolish and scandalous attachment of salvation to a name, to this name in particular? As I have already pointed out, this identification brought the first Christian missionaries into direct conflict with the basic rules of the contemporary "market" in religions and philosophies. This brings us to the main question to be dealt with in this present chapter on the credal words: "and in Jesus Christ."

The first point to be made is that it is not easy for us today to understand the biblical respect for names. In contrast to the realistic Platonic approach which assigned to words and even names an important metaphysical status, we today approach this biblical interest in names with a nominalist prejudice. We tend to regard words and names as merely conventional means of expression and communication. Biblical thinking is neither realist nor nominalist here, but it does have a profound awareness of the significance of the name. The name is much more than an arbitrary vocable. It is laden with the mystery of its bearer's unique personality, and in many important instances with a good deal more besides: it can embody the life-calling and program of the person named. For biblical thinking, the name is prognostic.

From the standpoint of the New Testament—and of the Creed—this is certainly true in the case of the name "Jesus Christ." This name

77

expresses in capsule form the key points of the Second Article. No exposition of this article, therefore, can dispense with an analysis of the significance of this name.

Adopting the sequence followed in the old Roman Creed (which reads here "and in Christ Jesus"), I begin with the designation "Christ." Although this is not the sequence followed in the Apostles' Creed or the Nicene Creed, it probably reproduces the more ancient form. The sequence "Christ Jesus" occurs frequently in the New Testament and still clearly reflects the recognition—important for our exposition of the Creed—that the term "Christ," which very early on was combined with the name "Jesus" to constitute a personal name, was originally and properly a title. The programmatic dimension already referred to becomes clearly visible here.

The title in question is an extremely important one in the history of religion. *Christos* is the Greek translation of the Hebrew word *mashiach*, meaning "anointed one." It denotes in the first place those dignitaries who, according to the Old Testament, were the anointed leaders in Israel—priests, certain prophets, and, above all, the kings. The anointed of Yahweh acquired a special significance in the promise of the eternal Davidic monarchy. The Messiah here gradually becomes the bearer of his people's eschatological hope. The messianic hope becomes especially intense and assumes extremely vigorous and sometimes violent forms, above all, in times of oppression. In the intertestamental period especially (for example, in the Psalms of Solomon)[5] the political and soteriological dimensions of this hope, the expectation of victory over Israel's enemies, and the glorification and sanctification of Jerusalem were welded together.

The striking thing in the synoptic Gospels themselves is the reticence of Jesus himself in respect of this title. He seems hardly to have used it at all. When confronted with it, he shows no readiness to accept it without further ado. To the direct question of Caiaphas (Mark 14:61f.), as in the presence of Pilate (Mark 15:2f.), his answer is ambiguous. In the important episode at Caesarea Philippi (Mark 8:27ff.), while not repudiating Peter's messianic confession, Jesus prefers in his own answer to use another title of honor, namely, "Son of man," just as he does in the presence of Caiaphas. Moreover, when Peter rejects the very idea of suffering that Jesus associates with this title "Son of man," Jesus rebukes him vigorously with the words: "Behind me, Satan!"

How is this reticence of Jesus to be explained? Oscar Cullman's answer is a convincing one.[6] What made Jesus uneasy was not the actual title "Messiah" but the notion of a politically victorious messianic figure which so many people associated with it, not only in the Psalms of Solomon but also in the popular expectations of many of Jesus' contemporaries. In view of the mailed fist of imperial Rome this notion was understandable enough, but from the outset Jesus radically rejected any interpretation of his mission in terms of power politics. The temptation narratives (Matt. 4:1–11 and Luke 4:1–13) make this very clear, and the decision recorded there underlies the action and suffering of Jesus throughout his entire ministry.

> If sovereignty is a constitutive part of messiahship, Jesus makes it a reality in service. If the Messiah's way to sovereignty is via struggle and victory, for Jesus the way marked out is one of suffering and defeat . . . In the kind of ministering sovereignty which follows from thinking as God thinks and which includes suffering . . . a new vision of messiahship dawns which prevents Jesus from accepting the designation of Messiah, because to have done so would only have encouraged people to misunderstand his mission.[7]

Precisely in this way, however, Jesus identified himself with the deepest Old Testament traditions concerning the true role and hope of the people of God, and concerning the coming of a kingdom that is modeled not on the tyranny of earthly kingdoms but on the rule of love and justice lived out in sacrificial solidarity with other human beings, above all with the poor and the oppressed. *This* is the kingdom Jesus represents, and with authority. In words and deeds of liberating love he embodies the will of God. In this sense he was— and certainly knew himself to be—the true Messiah, the one in whom the promises of salvation history are fulfilled. It was altogether natural, therefore, indeed almost inevitable, that the disciples, after the events and experiences of Easter, should have ascribed to Jesus the title of Messiah, a title rarely if ever used by Jesus himself but one that he had nonetheless refined and purified. For the promise of God's eschatological presence, long invested in the Messiah, had indeed been fulfilled by this same Jesus. More and more clearly, therefore, the message of the New Testament and of the first Christian communities comes to be crystallized in the simple affirmation "Christ Jesus"—the Messiah is Jesus! And in the end the terms become completely fused into the personal name Jesus Christ.

What does this title "Messiah" tell us about the character of Jesus' mission and about the Christian life based on that mission? So far as the mission of Jesus is concerned, the first point to be noted is the intimate connection between this title and the expectations of Israel. Jesus is viewed in the context of the history of salvation already profiled in the Old Testament—in the context of the covenant between Yahweh and his people. God's salvation comes "from the Jews" (John 4:22). Jesus is heir to the promises of salvation made to Israel; he is the mediator of the new covenant. He comes to bridge the yawning chasm that throughout the history of the covenant opened ever more widely because of Israel's faithlessness. He himself becomes the victim of Israel's disobedience, but by his own faithfulness he bridges the gulf between God and his people. When Christians confess: "I believe in Christ Jesus" it is into this history—into their Jewish roots—that they are "engrafted."

That in itself already indicates that the title "Christ" defines not only the mission of Jesus, but at the same time the nature of the Christian life. As the etymology of the word itself suggests, "Christianity" is by definition to be understood in terms of Christ. Being a Christian means living with Christ as basis and Christ as goal, or—more emphatically and in New Testament terms—being "in Christ," to use a significant New Testament formula. This phrase is frequently used by Paul in a variety of contexts to emphasize the intimate solidarity between the Christian and Christ. Paul refers, for example, to "speaking" in Christ (Rom. 9:1), to his "handiwork" in the Lord (1 Cor. 9:1), of "joy in the Lord" (Phil. 3:1), of his "ways in Christ" (1 Cor 4:17) and, comprehensively, of "life . . . in Christ Jesus" (2 Tim. 1:1). This varied use of the phrase "in Christ" reflects a datum which is fundamental for the New Testament and, of course, for the Creed as well: The Christian life in its distinctive dimension is rooted in Christ. In the final analysis, Christ and our life in faith are inseparable; our "life is hid with Christ in God" (Col. 3:3). Christ is "our life" and this in a comprehensive sense, as is impressively shown by the diversity of contexts in which the "in Christ" phrase is used. Christ's relationship to us and ours to him is not confined to the spiritual realm, to the soul and the beyond, but embraces the whole life of every Christian and leaves its mark on all their words and actions.

This means that the Christian view of life rejects all attempts to interpret human life, and above all, to deal with human beings, "as if there were no Jesus Christ." It rejects every temptation to take a positivist or technocratic attitude toward other people with a view to controlling or manipulating them. "In Christ," human beings are clearly not just objects or passive creatures of circumstance. In Christ, our life is no longer imprisoned in a world of blind facts, an unalterable fatalism of circumstances and processes. Life is shifted rather into the horizon of promise and opportunity that already affirms and upholds us because of Christ. We can never say of our own or of another human being's humanity: "That's all there is to it; there's nothing more!" In Christ, there *is* more to it than that. There is the "moreover" of grace and salvation. This is why we can never make a fetish of present circumstances and conditions. Here, I believe, is a fundamental and liberating "anthropological" component of the Creed and of most of its clauses, especially of this central reference to the name of Christ.

The Significance of the Name "Jesus"

We now turn to the other—the first—name mentioned in this central section of the Creed, Jesus. We descend, so to speak, from the lofty heights of the messianic tradition and of our exploration of the title *Christos*, to the very ordinary level of Jewish daily life. "Jesus" was already a common name in the Old Testament and even in the days of Jesus of Nazareth. It is the Greek form of the Hebrew Joshua, which had become Jeshua in late Hebrew and Aramaic. A whole series of Old Testament characters bore this name. The most outstanding of them was undoubtedly Joshua the son of Nun, who brought the Exodus to a successful conclusion by the entry into the Promised Land, and after him the high priest Joshua, son of Jehozadak, who accompanied Zerubbabel back from exile. The name continued to be a popular one right down to the beginning of the second century in the Christian Era. Three of the seventy-two translators of the Septuagint, for example, bore the already Graecized form of the name. The situation in the New Testament is similar; others besides Jesus of Nazareth were also called Jesus.

In the circumstances, therefore, it might seem rather artificial to inquire into the theological significance of this commonplace name. Yet it is precisely this most obvious feature of this name, its commonplace character that is significant. What is affirmed in this name, with all

81

its echoes of cultural and religious history, is the complete and unabridged humanity of the Savior and also, therefore, the concretely historical character of salvation: the "Christ," the "Son of God," the "Lord" appeared in the historical person who bore this ordinary name. Indeed, beyond that: the one familiar to us under these titles of majesty is none other than, is identical with, this historical man from Nazareth.

This affirmation was what distinguished the faith of the apostles from that of the Gnostics, and the Creed too is obviously bent on distancing itself from Gnostic mythology:

> There is no divorce here between an earthly body and a Christ who puts on this body, as there was in Christian gnosticism. *Iesous* is *ho kyrios* (the Lord) and not something apart from him. The gospels, therefore, and the missionary preaching of Acts and Paul (Gal. 3:1), present this Jesus of Nazareth and declare that God has made this man the Lord and the Judge: *en andri ho horizen*—"by a man of His choosing" (Acts 17:31).[8]

We said earlier that the distinctiveness of the Christian faith is bound up with the "in Christ." We can now equally well say—since the two names are inseparable in the view of the apostles (and of the Apostles' Creed)—that the Christian faith is also indivisibly bound up with this particular name Jesus, with the historical human being quite specifically identified by this name—with Jesus the Christ. Salvation has the unmistakable historical features of this particular human life, a fact that is important not only for doctrine but also, and above all, for ethics. Because this is so, the direction of Christian faith and life is not left to chance, to an arbitrary, nonobligatory choice. The title "Christ" is not just a variable cipher to which we are at liberty to attach any meaning we like in accordance with whatever theory of life we may happen to favor at any given moment. No! Christ is Jesus, and life "in Christ" is a life that is necessarily one of discipleship, following in the footsteps of Jesus. The name "Jesus" establishes and shows us the direction for our discipleship. This is the doctrinal and ethical significance of this ordinary name at the very heart of the Christian Creed.

But there is yet another fundamental aspect. According to the gospel witness, this quite common name Jesus has in the case of this quite specific person a very specific significance. I remind you of something I stressed earlier in this chapter: in the biblical view, a name is not just an accidental and unimportant vocable. Names can take on an almost prophetic and programmatic character. According to the Gospels, this was so in the case of Jesus of Nazareth:

> According to Mt. and Lk., the name *Jeshua-Jesous* is not accidental. It is given to the child of Mary by virtue of the divine promise. Mt. 1:21 explains this as follows: "You shall give him the name Jesus (Savior), for he will save his people from their sins."9

Occurring as it does in the prologue to Matthew's Gospel, this theological statement is meant to provide, in condensed theological form, an omen, a keynote for the following account of the life of Jesus of Nazareth from the standpoint of faith. There are at least three reasons why we should keep this theological statement in mind:

1. The man from Nazareth is taken at his word, indeed, at his nominal value. His name is his program. The name "Jesus" means "Yahweh is Savior"—a central article of Israel's faith. This means that, for all its contingency as an unvarnished human history, what begins with this name is part—or, more precisely, the center—of the history of salvation. The final seal is now set on the covenant of salvation that was rooted and grounded, but also repeatedly called in question, in the Old Testament history. This is, from the very beginning, the meaning and goal of this history connected with Jesus.

2. What is at stake in this history, in salvation history, is the deliverance of the people of God, indeed, the deliverance of the nations. What is at stake in the faith in Jesus and in the salvation that he brings is our liberation. While not exaggerating the importance of the motif, it is also theologically important here to note the possible allusion to the Joshua of the Old Testament. The Joshua-Jesus of the New Testament completes the journey of the Old Testament Joshua. In Jesus' name there begins and continues the new and final exodus of God's people from the house of bondage that is our human alienation. The credal confession "I believe . . . in Jesus" reminds the Christian of this history of deliverance.

3. Although this history of deliverance is undoubtedly one of liberation within history, the history of an exodus toward greater justice and freedom here on earth both individually and socially, it nevertheless points beyond itself and surpasses by far all levels attainable on earth and in society. Its goal is not only to make possible the

relatively better (that too, of course!), but also and above all to over-come radical evil in a way that no act of historical deliverance or social achievement could do. This aspect finds expression already in the explanatory comment on the name "Jesus" in Matt. 1:21: "for he will save his people from their sins." As Julius Schniewind points out in his commentary on Matthew's Gospel, "Both in the Old Testament and in the New, the forgiveness of sins summarizes God's salvation in its entirety. The forgiveness of sins means much more than the erasing of specific evil deeds; it means the abolition of the divorce between God and humanity."[10] When Christians recite the words of the Apostles' Creed, "I believe in Jesus Christ," they are being summoned to praise and practice this deliverance.

8

His Only Son, Our Lord

What It Means
to Confess "the Divinity of Christ"

The lofty theme of "God," far from being left behind in the transition from the First Article to the Second, is taken up once again in an even more concentrated way and with an unprecedented concreteness, as was shown in the previous chapter. Both the trinitarian pattern of the Creed and the significance of the name "Jesus Christ" point unmistakably in this direction. Only in the next two designations, however, "His only Son, our Lord," is the position made clear beyond all doubt. It is significant that of all the christological titles found in the New Testament these two were chosen. These two titles bring out most clearly the unique presence of God in the history of Jesus of Nazareth, indeed, God's identification with this history. "Lord" recalls the term "Kyrios" used in the Greek version of the Old Testament for the name of God in Israel—Yahweh. "Son" expresses the especially intimate relationship of Jesus to the Father.

Does this mean that "divinity of Christ" is made the theme of the central section of the Creed? Before we can answer this question, we must first all consider carefully how and in what context the divinity of Christ becomes a specific theme. In other words, we must first of all examine the meaning of the two designations "Son of God" and "our Lord." Only in this sense can the divinity of Christ be the basic theme of this chapter. My provisional answer to the direct question at this point would be both Yes and No. *Yes*, in the sense that the whole dynamic of the two designations "Son of God" and "our Lord" as well as the whole course of the history of doctrine right down to the emphatic "true God" of the Chalcedonian dogma both point unmistakably in the direction of an affirmative answer. *No*, to the extent that a fixed textbook definition is implied. No such definition is given in the Creed. In this respect, the Apostles' Creed differs from the Nicene Creed which, precisely at this point, extends the affirmation in a particularly emphatic and expansive way: "the only-begotten Son of God, begotten of his Father before all ages, God from God, light from light, true God from true God, begotten not made, of one substance with the Father, through whom all things came into existence."

An impressive flood of doxological affirmations! Liturgically and dogmatically, we are almost overwhelmed, inundated, and carried away by the stream! It is almost as if the Nicene fathers wanted to make everything finally clear, to leave nothing vague and imprecise, no obscurities, particularly on this one point—the complete divinity of Jesus Christ. In the encounter with Jesus Christ, we meet none other than the one God of Christian faith. So the dogmatic colors are laid on heavily rather than lightly: "God of God . . . true God from true God . . . of one substance with the Father . . ."

The Apostles' Creed is strikingly different here. Poorer? Perhaps. But there could also be a positive aspect to this difference. Am I mistaken in thinking that it could perhaps be precisely these heavy underlinings of the Nicene Creed—for all their doxological brilliance —that keep many of our contemporaries from appreciating the underlying concern of the fathers? Make no mistake, I fully share this underlying concern. I can also understand why, precisely at this point in his expositions of the Creed, Karl Barth vents his wrath on the modern despisers of this christological enthusiasm of the ancient church:

> Modern theologians who make fun of the people of Constantinople for their fierce disputes as to whether Jesus Christ is only *like* God or actually *is* God Himself, only prove thereby their own greater stupidity.[1]

Or again:

> This inveighing against so-called "orthodoxy" is something we should have no truck with even as educated persons, for there is something barbaric in this scolding of the fathers. . . . There really had to be a tussle over the *iota*, over whether this was God Himself or a heavenly or earthly being. That was certainly no trivial question. The whole gospel was at stake in this *iota*. In Jesus Christ we are confronted either with God Himself or with a creature.[2]

There can be no quibbling over this warning. It must be taken seriously. The question nevertheless remains—not a question to the church fathers of that time but one concerning our own situation today. In expounding today the theme of the divinity of Christ, might not a reduced dogmatic definitiveness actually accomplish more? Might it not be helpful if the dynamic theme were not frozen in static concepts such as substance (and later on natures)? The liturgical and doctrinal enthusiasm of the early church undoubtedly helped to establish faith in God's unique presence in the history of Jesus Christ. It created clarity at a time when the New Testament faith was endangered by religious myths that threatened to swallow up the name and history of Jesus Christ in the general religious processes of Gnostic mythology. Today, however, this doxological inundation, which at that time helped to clarify the faith, could be counterproductive. In that case, the more frugal text of the Apostles' Creed could offer us a potential advantage. For here, while the theme of the divinity of Christ is unambiguously attested in the two central affirmations, its eschatological dynamic is left open; it is not at once defined conceptually. I turn now to look at the meaning of the two designations: "God's only Son" and "our Lord."

God's Exodus in the Mission of the Son

In using the term "Son of God," the Apostles' Creed adopts a theological concept that plays a rich variety of roles not only in the New Testament but also in the general religious history of the New Testament world. For the origin of the concept we must of course, turn to the religions of the ancient East, above all to the history of Egyptian religion. There, the rulers—the Pharaohs—were revered as sons of Re, the Sun God. But the title "Son of God" was also found outside Egypt, in the context of political religion, in the apotheosis of the ruler and an ideology of power. In the course of the Hellenistic period, this tendency was established even in Rome. The Roman emperors welcomed attribution to themselves of the title *Divi filius*.

A limited "democratization" of this essentially autocratic title took place, certainly, in the Hellenistic world, where it was applied to exceptional persons outside the dominant political class, and above all to various miracle workers who were described as "divine men." Anyone with access to "divine powers" could claim this title. The

"Son of God" theme thus became a widely used and familiar one in the Hellenistic milieu of the New Testament.

In these circumstances some New Testament scholars, not surprisingly, have championed the theory of a Hellenistic derivation for this title, even in the case of the New Testament and the Creed. A particularly impressive case in point was W. Bousset in his major work *Kyrios Christos* (1913). He was followed by many others, including Rudolf Bultmann who adopted a similar position in his *Theology of the New Testament.* In the light of the studies conducted by Oscar Cullmann, however, I find this theory not entirely convincing. Certainly it is hard to sustain in the case of the synoptic Gospels.

> The only story in which Jesus is called "Son of God" in a sense which corresponds to the Hellenistic concept is Matthew's version of Jesus' walking on the sea, after which the disciples cry out, as a result of the miracle, "Truly, you are the son of God" (Matt. 14:33).[3]

Apart from this single instance there is no other indication that the divine sonship of Jesus was that of the Hellenistic miracle worker. On the contrary, precisely this assumption is consistently challenged by the witness and the practice of Jesus himself. For our present context the story of the temptation of Jesus provides a very illuminating example. In this test of his divine sonship, the current Hellenistic conception is vigorously and clearly rejected as a diabolic temptation. It is rejected, moreover, in both its forms: as the temptation to worship power in the manner of the imperial *Divi filius*, but also as the craving for miracles in the manner of the "divine men" who make a display of their powers. Jesus firmly rejects both temptations on one and the same decisive ground, namely by an appeal to the Word of God in the Old Testament tradition.

This appeal to the Old Testament tradition is also of vital importance when we seek to understand the significance of the "Son of God" motif. The Jewish background has to be taken into account. For the "Son of God" motif indeed appears at important points in the Old Testament narrative. Let me mention just three of these. First, in the story of the Exodus, Moses is sent to Pharaoh to tell him: "Israel is my first-born son" (Exod. 4:22f.). Next, Hosea's announcement of the divine word: "Out of Egypt I called my son" (Hos. 11:1), which is later repeated in the New Testament. Finally, in a royal psalm (Psalm 2, which is also cited frequently in the New Testament),

Yahweh tells the Davidic king: "You are my son, today I have begotten you" (Ps. 2:7).

These and many other Old Testament passages furnish a radically different frame of reference for the idea of the "Son of God" in comparison with that of Hellenistic traditions. What is fundamental here is the act and promise of divine election, which is revealed to the people of God in its history of deliverance and at the same time requires proof of the freedom thus bestowed in the form of free "filial obedience." We can only endorse the conclusion of Oscar Cullmann:

> The Old Testament and Jewish concept of the Son of God is essentially characterised, not by the gift of a particular power, nor by a substantial relationship with God by virtue of divine conception, but by the idea of *election* to participation in divine work through the execution of a particular commission, and by the idea of strict obedience to the God who elects.[4]

When we turn to the world of the New Testament, it soon becomes clear that the "Son of God" motif is interpreted and presented primarily in its Old Testament and Jewish context, not only by Jesus himself but also by the apostolic witnesses (and hence also in the Creed). In what follows, let me emphasize three clearly defined strands in this interpretation which, although given different weight in the various New Testament witnesses, are nonetheless inseparable.

1. What is expressed, first of all, in the "Son of God" motif, is the inner dimension of the history of Christ, the unique relationship of Jesus to the Father. This is a central theme in the Fourth Gospel and is there dealt with in detail—the identity of will, action, and even of "substance" between Jesus and his heavenly Father. Jesus is the Son, and this is a unique and incomparable sense—the "only" Son. He is in the Father and the Father in him. He can even say of himself: "I and the Father are one" (John 10:30).

This Johannine position, of course, is not simply to be read into the self-understanding of the synoptic Jesus. On the other hand, neither is there any sharp discontinuity here between the fourth evangelist and the synoptic Gospels. This is clear not only from such isolated passages as Matt. 11:27 ("No one knows the Son except the Father, and no one knows the Father except the Son") but also from the way in which the whole ministry of Jesus is consistently presented in the synoptics. For the synoptic Jesus, too, the conviction is fundamental that in his own actions and sufferings God's work is being done, that in himself the kingdom of God comes into our midst. This conviction is not stridently and obtrusively publicized; Jesus does not advertise his divine sonship on every street corner. But neither does he timorously conceal it. At key moments in his ministry—for example at his baptism or again at Caesarea Philippi—the "Son of God" motif is clearly audible and is accepted by Jesus, not rejected. While we must certainly be careful not to indulge in speculations about a "messianic" or "Son of God" secret retained by Jesus, it seems to me not unwarranted to conclude with Cullmann:

> The conviction that in a unique way he was "God's Son" must belong to the very heart of what we call the "self-consciousness" of Jesus.[5]

This "son" believes and knows that the way he goes is not just one of his own choosing but rests on the election of his heavenly Father.

2. Not only the inner dimension of the history of Jesus but also its external dimension in relation to the world—his mission and his ministry—is determined by the "Son of God" motif. Just as Israel's election is not an end in itself but at the same time the requisitioning of Israel—as representative of the nations—its summoning to witness and service, so too, in the case of the Son of God in the New Testament, his consciousness of sonship is not self-centered but has an imperative outward dynamic and becomes a mission and a task.

This aspect is captured magnificently in a key passage in the New Testament to which we shall have occasion to return when we come to speak of the title *Kyrios*:

> Though he was in the form of God, he did not count equality with God a thing to be grasped, but emptied himself, taking the form of a servant, being born in the likeness of men . . . he humbled himself and became obedient unto death, even death on a cross (Phil. 2:6ff.).

Note simply the main ideas here: he "emptied himself," "took the form of a servant," "humbled himself," "became obedient unto death"—all these expressions indicate the basic tendency in the New Testament interpretation of the "Son of God" theme. It indicates the movement of God outwards, indeed "downwards" ("into the far country," as Karl Barth chose to define a central theme of his doctrine of reconciliation), in sacrificial ministry to humanity and in obedient service even unto death. In the synoptic Gospels we have a vivid concrete account of this way into the far country. The synoptic account of the history of the Son moves precisely in this direction. At central points—I refer again to the baptism, the transfiguration (Mark 9:2–10 parr.), and Peter's confession—it repeatedly combines the "Son of God" motif with that of representative suffering. This standpoint finds particularly clear expression in the Letter to the Hebrews, in its theological meditations on the kerygma. Nowhere is the obedience, testing, suffering, and self-sacrifice of the Son of God more clearly attested than in this letter. In all the diverse testimonies to this christological title "Son of God," this is clearly and constantly the basic theme: The "Son of God" does not remain in some absolute and autocratic height but plunges into the depths; he is not preoccupied with the vested interests of a complacent and self-sufficient divinity but addresses himself with the utmost seriousness to the essential interest of suffering humanity.

3. This brings us to the third strand in the New Testament deployment of the "Son of God" motif: the mission and destiny of the "Son of God" are indissolubly bound up with our human destiny. To speak of the "son" means to speak of "sons"—and "daughters." The "only" son does not remain solitary. "The son of man came not to be served but to serve, and to give his life as a ransom for many" (Mark 10:45). This is how the synoptic Jesus understood his mission. The apostle Paul too develops his doctrine of reconciliation on this same foundation: God sent his son "that *we* might receive adoption as sons" (Gal. 4:5f.); through the "death of his [God's] son," *we* are reconciled (Rom. 5:10). Indeed, we can go even further: The goal of reconciliation is that we too should become "sons" in the full sense, by which Paul means free human beings, no longer enslaved. "Emancipation" is the ultimate purpose of the sending of God's son. The purpose of his journey into the far country is our deliverance from our present state of tutelage and alienation. Reference is made to this purpose at the end of the eloquent christological doxology in the Nicene Creed, where confession is made of him "who for us men [and women] and for our salvation, came down from heaven." The fish symbol of the ancient church also reflects this emphasis: ICHTHUS—Jesus Christ, Son of God, is our Savior. There is no doubt that in the mission of the Son of God what is at stake is our cause, the destiny of humanity.

These reflections on the theme of the "Son of God" suggest a provisional answer to the question of the divinity of Christ. The divinity of Christ is affirmed not as a matter of doctrinal speculation but as a testimony to faith in the dynamic presence of God in the history of Jesus of Nazareth, faith in the personal initiative of God in his search for us, his exodus toward us—and, indissolubly bound up with this, our own "exodus," our own reconciliation and liberation both in the midst of life and at life's end. It is for *this* reason, with this interest in salvation and not out of any purely intellectual concern, that the Creed confesses the divinity of Christ. It formulates its affirmation, therefore, not as an equation: "Jesus=God" (nor are we offered any such equation even in the New Testament) but in the form of the confession of Jesus as God's only son, God on his way toward us, the God of this particular history of his son. Only here, in this specific context of *faith*, does the question of the divinity of Christ arise in the sense intended in the Creed.

Here, however, in this specific context, the question of the divinity of Christ is answered unambiguously: In Christ what we do in fact encounter is *God* on his way toward us. The one who is at work here or suffers here is none other than God. This is the point at which the doctrinal struggles of the ancient church really begin, and with appropriate passion. Here every iota has to be contended for, not because of the so-called rage of the theologians intoxicated with their own ideas but because at stake here are the most central concerns of salvation and faith. At question here is the very basis of salvation. If Christ is only *like* God, his history is not God's exodus toward us but just another of the many divine-human myths that flourished in the world at that time when the ancient church was born. The statement that Christ is God's "only son" erects a defense against this temptation of mythology.

The Lordship of Jesus—
A Radical Critique of Power

We turn now to the other key title in the Christology of the Apostles' Creed: "our Lord." The contemporary background to this title of majesty is much the same as in the case of the title "Son of God." We encounter the term *Kyrios* not only in the New Testament but also in the history of religion. Indeed, it was perhaps even more widespread in the Hellenistic world than the term "Son of God." Hellenistic rulers—Ptolemy and Cleopatra, for example—were referred to as "Lord, God, Majesty," while the Roman emperor was often addressed as "Our Lord and God." The term "Lord," therefore, was one of the most popular titles of the ruler cult in Hellenism.

The theory that this title originated in Hellenism has therefore, not surprisingly, been even more widely and tenaciously held by modern scholars than in the case of the title "Son of God." Mainly under the influence of the classic study of this question by W. Bousset, *Kyrios Christos*, it was almost unanimously accepted by specialists in the history of religion. According to this theory, the title is foreign to the oldest strata of the gospel tradition. Its intellectual milieu is to be sought primarily in the Antiochene and other Hellenistic communities, from whence it infiltrated into Christian piety under the powerful influence of the Hellenistic *Kyrios* cult.

To an even greater extent than in the case of the "Son of God" title, this theory calls for correction. Its chief weakness is that it ignores the Old Testament background, which was so much closer to Jesus' immediate milieu, and of course to Jesus himself, than was the Hellenistic background. The *Kyrios* title was familiar to every reader of the Greek Old Testament as the Greek rendering of Yahweh, the Hebrew name of God. In the light of recent discoveries, it is also probable that it played an important part in the Aramaic background to the Gospels. The Aramaic term *Maranatha*, for example, can be interpreted as an imperative, *Maranatha* "Our Lord come!" (1 Cor. 16:22) equivalent to the Greek *erchou kyrie*, "Come, Lord!" (Rev. 22:20). If the comparison is valid, the *kyrios* title goes back to the oldest Palestinian strata of the gospel tradition, in which case the theory of its Hellenistic derivation is radically called in question, as are the supposed Hellenizing consequences of this derivation.

In the New Testament it was Paul (though by no means he alone) for whom the confession "Jesus Christ is Lord" became the core of Christology. The classic expression occurs in Rom. 10:9: "If thou shalt confess with thy mouth the Lord Jesus, and shalt believe in thine heart that God hath raised him from the dead, thou shalt be saved" (KJV). This passage is already of great interest for its description of the form in which the act of confession occurs.

Paul expressly connects "confession with the lips" and "faith in the heart." It is significant that "to confess with the lips" quite self-evidently refers to this one confession, "Jesus is Kyrios." This is without doubt *the* confession, the "original confession" which includes all others.[6]

As for the *substance* of the confession, three aspects of the *Kyrios* motif are important for New Testament Christology. First, it is in the presence of the risen Christ that utterance is given to the confession: "My Lord and my God" (John 20:28). The reference, of course, is not to some anonymous power but specifically to the crucified and risen one, the Savior whose name is Jesus of Nazareth. It is his specific life story, as we shall soon see, that is vitally important for the concrete definition of his lordship. Quite plainly, however, the attribution of the title "Kyrios" is connected with the Easter events: "God has made him both Lord and Christ, this Jesus whom you crucified" (Acts 2:36). This was what Peter proclaimed in his first sermon, referring directly to the resurrection.

Second, the confession of Jesus as *Kyrios* primarily defines Christ's present time—and the present time of Christians, of course! But once again, not exclusively. The classic confession: "Come, Lord Jesus!" not only points back to a definite past, that of Jesus of Nazareth; it also points forwards to a definite future, that of the coming Christ. Above all, however, it is the present time of the confessing Christian and of the church that is, according to most New Testament passages, brought liberatingly and authoritatively into the light of the confession of faith.

Third, it is not just the life of the individual Christian and of the church that is illuminated by this horizon, but at the same time the whole cosmic situation of humankind, and indeed of all creation. It is significant that when Paul confesses this "name that is above every name," he bears witness to Christ's lordship over "all power in heaven and on earth," over all natural and supernatural powers—and this not only as our "comfort in life and in death," but also at the same time as our authorization to undertake public action to change the world.

These three aspects of the confession of Christ as *Kyrios* bring out the fact that the Christian life is firmly connected with reality. Faith in Jesus as Lord is totally different from any of the Hellenistic private religions, from the Gnostic cults and mystery religions with their concentration on the religious needs of the individual or group and their facility for compromise with other cults and saviors. If Jesus is Lord, witness must be borne to his lordship in every area of life, including emphatically the field of politics. This corollary led to conflicts with the political powers of the time, above all with the official emperor worship. The empire confronted Christians not only with a reality whose sovereignty over all political matters was a palpable daily experience—as can be seen for example in both the theory and practice of the apostle Paul, Christians fully acknowledged the role of Rome in government—but also with a religious and ideological apotheosis, and here Christians refused to conform.

The response of their contemporaries to this refusal was first astonishment, and then hatred and persecution. This is vividly illustrated in the *Martyrdom of Polycarp* (from the second half of the second century).[7] Here the representative of Rome asks the martyr what harm there is in saying "Caesar is Lord?" Almost all the adherents of other "lords" were quite ready to do so. But such an attitude was impossible for believing Christians. The lordship of Jesus was unconditionally binding—here and now in the given social and political situation. If Jesus is Lord, it is impossible to believe in him and, at the same time, accept partial confessions and religious reservations. Faith in this Lord goes all the way. Polycarp and countless other martyrs like him preferred to die rather than deny the lordship of Christ in certain areas of life, above all that of politics, and to abandon these areas to the arbitrary and autocratic pleasure of other "lords." This is why the Johannine apocalypse, which vividly illuminates the character of the Christian confession of faith as protest and conflict in the confrontation with pseudo-divine "apocalyptic beasts," speaks of Jesus Christ with complete clarity as "Lord of lords" and "King of kings" (Rev. 17:14).

It was no accident therefore that the emphasis on the lordship of Christ, and the corresponding doctrinal emphasis on Christ's royal office, was again and again accompanied by an insistence on the ethical and political responsibility of Christians. This is illustrated, for example, by the Czech Reformation, not only in the passionate concern of the Hussites for social justice but also in the insistence of the Czech Brethren on the need to proclaim and obey Christ "not only as a prophet of the pulpit, not only as priest and bishop of the altar, but also as the sceptred king on the throne who exercises judgment on the disobedient."[8] But this is also true of recent and present ecumenical

95

history. One of the essential inspirations of the ecumenical movement, including its efforts in the field of social ethics, was the rediscovery of "the kingship of Christ."[9] This motif also played an important role in the struggle of certain churches against totalitarian pretensions, for example in the German church struggle of the 1930s and 1940s.

Descent into the Depths

It is necessary now to fill in more precisely the content of this social and ethical dimension of this lordship of Christ, which is not simply an abstract and general term to be used in any way we please. We need to heed A. Ritschl's warning: "Unless its content is supplied from the specific features of his historical ministry, the notion of Christ's present lordship remains either a worthless slogan or simply an excuse for every sort of fanaticism."[10] That warning is still true today, and not only with respect to possible misunderstanding on the part of those contemporaries of ours for whom the term "kingship" may have authoritarian connotations that are clearly suspect in a democratic age. The fuller specification of Christ's lordship is needed also because of certain traditional ideas bequeathed to us from church history, where "Christocratic" concerns have often been equated with general theocratic and even ecclesiocratic programs, with cultures and societies kept subservient to church policies pursued under the banner of "Christ the King."

Misunderstandings of this kind can be avoided if we reflect carefully on the New Testament basis of the lordship motif. According to the New Testament, as seen particularly in Paul, the lordship of Christ is rooted in the concrete history of Jesus of Nazareth. The key passage, cited earlier in this chapter, is Phil. 2:5–11. You will recall that it describes the journey of the "Son of God" into the far country, his "descent into the depths" in devoted and sacrificial service. The "name that is above every name," the title *Kyrios*, is inseparably connected with *this* journey. In other words, the "Lord of lords" rules not in the manner of other lords, as an authoritarian despot, but in a freely serving love. Conversely—and this has consequences for our critique of society—no earthly (or heavenly) ruler, however bristling with power, is the real lord. The true Lord is the serving man from Nazareth. The way he chose, and the way he directs us to take, involves not the love of power but the power of love. Christians and the church itself can convincingly bear witness to and act in the name of Christ's lordship only by ethically and politically conforming to *this* way, the way of solidarity, for others, the way that leads downward, not by an upward drive for sovereignty and power.

We have to differentiate—but without separating—two stages, two modes, in the witness to and discipleship of *Kyrios* Jesus: the sphere of the church and sphere of the world. The confession "Jesus is Lord" is related to reality, to life, in a concretely structured way. The lordship of Christ is not simply there in some abstract sense but is primarily connected with Christians and the church. The Apostles' Creed speaks plainly of "our Lord." In doing so, it reproduces a vital element of the New Testament witness. In the original form of the confession of Christ as Lord, Jesus is confessed to be the Lord of the church. As we have seen, "Our Lord, come!" is one of the earliest prayers (still in Aramaic!) of the praying community. "Our Lord" refers primarily not to some ruler of the whole cosmos but to the Master of the disciples, to the one who is "Head of his body," not of the world in general but of his church. It is here in this specific place, in this inner circle, in personal decision and relationship, that the lordship of Christ is known, confessed, and—in faith—validated. This is where the first stage is to be found, the first mode, the primary horizon—in faith in the lordship of Christ.

But the second stage follows immediately. The apostolic vision of the lordship of Christ, while it certainly has a pneumatological and ecclesiological starting point, nevertheless transcends the sphere of the church. The Lord of the church is "the head of *all* rule and authority" (Col. 2:10); he is Lord of the world. To assume a cosmological starting point for this confession of faith would be a mistake; yet there is no denying its cosmological horizon. This, at any rate, is the logic of the New Testament statements. Firmly anchored in the community of the disciples of Jesus, these statements have an inherent dynamism in the direction of the world. When the Christian community confesses "Jesus is Lord," all other powers totter and fall—at least in the sense of being denied any ultimate legitimacy, or any totalitarian claim. As we have seen, this logical extension soon leads to conflicts which, far from being concealed, are endured even to the point of martyrdom. This dynamic thrust in the direction of the world leads not to some kind of conflict strategy but to a

97

liberating vision of other human beings—all of them without exception—indeed a vision of all creation. Nor is it simply a matter of vision. The Christian community is at once led, in its practical life too, to fulfill its mission to go into all the world. When it is really faithful to the confession of "Our Lord," the Christian enterprise has about it the flavor not of a self-centered pressure group but the bracing ecumenical "fresh air of the great wide world." For the one confessed as "Lord" is none other than "God the Father almighty, maker of heaven and earth," he who is present in Jesus Christ.

This brings us back once again to the divinity of Christ, the basic theme of this whole chapter. Here as we conclude our exposition of the title "our Lord" we ask, as we did in concluding the section of the title "Son of God": what does all this mean for the divinity of Christ? I single out one aspect, which, while it connects up with the line of argument just developed, also develops it further in one particular direction. The affirmation of Christ's divinity is certainly no theoretical, clinical declaratory definition of Christ. Its native air is existential, practical, indeed political, and its truth is experienced and demonstrated doxologically and ethically. Indeed doxology and ethics are its two important dimensions. Doxologically it is praise of the divine grace, that grace which in consequence of this "Son of God, our Lord" makes us—who are tempted, assailed, and alienated human beings—God's beloved sons and daughters so that we are no longer slaves. We are no longer strangers but adopted children. "If God is for us, who is against us?" (Rom. 8:31)—this is the question Paul raises in light of the destiny and history of Jesus Christ, and in praise of this grace. But at the same time, ethical response, indeed political response in the form of practical work for God's kingdom and God's justice is the appropriate response to this grace for disciples of this Lord.

It is in this sense that Leonhard Ragaz, in his exposition of the Creed, interprets the affirmation of the divinity of Christ, providing at the same time a number of practical examples that are still relevant today. I offer them here as a succinct summary, worthy of consideration:

> Even today, of course, it is right and we have a duty to affirm the truth of the divinity of Christ, to confess it and bear witness to its truth. In opposition, for example, to the new Baal, the deification of blood and soil, the idolatry of race. In opposition, for example, to the modern

Caesar, the deification of the State. In opposition, for example, to the divinity of the machine and of technology. In opposition, for example, to the tyranny of Mammon. In opposition, for example, to the Moloch of militarism. When, in opposition to these powers, we affirm the other person, the soul, the spirit, humanity, together with justice and love, we are actually affirming the divinity of Christ *today*. For that is *his* spirit, and *his* truth. When, in opposition to every glorification and deification of nature, every enslavement to it, and when in opposition to any merely aesthetic attitude we stress the seriousness of sin and guilt, then we are actually confessing the divinity of Christ; or, more precisely, when modern men and women awaken to the utter seriousness of sin and guilt, then they are actually acknowledging Christ as Lord. When in the name of conscience we resist every new Baal idol or Caesar idol, along with the other idols of our time, then we are actually confessing our faith in "God in Christ." Today we have so many, many opportunities for confessing Christ as Lord in a new way.[11]

9

Conceived by the Holy Spirit, Born from the Virgin Mary

Taking the Tension Out of an Old Dispute

This clause is one of the most disputed statements in the Apostles' Creed. The dispute is a real one, involving sharp differences of opinion. In some churches when the Creed is recited it is the custom at this point for worshipers to cross themselves as a sign of reverence for the mystery indicated by these words. Other Christians, however, have problems with the formulation·and are even troubled by it.

While the differences of opinion do not quite follow confessional boundaries, it can be said, broadly speaking, that whereas great importance is attached to this article in Eastern Orthodoxy—and whereas it is also central in Roman Catholic piety and theology especially—on mariological grounds, in Protestant circles the prevailing attitude in recent times seems to have been one of reserve toward and even outright repudiation of this article. There are nevertheless overlappings on this score, especially at present. Among some Protestants there is a special interest in this credal clause; on the one hand, for example, some fundamentalist groups accept it as a test of basic orthodoxy, and theologians like Karl Barth who focus sharply on Christology have repeatedly cited these words with approval as expressing the great "mystery of Christmas." On the other hand, there are also modern Catholic theologians who remain surprisingly aloof, more or less silently ignoring the theme, as in the authentically Catholic Christology of Walter Kasper's *Jesus the Christ*[1] or else frankly rejecting it or interpreting it symbolically, as in the case of the Dutch Cathechism and the Swiss theologian Hans Küng.

Usually, of course, it is only when we come to the second part of this article that the controversy flares up, and even here the point at issue is not so much the underlying doctrinal intention as the specific way in which this intention is carried out in the virgin birth motif. At this critical point people seem to discover something particularly mysterious or something particularly disreputable, and they pounce on it with their arguments and counterarguments. I counsel strongly against this way of proceeding, which for quite understandable and very human reasons is of course a very tempting procedure. The special attraction lies in the idea of parthenogenesis, in the appeal of its biological and sexual associations to our imagination, whether in the modern liberal mold or a suppressed ascetic mold. Once we embark on this path, however, isolating the virgin birth motif from its context and assigning it a central place on its own, we are in danger of missing the true center of the whole clause and failing to understand the real underlying theological intention of the virgin birth confession. This is no way to do justice to the essential content of the Creed.

The Two Dimensions of Christology

But what is the center of gravity here? Where is the main emphasis in this clause? As I see it, the main concern is to bear witness to the divine incarnation, God's assumption of our humanity. The event that dominates the prologue to the Fourth Gospel—"And the Word became flesh and dwelt among us" (John 1:14)—also dominates the christological prologue of the Apostles' Creed. Its central theme is the incarnation of the Word, the Spirit's adoption of our humanity.

A comparison with the text of the Nicene Creed is instructive here. Not only is the corresponding section there much fuller; it is also set in the dynamic context of the question of our salvation and of the divine condescendence: "Who for us human beings and for our salvation came down from heaven and was incarnate from the Holy Spirit and the virgin Mary." The central theme is explicitly defined here by the classic term "incarnation." It is probably no accident that this term is not employed in the Apostles' Creed. In Eastern piety and theology the theme of the divine incarnation is unquestionably central whereas—and the Creed shows this—the Western church concentrated more on the passion and resurrection of Christ. We have to be careful, of course, not to set up false antitheses here, where what is really involved is rather a matter of divergent emphases within one

102

and the same common ecumenical witness to Jesus Christ. What the Eastern church emphasizes is certainly not absent in the Western church, and, of course, vice versa. The major theme of God's assumption of our humanity is fully present in succinct form in this clause of the Creed.

How is the incarnation attested? The first point to be noted is the bipolar structure of the clause. On the one hand, the Creed speaks here of the Holy Spirit; within its trinitarian framework the Creed speaks of the Creator's presence. On the other hand, it speaks also of a human being, identified by the name Mary—a specific historical person. In this article of the Creed, therefore, God and humanity stand side by side together. The christological significance of this point is fundamental. It is impossible to do justice to the person and history of Jesus Christ—and this is what the whole Second Article is about—if we insist on understanding and confessing them one-dimensionally, by reducing them to one dimension or the other. What is made quite clear already by this christological prologue is that in Christology proper God and humanity are both present together.

This, we know, is not a self-evident truth. It is not so today and it was never so throughout the entire history of the church, certainly not in the period when the Apostles' Creed came into existence. At that time especially, the struggle for an unabridged christological confession of faith was the *main* credal problem; Christology was that article of faith on which the very existence of the church depended. The New Testament message of the divine incarnation in the person and life of Jesus of Nazareth was repeatedly assailed from within and from without. It was regarded as foolish and scandalous, ambiguous and obscure, even exasperating, because of the two-dimensional character of its covenant history, that covenant between God and humanity. "God *and* humanity"—what on earth does that mean? This was surely far too ambiguous and obscure a message! It needed simplification in clear concepts, clearer connections! What was meant by "clarity" here, of course, was the elimination of the bipolarity, the double dimensionality, and the advocacy of a more or less ruthless reductionism as regards the doctrine of Christ.

This reductionist approach presents a constant temptation for any reflection on Jesus Christ both inside and outside the church, not one that is confined to the period when the Creed took shape. Tendencies to Monophysitism, whether of a crude or sophisticated kind, are found throughout most of the church's history. Monophysitism attempts to reduce Christology to a single dimension or "nature" of Jesus Christ (to use the not altogether felicitous language of later christological dogma). I would prefer to speak of two forms of Monophysitism—the one "from above," the other "from below." The monophysitism from above is what endangered the Christology of the ancient and medieval periods, and even the later periods of "orthodoxy"; here the full humanity of Jesus takes second place to his divinity. The Monophysitism from below is what threatens Christology in the modern period; here the divine initiative and presence in the history of Christ are minimized or explained away altogether and Christ is reduced to a mere example or a code word for potentialities that are found in all humans in general.

Both kinds of Monophysitism trivialize and truncate the New Testament witness to Christ. In our present context this means concretely that they rob the divine incarnation of its reality and significance. For when either aspect of the Christ event—the true divinity *or* the true humanity—is minimized or eliminated altogether, the scope and relevance of this central message is threatened and diminished. According to the witness of the New Testament, the very basis of our salvation, the very ground of our hope consists in the fact that we are permitted to believe, know, and confess the authoritative presence of *God* in the *human* life and destiny of Jesus of Nazareth.

Speaking of the resurrection of Christ, the apostle Paul formulated this axiom: "If Christ has not been raised, then our preaching is in vain and your faith is in vain" (1 Cor. 15:14). It is surely legitimate to venture a similar formulation with respect to our present theme and say: "If God was not incarnate in Christ, then our preaching is in vain and your faith is in vain." That, at any rate, was what the ancient church believed. The very foundation of salvation depends on these two pillars of the Christ event remaining intact and in place. When either is whittled away or collapses, the very foundation of our faith is also shaken.

If it was not God who acted and suffered for us in Christ, then we with all our guilt and hope are left solely to our own devices, or rather left at the mercy of the principalities and powers of this human world. To use Paul's words again, we are therefore "still in our sins" (1 Cor.

15:17), "having no hope and without God in the world" (Eph. 2:12). But the converse is also true and no less important: if in Jesus Christ God did not become completely human, did not really become one of us, then his salvation did not fully reach us; it shines (or dawns) ineffectively above our heads, instead of really affecting us right here where we live and suffer, right down here in the very midst of and over the whole range of our human life and destiny.

This, then, is why the ancient church conducted its battle on two fronts, against the Monophysitism from above and the Monophysitism from below—not because of any merely speculative concern for neat conceptual symmetry, but because of its vital interest in salvation. Though tedious and often confused, the struggle was of ultimate importance for salvation and for life. It ended with the achievement of the Chalcedonian formula: "truly God and truly human . . . one and the same Christ in two natures, without confusion, without change, without division, without separation." We may be put off and perhaps even shocked by such dry intellectual language. Even so, we should be foolish to ignore the throb of vital concerns and decisions of faith that pulses beneath the conceptual crust of this Chalcedonian formula, which was an attempt, however halting, to remain faithful in the face of all opposition and to do justice to the mystery of salvation involved in God's assuming of our humanity.

This is the central concern of the clause "Conceived by the Holy Spirit, born from the virgin Mary" in the Apostles' Creed. This formulation too, like that of Chalcedon, is incomplete, imperfect, open to misunderstanding. It too can only announce and signal but never adequately express much less exhaust its essential theme, the incarnation of God, by its reference to the two dimensions. Here, too, we are not required to swear by the precise wording, provided we adhere to its substance. In a real sense, however, the statement of the Apostles' Creed has an advantage over many other doctrinal formulations, including the Chalcedonian formula. As said early in the previous chapter (with reference to the divinity of Christ), the Apostles' Creed does not freeze its dynamic theme in static concepts (such as the "natures" of Christ) but points unmistakably to an event, a history. In so doing it is faithful to the dynamic character of the reality to which it points, namely, God's *becoming* incarnate, his assuming of our humanity.

Christmas Is
the "Conception" of the Holy Spirit

The dynamic event referred to here in the Creed is a specific one, the one recounted in the Christmas story. This also means that the main biblical background of this credal clause is obviously the Christmas narratives of the Gospels, in particular Matt. 1:18–25. We shall have occasion repeatedly to refer to these narratives as we deal with the two parts of our article.

The question envisaged and answered in the first brief clause, conceived by the Holy Spirit, is the question of the origin of Jesus of Nazareth. Obviously this is a question that can be answered in a number of ways—with reference to the biological, geographical, or sociological provenience of Jesus. There can be no objection in principle to such approaches; they too are grounded on the complete humanity of Jesus. According to the Fourth Gospel, for example, Jesus' contemporaries discussed the question of his origin and birth, and used the fact that he came from Nazareth as proof that he was not the Messiah. Everyone knew Jesus' origin: "We know where this man comes from; and when the Christ appears, no one will know where he comes from" (John 7:27). Speculation is likely to run wild in the answering of such questions, given the difficult state of the historical sources. The biological question has often assumed the greatest prominence in this connection (nor surprisingly in view of the virgin birth motif in the second part of our article), with the major question being Who was the Father of Jesus? Anti-Christian propagandists took a certain delight in pursuing this question. Rumors circulated already in the period of the early church to the effect that the father of Mary's child was a Roman soldier named Ben Panthera. The rumor is occasionally repeated even in our own day. I am reminded of a court case in Yugoslavia in 1966 when an antichurch poet was found guilty of religious intolerance for having used ambiguous words to ridicule the story of Jesus' parentage: "The Holy Spirit lay down on Mary, the Virgin kissed the Holy Spirit, kissed His mighty hands . . ."

Questions and answers of this sort are indeed possible, and Christians should not be quick to take offense (or appeal to the civil courts for protection!). He who is Son of God and son of man was also delivered into human hands that were not exactly clean; that is part

106

of the risk he took in becoming human. But the questions put and the answer given by the Creed are quite different. The Creed is concerned not with Jesus' immediate background but with what lies behind it, with his derivation, where he came from, with his provenience not in any relative sense but in the absolute—or theological—sense. The ambiguous term "conceived" points not to biological realities but to the origin or beginning in the radical sense. It focuses attention on the deepest, the ultimate conception of this history of Jesus of Nazareth, on its true initiation, beginning or "genesis" in the specifically biblical sense.

Despite all the ambiguity of the images used, the New Testament passages are quite unambiguous about this theological context. In the Christmas narratives particularly they utilize a whole series of Old Testament themes. The prominence given to the theme of the Spirit in these narratives itself establishes richly significant links with the Genesis account of the beginnings. The Spirit of God is the power of creation (Gen. 1:2) and also that of the "new creation," that is, of God's becoming human. What takes place is the beginning of the life of Jesus, therefore, is in fact the new "genesis"—this is actually the Greek word that appears in the title of Matthew's narrative (translated as "birth" in Matt. 1:18). John too adopts the same point of view in his prologue; he answers the question about Jesus' origin by pointing to the eternal creative Word of God that now becomes flesh.

This is the question that receives an unambiguous answer in the affirmation "conceived by the Holy Spirit." The origin and beginning of Jesus are due not to the decision of an individual human being, or to some accidental combination of circumstances, but to the promise and election of God. No other conception—or absence of conception—is disclosed in the history of Christ, than the conception of God. No other seizes the initiative than God's Spirit. The creative power that presses toward incarnation is none other than the Creator Spirit. The only love at work in the coming of God's son is the love of the Father for the Son in the Holy Spirit. "The subject of the story of Jesus Christ, therefore, is God himself, as truly as a human being there lives, suffers, and acts."[2]

For the Apostles' Creed—which here is simply following the Gospel—the important point to be clearly grasped is what might be called the movement, direction, trend, or inclination of the incarnation, of the Christmas story. Christmas involves both God's history and human history. Neither of the two may be overlooked—not even the human side. The human lovingkindness, generosity, and the good will that mark the celebration of Christmas, even where the event that the festival celebrates has been watered down or forgotten, are not just part of a misunderstanding. In its interpretation of that event, however, the Creed insists on clarity: let it be understood that the good will involved here, the lovingkindness and generosity, is that of God (cf. Tit. 3:4). In God is to be found the beginning, the origin, and the foundation of Christmas joy. To be sure, that joy radiates outward and is reflected in the purely human sphere—thank God it does—but that radiation and reflection proceed exclusively from the direction of God, on the basis of their "origin" in his "conception."

It is in this sense that our reflection on the two sides of the Christ event, on the two poles of God's becoming human, must be given greater theological specification. I spoke earlier of the "two pillars" on which salvation rests in any authentic interpretation of the incarnation. There can be no going back on that. At the same time, we need to guard against a possible misunderstanding: there is no fifty-fifty distribution of weight between these two pillars. The history of Jesus is not half-human and half-divine; it is one-hundred-percent divine history and one-hundred-percent human history—but in an irreversible direction, namely, from God to us, from heaven to earth, from the eternal origin downwards into our time.

In its Christology the church has made every effort to remain faithful to this vital aspect of the Christmas story. It has taken great pains to stress the divine initiative in the act of the incarnation. I am thinking here particularly of the doctrine of the anhypostasis or enhypostasis of the humanity of Jesus Christ—the doctrine that the "human nature" of Jesus Christ has no independent existence but that its human history has clearly been taken up into the history of God. This doctrine is undoubtedly one of the bugbears of the dogmatic tradition, which seems here to have produced one of its most speculative constructions. While we cannot enter into the details of the doctrine here,[3] it is important to note its central positive thrust, that in the incarnation of God the humanity of Jesus Christ—and through him our own humanity—does not act on its own; it is not self-subsistent, in isolation, but is securely encompassed and carried in God. Salvation originates in God alone!

Mary and the Relativity of the Miracle

This salvation, nevertheless, does come into our human world! Far from remaining suspended somewhere between heaven and earth, it seeks us out here, in our real history, both personal and collective. At the heart of the self-giving of the son of God is his unconditional solidarity with us, indeed his utter identification with us, his *becoming human* not just in some metaphorical or symbolic sense but really and truly, in the full sense of the word "incarnation." To emphasize this is, in fact, the whole point of the second part of our credal clause—"born from the virgin Mary." We must beware of becoming too easily fascinated—or irritated—by the virgin birth motif. We must beware of allowing our attention to be all too quickly diverted from the primary fact that what the Creed is speaking of here is quite simply a human being, a particular human being, a specific Jewish woman named Mary. In one of his central christological passages, the apostle Paul speaks of the incarnation as follows: "When the time had fully come, God sent forth his Son, born of a woman, born under the law" (Gal. 4:4). What he enumerates here are the main dimensions of our human existence—the dimension of history and of salvation history, the biological dimension, and the religious and cultural dimension. The Son of God shares in all these dimensions; nothing human is alien to him. The central fact of the incarnation—and the primary and central article of faith confessed in the Creed at this point—is that Jesus comes into the world in the way that is common to us all: he has a flesh-and-blood woman as his mother; he is conceived in the womb and brought to birth.

> then
> when in the cry of birth God
> smashed the idols
> and
> between Mary's thighs
> the child lay
> wrinkled and red[4]

Blood and tears cannot be expunged from the Christmas story without trivializing and distorting our remembrance of the "then"—*and* our Christmas celebration here and now. There is no evading "the child"—"wrinkled and red" like countless other newborn infants. Here we have the very heartbeat of the apostolic affirmation.

Only after this has been made quite clear is our attention drawn secondarily, but nonetheless seriously and with emphasis, to the parthenogenesis motif. The Apostles' Creed unquestionably speaks of the mother of Jesus as a virgin: "from the virgin Mary." I attach great importance to this sequence of primary and secondary. It seems to me to be of real help in avoiding all the tensions and controversies that have accompanied the doctrine of the virgin birth down through history. I regard it as a tragedy that just at this particular point in the Creed the battle lines should be so sharply drawn and people forced to decide one way or the other.

For example, I have serious problems with Protestant critiques of parthenogenesis that consider the doctrine almost a complete distortion of the authentic christological message, one that renders it obscure and unacceptable to the modern mind. Some such attitude can be detected in the polemics of Emil Brunner, who describes this credal clause as "a biological interpretation of the miracle" and refers to it as to a form of "little faith."⁵ Not surprisingly, this provokes from the Orthodox side, and from no less important a spokesman than Nikolas Berdyaev, an equally categorical and certainly overstated reply:

> I read Brunner's book [*The Mediator*] with tremendous interest, because I felt in him tenseness and acuity of thought, religious sensibility. But when I reached the passage in which Brunner confesses that he does not believe in Jesus Christ's birth of the Virgin, or at least confronts it with indifference, my mood became sad and the matter grew tedious. For it seemed to me as though everything had now been cancelled, as though everything else was now pointless.⁶

I have spoken elsewhere of the "relativity" of this doctrine and given my reasons for doing so. Here too I want to use the same descriptive term, and not simply to refer to the fact that the statement "born from the virgin Mary" is very sparsely attested in the New Testament. It is of course referred to only in the nativity narratives of Matthew and Luke, and even here somewhat ambiguously in that the Greek word for "virgin" is itself a translation—used already in the Septuagint—of the Hebrew word *almah* which simply means a "young woman." Moreover, the theme of parthenogenesis is absent altogether from the Johannine and Pauline writings. This almost total reticence of the apostolic preaching on the topic of parthenogenesis needs to be taken seriously in our doctrinal reflections.

What I have chiefly in mind, however, when I speak of the "relativity" of this doctrine is the basic fact that the virgin birth is an "interpretative dogma." That is to say, the credal statement is not an independent affirmation of something that stands alone, on its own. It represents not a dominant motif but a subservient motif in the Christian testimony. It exists to serve the more important kerygma—indeed the real christological kerygma—of God's assumption of our humanity. It is to be attested only in relation to this message—as its "sign" (as Karl Barth liked to call it). But if this is the case, then the battle lines lie elsewhere, and the virgin birth is useless as a test of orthodoxy or of intellectual integrity. Only the reality itself, God's assumption of our humanity, is the article on which the very existence of the church depends, not the virgin birth as its specific interpretation.

Within this frame of reference, given this relativity of the virgin birth as a secondary and not a primary theme, the motif itself certainly merits theological attention. Its purpose is to serve that which is greater than itself, just as John the Baptist, for example, points away from himself to the Coming One. Another analogy may be the way in which the angels appear in the gospel narrative at precisely the moment of some radical new beginning—specifically in the Christmas and Easter narratives. So too the theme of the virgin birth—in which the angels also play a vital role—is intended to signal to the presence of a mystery. This analogy with the angels may suggest yet a further clarification: Just as it was unwise for theology to have gone beyond the witnessing function of the angels and turned that theme into a discrete element within a general picture of the world, and developed a whole ontology and even a physiology of the angels, so too it is unwise to treat the virgin birth motif as a discrete biological and even a gynecological theme.

That misunderstandings should have been possible and even inevitable from the beginning on this score is not at all surprising when we recall the importance of the parthenogenesis theme in the general history of religion. Here it crops up most often in connection with various divine marriages between gods and virgins. Ascetic and secular fantasies too might have led to misunderstandings, for they were easily triggered and fueled by the notion of a virgin birth. The point to be emphasized here, however, is that factors such as these were not the matrix for the Christmas narratives of the Bible, nor of the doctrine itself. As Lohmeyer rightly says in his commentary on Matthew, the idea of the virgin birth is a "theologoumenon that establishes a religious hope, not a myth that satisfies a devout curiosity."[8] In its original meaning the biblical text has virtually nothing to do with biology and physiology, either in an affirmative sense (as glorification of sexuality such as was known among pagans in their divine marriages) or in a negative sense (as a basic distrust of human sexuality). Its intention is strictly theological.

Can we define this intention more precisely? Yes, I think so. Indeed I would be inclined to pursue such a sharpened definition by developing and sharpening the concern that emerged at the close of the previous section—that salvation originates in God alone. In the words of Karl Barth: ". . . that God stands at the start, where real revelation takes place—God, and not the arbitrary cleverness, capability or piety of a human being."[9] The parthenogenesis theme achieves the sharpening by specifically excluding the male. It excludes him not so much as a member of the male sex but rather as the typical human being who throughout most of human history has by his self-assertion set himself up—over against the "weak" female sex—as the "strong one," the chief actor in history and the prime shaper of civilization, the "lord of creation." *This* human being, this patriarch, this head of the family, this Mr. Fix-It—is by the parthenogenesis theme— unmistakably set aside.

"Born from the virgin Mary" is concerned to make one point quite clear, that in his work of salvation, God needs no coequal agent, no coworker, no dynamic collaborator, no coredemptor or coredeemer. In the act of God's becoming human, humanity is involved in only one way—in the figure of the "virgin Mary"; in other words, in the form not of a primarily creating, controlling, self-assertive, self-glorifying humanity but of a primarily listening, receiving, serving, and blessed ("graced") human being—as Mary is impressively described in the Christmas narrative.

These characteristics of Mary are not to be confused with a basic passivity or with an ideology of patience, much less with the usual distribution of sex roles. The New Testament itself warns us against all equations of this kind. The evangelist Luke puts one of the most revolutionary utterances of the New Testament into the mouth of Mary as her response to the initiative and deeds of the divine grace: "My soul doth magnify the Lord . . . for he has cast down the mighty from their seats and exalted the humble and meek; he has filled the hungry with good things and the rich he has sent empty away" (Luke 1:45, 53). In a sermon preached in the year 1933 (certainly with the Nazi takeover of his homeland in mind) Dietrich Bonhoeffer comments: "The Mary who speaks here is not the gentle, tender, dreamy Mary portrayed by the painters, but the passionate, rapturous, proud, and enthusiastic Mary."[10] As is clear from Mary's Magnificat, however, this committed response is not a matter of arbitrary self-help by a take-charge person; it rests rather on the dynamics of grace. It is the response *not* of a graceless humanity but of a humanity under grace. This is the point that the Apostles' Creed would make when it declares that Jesus Christ was "conceived by the Holy Spirit, born from the virgin Mary."

An Ecumenical "Dialogue of Angels"

An ecumenical dialogue on this article, while difficult, is not impossible. I would raise two questions for ecumenical discussion, first a question and then a counterquestion.

First, in view of the arguments just presented, I would ask Protestant theologians to consider: Have we not been much too easily inclined to ignore the virgin Mary and not take seriously her presence in the Creed? The history of the church, of course, provides real grounds for a certain theological reticence here, in view of the sometimes excessive mariological elements in Eastern Orthodox and Roman Catholic spirituality. We must nevertheless face up to the question whether in Protestant dogmatics and ethics we do not pay too little attention to the human example provided us in the Mary of the Gospels and the Creed—and, of course, in Mary herself—as the listening, receptive, and "graced" human being who of course is then also determined to obey and serve.

I am reminded in this connection of an anecdote told me in the Russian Orthodox monastery in Zagorsk in explanation of an ancient icon. The icon depicted a saint working away at his translation of the Bible. He is about to translate Isaiah 7, when an angel intervenes to say: "Don't write 'young woman,' write 'virgin,' for heaven's sake!" The Eastern church's concern for parthenogenesis must be ecumenically considered, and with discretion accepted, in Protestant circles.

At the same time, however, and in the same ecumenical spirit, a "Protestant" question, so to speak, must be raised for Eastern Orthodox and Roman Catholic consideration: Is not too great and one-sided an emphasis being placed on the mariological and par-thenogenesis motif when it is construed not simply as a relative and subservient theologoumenon but as *the* miracle, the heart of the divine incarnation itself? Two matters seem especially open to question.

First, does not Mary become too easily the leading lady in the drama of salvation—not just "the handmaid of the Lord" but also the "queen of Heaven?" But this would certainly obscure rather than clarify the *theological* intention of the virgin birth, which is to point away from itself toward God alone. The development of mariological dogma in the direction of attributing to Mary the title "coredeemer" gives us pause. I regard this tendency, though not mariology in its entirety, as a distortion of the apostolic virgin birth motif.

The other question is closely related: Does not the independent emphasis given to the virgin birth in mariology, the concentration of attention on the matter of the virginity, almost inevitably bring into play those erotic and biological motifs to which we have referred? If what is emphasized symbolically in the term "virgin" is not just the initiative of the Holy Spirit but also the exclusion and ascetic suppression of human sexuality, attention is all too easily diverted from the central theological intention. Here a Protestant counterquestion needs to be put, as an invitation to reconsideration. Today a Protestant angel—and why should there not be such?—would have to issue a different warning to the Bible translator: "Don't write 'virgin,' write 'young woman,' for heaven's sake!" Theologically, this possibility is quite open to us—particularly since, far from abandoning the central intention of the dogma, it emphasizes all the more clearly the constitutive relationship of the virgin birth to that which is "greater" than itself, namely, the mystery of God's becoming human.

Is it just my imagination or are there really opportunities today for such an ecumenical "dialogue of angels?" Be that as it may, I would like to give the last word in this chapter to the eminent Catholic theologian and dignitary Josef Ratzinger:

> The virgin birth is not a chapter in ascetic theology, nor is it directly part of the doctrine of the divine sonship of Jesus. From start to finish it is a theology of grace, a message telling us how salvation comes *to us*—namely in the simple act of receiving that wholly gratuitous gift of love which redeems the world.[11]

10

Suffered Under Pontius Pilate

Salvation with a Human Face

To sum up in a phrase the main theme of this clause, "Suffered under Pontius Pilate," I would say it is concerned with the complete humanity of Jesus Christ. Following confession of faith in the complete divinity of Christ ("His only Son, our Lord") and in the divine incarnation ("Conceived of the Holy Spirit, born from the virgin Mary") we now have as a third main christological theme that of the true humanity of Jesus Christ. These three themes are inseparable, of course, and none of them is to be emphasized at the expense of the others. The essential character of the history attested in the Creed, the integrity of the christological article, depends on all three themes, the present one no less than the previous two.

Recognition of the complete humanity of Christ and confession of its significance for salvation were not something that could be taken for granted in the ancient church. Indeed, it was only through costly struggle that this recognition and confession came to be clearly and unambiguously secured. The New Testament writings themselves should remove any doubt about the fact that the history unfolded here is a human one. The synoptic Gospels provide a vivid down-to-earth account of the teaching and ministry of Jesus. The Pauline corpus witnesses to the Son of God who in the fullness of time was "born of woman, born under the law" (Gal. 4:4), and who, above all, was crucified under Pontius Pilate. John too asserts that there is no worse misunderstanding of the history of Jesus than that of those who cast doubt on his coming "in the flesh"—in a truly human body, sharing completely the human condition (1 John 4:1ff.).

In fact, however, doubts were already there in the background of the New Testament texts, and these doubts, so far from weakening, were actually reinforced as time went on. Given the intellectual climate of that time, it was no easier to affirm the full humanity of Jesus Christ than it was to affirm his divinity as Son of God. Despite the rich variety of divine sons and divine saviors in the religious currents of the time, in no case was any of them identified with a unique individual and a unique history. Mythology and Gnosticism, which dominated the religious scene, tended to remove salvation—and therefore the Christ event too—from this world and its history, and hence from the human sphere as well. In these circumstances, the message of the divine Logos sounded less offensive to pious ears—both inside the church and outside—than did the message of the incarnation. To become "Docetist," that is, to water down the tangible historical and personal human realities of the history of Jesus, became perhaps the most insidious temptation of the Christology in the ancient church.

The Creed resolutely rejects this temptation. It does so unmistakably when it affirms that Jesus "suffered under Pontius Pilate, was crucified, dead and buried." This series of short staccato statements rules out all flight into mythology and symbolism. What is attested here is not a rationalized dream or semblance but the harshest of harsh human realities—suffering, dying, and being dead. The living and dying of a suffering human being is the bitter horizon to which the apostolic faith in Christ refers.

The underlying interest here, in recognizing and confessing the humanity of Christ and its significance for salvation, is not simply historical; it is not concerned, for example, simply to prevent the historical core of Christianity from being dissolved without remainder into religious mythology or Gnosticism. The concern from first to last is with something absolutely vital to Christian faith. Here again, we could adapt Paul's words about the resurrection and say: If Christ did *not* become fully human, if he did *not* suffer, was *not* crucified, did *not* die and was *not* buried, then our faith is utterly in vain. The down-to-earth realism of the Christian faith depends completely on the full humanity of Jesus Christ, on God's having really become *human*. There are at least two senses in which this is true and both are concerned with the two supremely important aspects of faith's connection with reality: the soteriological aspect and the ethical aspect. Let us look briefly at these two aspects.

The ancient church had already given a convincing answer to the question of the soteriological significance of the full humanity of

Jesus: "What has not been assumed has not been redeemed."[1] If Christ was not fully human, the salvation revealed in him has not come all the way to us, has not really reached us. In that case, there are areas of human life, indeed of creation, that remain unaffected by salvation, utterly "hopeless" areas. This view is a prevailing one in the history of religion. In particular, the physical, material, and historical dimensions of human life and of the world are held to lie beyond the reach of salvation. But Christology, by its witness to the full humanity of Jesus, resists this restriction imposed by religious idealism. In traditional theology, the term "among us completely" was coined to counter this restriction. In other words, nothing human is alien to God. In his work of salvation God abandons no part of his creation. No sphere of our human reality is excluded from the encounter with Jesus. According to the witness of the New Testament, this is precisely what Jesus' contemporaries experienced in their dealings with him. Neither in his dealings with them nor in his message to them did Jesus impose any prior conditions on them. He did not pressure them into religiously stereotyped roles—for example, by insisting on a certain religious or ascetic style of life—but summoned them instead to hope and repentance in the diverse circumstances of their concrete human existence. Salvation as the apostles bear witness to it, because it is rooted in the human Jesus, is salvation with a human face.

This has ethical consequences—and here we come to the other aspect of the Creed's connection with reality. Two points call for emphasis, one general and the other specific.

First, the general point: Since by its reference to the complete humanity of Jesus the apostolic witness to Christ leads us to the very heart of human reality, it establishes at the same time, as a central and indispensable dimension of this witness, our ethical (and political) responsibility. Since the salvation opened up in Christ is indivisible, the responsibility anchored in this salvation is also indivisible. Since our hope of salvation is connected with "the center of time," and accordingly has to do with *history*, it therefore really *has to do* with history; salvation must relate to what is going on and cannot be divorced from the shaping of historical circumstances. We are not at liberty, therefore, to exclude ethical and political practice from the legitimate and necessary concerns of Christian discipleship. Ethics is an inseparable part of the "business of faith."

But the confession of faith in the complete humanity of Jesus has

117

concrete ethical implications as well as general ones. The concrete features of the historical life and ministry of Jesus are vitally important, especially in the ethical context. They give shape to Christian existence, indicating the direction and path of discipleship and stamping Christian faith as necessarily a way of life. The possibilities for the Christian along this way are not unlimited, if by this we mean completely arbitrary. In the human existence of Jesus, Christians are provided with a model, not one to be slavishly imitated but certainly one to which we must conform—in his light and in obedience to his teaching and example. Emphasis on the humanity of Jesus gives concreteness to faith's relevance for daily life.

A Profane Figure in the History of Salvation

The basic content of this credal clause is unfolded in two specific emphases: "suffered" and "under Pontius Pilate." Careful attention must be paid to both statements. We begin with the second.

The appearance of the profane figure of Pilate at the very center of the event of salvation attested in the Apostles' Creed has always surprised and even shocked many people. This surprise has even left its imprint in the proverbial wisdom of the Christian traditions. The Czechs, for example, have a saying: "He's as out of place here as Pilate is in the Creed!" For understandable reasons, people have taken offense at the basic incongruity. There is nothing incongruous, of course, about the Creed naming a human being in this Second Article. In a history taking place among human beings and for human beings, this is only to be expected. There is no objection to the presence of Mary in this history. What *does* bring us up with a jolt, however, is that alongside the grace-filled figure of Mary, the woman who found favor with God, alongside the spotless virgin, there should appear the patently "grace-less" figure of Pontius Pilate, a disreputable opportunist.

As we know not only from the Gospels but also from other historical sources, Pontius Pilate was a shady as well as a shadowy character. An imperial procurator in a remote province of the Roman Empire, he was obviously not much respected in Rome. Because of his office, as representative of the occupying power, he was certainly feared and hated by the people in Palestine. In the exercise of his office Pilate distinguished himself as a brutal governor (one of his pitiless draconian acts is described in Luke 13) who also gave the impression of being a rather weak and spineless bureaucrat. He comes into Jesus' history at the decisive moment of its final crisis. The Gospels tend to play down his role. It is rather the religious authorities who are the moving spirits in the trial of Jesus. The very reticence of the Gospels, however, throws Pilate's failure as a statesman into an even more shocking light. Against his better judgment he bends the law; with only slight hesitation he yields to Jesus' enemies in a very cowardly way for purely opportunistic reasons. His last act—the release of the murderer Barabbas and the execution of the innocent Jesus—overturns the very principles of his own Roman justice. It was a lamentable dereliction of duty, a squalid business.

Thus does a man of this kind come to be mentioned in the Creed—and hence become one of the most frequently named persons in the entire history of the church and of civilization. (In her 1943 radio play cycle *The Man Born To Be King*, Dorothy L. Sayers offers an interesting explanation of the dream attributed in the Gospels to Pilate's wife. Sayers suggests that Pilate's wife interceded with her husband on Jesus' behalf because in her dream she had heard the unending chorus of voices reciting endlessly in all languages that one phrase: "suffered under Pontius Pilate.") A profane figure at the very center of the history of salvation? That is an offense in and of itself!

But this was one affirmation to which the ancient church stuck firmly, persistently, and with amazing unanimity. On this point all three creeds agree, and that cannot have been accidental; it can only be explained as the result of careful theological reflection. There are good reasons why we should take this decision of the creeds seriously and respect its underlying motives. Unless I am mistaken, these motives are still relevant for us today.

The context in which the credal reference to Pontius Pilate is primarily to be understood is the ancient church's struggle against the attractions of Docetism. I have already pointed out that the church was tempted by various religious and philosophical currents of that time to water down the offensive historical character of its Easter message and to adopt instead a more spiritual symbolic interpretation—one that would prevent the honor of its central savior figure from being sullied by direct contact with the "polluted" realm of human, all-too-human history—and ultimately transform the history of Christ into "the myth of Christ" (to use a term made notorious in

119

the nineteenth century by thinkers such as Arthur Drews). In the words "under Pontius Pilate" the Creed provides a clear defense against such a fatal temptation. To put it positively: these words confirm the full humanity of Jesus Christ and therefore the down-to-earth realism of Christian faith. They do this in two specific ways: by their reference to the realities of history and of politics.

The specific reference to Pilate by name indicates, in the first place, the historical dimension of the Christian faith. From start to finish, but with particular clarity in the Second Article, the Creed affirms that the Christian faith is not a matter of general ideas but the narration of something that actually happened. The person who confesses the faith—more specifically, the candidate for and recipient of baptism—is not just spiritually and intellectually "enlightened" but actually taken up into a history, the history of the covenant and salvation, the history of the liberation of the people of God. What is now stressed in addition, here in the reference to Pontius Pilate, is that the locus of this history of salvation is not some insulated and safe ideal realm outside of world history but right here in the very midst of the circumstances and conditions of daily life.

Although Pilate is only a very minor figure in world history, his presence in the Creed establishes the fully historical dimension of the faith. It does this in the first instance simply by dating the history of Christ, by giving it a specific location within world history. The theologians of the early church displayed astonishing clarity of vision when—on theological grounds—they recognized and articulated this historical concern. Rufinus (d. 440), for example, declares:

> Those who handed down the Creed showed great wisdom in underlining the actual date at which these things happened, so that there might be no chance of any uncertainty or vagueness upsetting the stability of the tradition.[2]

But the dimension of complete historicity secured by this reference to Pilate in the Creed is far more than a matter of the datability—or even the actual dating—of the history of salvation. The important thing about this particular history that is associated with this particular name is not just *that* it happened but also *how* it happened. I am thinking here of the shadowy, questionable character of Pilate. The credal reference to Pilate surely emphasizes that the biblical history of salvation is concerned not just with outstanding people, or even just with respectable people, but also with quite ordinary people as well. It is not only the spotless virgin but also impure and unholy people who come within its purview; this can be seen also in the not-always-flattering genealogical tree of Jesus (Matt. 1:1–17; Luke 3:23–38), which includes among his ancestors some less than illustrious men and women. The history of salvation clearly is not some bourgeois "living room," to which only clean or apparently clean and respectable people are admitted, with all others invited on principle to stay away. Christian faith exercises no censorship over history. It does not invent a Docetic world of reverie and semblance but takes the world and history as they are—in order, of course, to confront them with Jesus Christ and shape them in accordance with his kingdom. The present relevance and permanent significance of Pilate's presence in the Creed, therefore, are to be found in this direction, namely, as an argument for the fully historical dimension of the Christian faith.

But there is a special reason as well for reference to Pilate. It not only brings into the purview of the Christian faith the field of human history. In the second place, and closely connected with this important historical dimension, it establishes the connection of faith with the field of politics. Pilate is not simply a general historical figure; he is also the occupant of a particular office, a political figure. It is as a public official that he plays his part in the gospel story. He plays it deplorably but he plays it, and his presence in the Creed must also be looked at from this angle.

It was Karl Barth who devoted special attention to this aspect of the story of Pilate. In his essay on "Justification and Justice" (1938) Barth started with the encounter between Jesus and Pilate in working out his own position on the relation between theology and politics. In his expositions of the Apostles' Creed, too, Barth emphasizes the political dimensions of the reference to Pilate. The whole drama and dialectic of Jesus' ministry and destiny comes to a sharp focus here. Jesus is neither a Zealot nor an anarchist. When brought before the procurator, Jesus makes no protest but accepts Pilate in his official role—though Jesus is under no illusions about how Pilate exercises his office. However ambiguous and questionable its forms, the political order is not something arbitrary and evil. It has its roots in the "divine order." According to John, Jesus tells Pilate quite frankly: "You would have no power over me unless it had been given you from above"

(John 19:11). Jesus takes seriously his own words, "Render to Caesar the things that are Caesar's" (Mark 12:17). In Romans 13 Paul's position conforms to the attitude of Jesus. Despite the misuse to which this chapter has so often been put—when at times the church has transformed it into an ideology of political authority—Paul's words still need to be taken to heart today.

But there is another aspect to the meeting between Jesus and Pilate—and to the tension-filled relation between theology and politics. The power given to Pilate "from above" is blatantly abused. Barth comments: "He [Pilate] does what politicians, by and large, have always done, and something which is undoubtedly a permanent ingredient in actual political practice at all times: he tries to save and maintain order in Jerusalem and, at the same time, to preserve his own position of power, by sacrificing the evident law he was actually appointed to defend."[3] By doing so, Pilate the politician and representative of the state ends up by acting contrary to the law, in opposition to the justification and justice of every true—every God-given and humanly just—political order. Another biblical passage, also a chapter thirteen, then comes into view: "In the person of Pilate, the state then deprives itself of its own basis of existence and becomes the 'den of thieves.' . . . This is the state as the New Testament describes it in the thirteenth chapter of the Book of Revelation: the beast from the abyss, accompanied by the other beast with the 'big mouth,' which continually glorifies and praises the first beast."[4]

Christians who lived in the time when the Creed emerged, realized with painful clarity that a good deal of the world's political history was governed by these two apocalyptic beasts. All the more to their credit, therefore, that in these conditions they did not take the easy way out and simply abandon the political realm altogether on religious grounds; they did not deny their political responsibilities, join in the disillusioned refrain of those who dismiss politics as a dirty game, and strike the name of Pilate from the Creed. Even in this very exposed territory, the Apostles' Creed helped to maintain the down-to-earth realism of the Christian faith, and in this sense too to conquer the temptation to Docetism.

Here we have the second basis for the permanent relevance of the reference to Pontius Pilate in the Apostles' Creed, a reference that at first sight seems almost scandalous. Indeed, this second aspect may be even more important today than the first. We are probably not much in danger today of forgetting that the Christian faith is anchored in history; on the other hand, our churches still have problems with the political dimension of their faith. Our problem today is not so much historical Docetism as political Docetism. Despite all the recent developments in political theology and despite the increased ecumenical concern for church and society, the political dimension of church theory and practice still seems underdeveloped. Many of the recent developments anyway are short-term and ephemeral, and therefore not likely to be of much use in the long run. What is long overdue and would really be helpful is a concentrated theological study of the foundations of the Christian faith—including, above all, the role of Pilate in the Creed—that would include intense reflection on its historical and political components. By being alert to the fatal danger of Docetism and—this would be the corollary—by resisting any reduction of the down-to-earth realism of the Christian faith, we would come closer than we might imagine to one of the fundamental concerns of the ancient church.

Christian "Masochism"?

The theme of the complete humanity of Jesus Christ is concretely developed and demonstrated not only in the adverbial phrase "under Pontius Pilate" but also in the preceding verb that it modifies—the little word "suffered." We now turn to this credal affirmation, both for its own sake and as a transition to the central affirmation that follows, the crucifixion.

Even this word "suffered" raises important exegetical questions. It can, of course, be interpreted in a very simple way—as a reference to the sufferings of Jesus at the end of this life and ministry, a summary of the passion narratives of the gospels. Although there is much to be said in favor of this simple interpretation, I regard it as inadequate. Throughout this chapter we have been considering the complete humanity of Jesus. When the word "suffered" is seen in connection with this larger consideration, we come to realize that in the Creed it actually stands for the entire life of Jesus from his birth to his death on the cross. We must look more closely into this.

Question 55 of John Calvin's Geneva Catechism reads: "Why do you go immediately from his birth to his death, passing over the whole history of his life?" Calvin gives the following answer: "Because the Creed is speaking here only of what properly belongs to the substance of our redemption."⁵ I have problems not only with Calvin's question, but also with his answer. The words "passing over" and "what properly belongs to the substance of our redemption" seem to suggest that, strictly speaking, the life of Jesus from his birth up to but excluding his final days and crucifixion is not an essential part of the saving events. In the last analysis, the whole theologoumenon of the divine incarnation, to the extent that it goes beyond the mystery of Christmas to include also God's solidarity with us in all the circumstances of human existence, would then take second place to the events of the cross and resurrection. I realize that this understanding is an option in Christology. Søren Kierkegaard, for example, opted for it quite deliberately when he suggested that the whole gospel could, in a pinch, be reduced to bare affirmations about the crucifixion of the Son of God. We find a similar tendency today in the indifference of certain contemporary existentialist theologians to the "historical Jesus."

I find it impossible to endorse this decision. For one thing, I am convinced that by neglecting a theme that plays so central a role in Eastern Orthodoxy, we would be painting ourselves into an isolated Protestant corner. There is an ecumenical concern here that should not be neglected.

However, there is an even more important reason, a central theological reason, why we should not choose this option. If the complete humanity of Jesus belongs to the very foundation of our faith, as Calvin insists, then—and here is where I part company with Calvin—the form which that humanity takes in the life of Jesus also belongs to this foundation. In principle, therefore, no phase of Jesus' life can leave me indifferent. More to the point, therefore, is Question 37 of the Heidelberg Catechism: "What do you understand by this little word 'suffered'?" and its answer: "That all the time of his life here on earth, but especially at the end thereof, he bore in body and soul the wrath of God against the sin of the whole human race."⁶ Or, again, as the English poet and preacher John Donne puts it in his Christmas sermon of 1626: "The whole life of Christ was a continual passion; others die Martyrs, but Christ was born a Martyr."⁷

But even if the position is formulated in this way questions still arise: Is it historically and theologically admissible to define the

whole life of Jesus in terms of suffering? Does not this smack of
"Christian masochism" and move in the direction of an ideology of
suffering? It can hardly be denied that the prominence of the word
"suffered" in the credal summary of Jesus' life could provide a
foothold for such tendencies. In expounding the Creed today,
therefore, it is vital that we should effectively correct such tendencies,
and do so on the basis of the Gospels. The history and message of
Jesus certainly offer little incentive for turning the good news into a
theology of suffering. It would be difficult to identify the man from
Nazareth and his message with a masochistic outlook on life. His life
has not only a dark side to it but a sunny side as well. It is not only
a "passion," a matter of things happening to him, but also an action:
he makes things happen. His appearance on the scene is connected
not only with sorrow but also with "great joy" (Luke 2:10). Think of
the Christmas message! Or think of the first miracle of Jesus as recorded in the Fourth Gospel (John 2:1–11); it is no accident that this
miracle has a wedding as its setting—the theme of the wedding feast
is repeatedly highlighted in Jesus' preaching of the kingdom of God.
Or, again, take the life style of Jesus. It certainly is not that of an
ascetic pointedly renouncing the world, suspicious of the joys of
human life, and bent on self-mortification. The reactions of the
people among whom he lived—and here the records bear the unmistakable stamp of historical authenticity—confirm the impression
that Jesus was not only a man of sorrows but also a man of freedom
and joy to whom nothing human was alien, indeed, one whose way
of life led some of his good religious contemporaries, on superficial
observation, to see him as a scandalous "glutton and drunkard"
(Matt. 11:19). Even today we can still learn from the man from
Nazareth how polyphonous, how rich and diverse life can be. His life
could hardly be called narrow and constricted. In this sense too we
must confess the full humanity of Jesus. So too must our interpretation of the word "suffered" move in this direction, though not exclusively so.

Once that is clear, we have to go on to take seriously the special ac-
cent implicit in that word. However rich and full, there is in Jesus'
life a somber fundamental theme. His path inevitably slopes in the
direction of his passion. Not that the Gospels pursue a one-sided
theology of suffering; many of their narratives indeed "breathe the

spirit of the resurrection" (as Bengel expressed it). Think of the transfiguration scene (Mark 9:2ff.), for example, or of the miracles of Jesus. At the same time, however, one would have to say that they also breathe the spirit of the cross. Kurt Marti understood this "takeoff point" of the biography of Jesus:

Flight to Egypt

not
Egypt
is
the takeoff point
of the flight

the child
is saved
for rougher days

the takeoff point
of the flight

is

the cross[8]

We are not to take this simply to mean that the life of Jesus also has a dark side in addition to its sunny side. That is certainly the case: his path leads from Herod to Pilate. But in the vision of the evangelists, the "takeoff point"—the cross—has a much deeper meaning. It means that the path of suffering is not simply a matter of tough luck, an unfortunate outcome; it is the fulfillment of a mission—the way of compassion, of suffering with and sacrificing for many. "The Son of man also came not to be served but to serve and to give his life as a ransom for many" (Mark 10:45). We cannot evade—nor should we wish to evade—the offensive idea that his is the way of "vicarious suffering," the way of the "suffering servant of God"; it is no accident that Isaiah 53 plays such an important role in the passion narratives. The Heidelberg Catechism captures something of this "somber note" that underlies all the Gospel narratives in the words already quoted: "He bore in body and soul the wrath of God against the sin of the whole human race." In this sense, suffering is in fact the basic theme of Jesus' life story.

Destruction of the Destructive

Is there then an ideology of suffering, a propensity to masochism, after all? No, the exact opposite is the case. As Karl Barth points out in his *Dogmatics in Outline*,[9] the word "suffered" is that point in the Creed where human sin and its consequences are spoken of. They are not mentioned in the First Article. They are dealt with here at this critical point in the Second Article, though even here only in the background, as it were. In other words, the wickedness of sin appears only in the light of God's saving action—in the context of the divine incarnation and of the ministry and suffering of the Son of God. Sin, therefore, together with evil and suffering, is clearly not a problem to be pounced on eagerly and enjoyed masochistically. Certainly we are confronted here with the somber reality of alienation, and with the wrath that is appropriate to it. But this confrontation occurs within the framework of God's countermeasures—the action of God that brackets sin and evil—and shows them to be already on the way to destruction.

This "destruction of the destructive" is still bad enough; it costs blood and tears. The way of Jesus is consistently and necessarily a way of suffering (as we shall show in more detail when we come to the word "crucified"). But this suffering is never to be viewed in isolation as an end in itself, much less as a glorious goal. What makes it necessary at all is the need to put an end to it. The goal is not the endurance of evil but the overcoming of it. It is in this sense that I interpret the somber reference to God's "wrath"—that divine protest, articulated in the suffering of Jesus, against the sin of God's creatures and the alienation of his creation. God's wrath is, as it were, the other side of the committed and active love of God.

This is what is really at stake in the credal term "suffered"—not a fetishism of evil and suffering, not a passive reconciliation with evil, but literally the "com-passion" of Jesus Christ, his suffering and sharing and struggling in solidarity with us. Ultimately it amounts to a word of promise: We are not alone in our suffering, not even in the sorrow that suffering causes us. Inasmuch as God's Son is with us and for us, God himself accompanies him on his way. God himself suffers in the suffering of his creatures. God is drawn into, moved to, the same "com-passion," uninsured against the risk because he is not an invulnerable or impassive God. This compassion of God really means the end of all masochism. It means the end, too, of all impassivity, all indifference to suffering, and especially all indifference to the people it strikes. Stated in positive terms, we are summoned here to solidarity, to suffering and sharing and struggling in solidarity with others—as disciples of and partners with him who "suffered under Pontius Pilate."

11

Crucified,
Dead and Buried,
Descended to Hell

The Hard Core

"We preach Christ crucified, a stumbling block to Jews and folly
to Gentiles, but to those who are called, both Jews and Greeks, Christ
the power of God and the wisdom of God" (1 Cor. 1:23f.). We referred to this central Pauline confession of faith already in chapter 7,
as we began our exposition of the Second Article, because Paul here
proclaims Christ as "the power of God and the wisdom of God." To
Paul's Greek and Jewish contemporaries, above all to the pious among
them, this confession of faith was of course scandalous and absurd
because it affirmed the incarnation of this divine wisdom and power
in a particular human life. But this scandal and absurdity reach their
peak at a quite specific point, where Paul confesses "Christ crucified."
If enlightened Greeks and law-abiding Jews were offended at the very
idea of a "God with a human face," then the idea of a God with *this*
face, the face of the *crucified* Jesus, was completely intolerable. In the
Greek world it was possible perhaps to imagine the radiance of divinity in beautiful human beings. In the Jewish world, the figure of a
condemned criminal who not only suffered but was actually crucified—and hence "accursed" according to the Jewish law (Deut.
21:23)—completely shattered the traditional images of the messiah.
So it was that confrontation with the crucified Christ brought to their
sharpest focus the scandal and folly of the Christian faith.

The apostle does not conceal this scandalous fact of crucifixion.
Neither does he glorify it, for example by sadomasochistically taking
perverse pleasure in the infliction of pain. Paul simply sticks to the
fact. He cannot do otherwise, knowing that here is the bedrock of the
apostolic faith and that he is simply articulating the foundational ex-

129

perience of the whole primitive church: "For no other foundation can any one lay than that which is laid, which is Jesus Christ" (1 Cor. 3:11). Certainly this foundation in Christ was established not only in the cross but in the entire history of Jesus Christ. Yet the cross is undoubtedly the hard core of this history. This is already clear from the exceptional length and the theological importance of the passion narratives in the Gospels. Luther's dictum that "the cross tests and confirms everything"—provided the cross is understood in the comprehensive biblical sense as connected with all the events leading up to and following it—faithfully reflects the view of the New Testament.

This very important fact is attested in a great variety of ways in the apostolic witness, and in the doctrinal developments to which it gave rise. A number of different "theologies of the cross" have been developed. We would do well to bear this diversity in mind and carefully weigh the differences, if we hope to avoid one-sided stereotypes and a reductionist theology of the cross. I would like to differentiate between at least three dimensions of the cross: the historical and biographical dimension, the eschatological and soteriological dimension, and the ethical and political dimension.

The Logic of Love

"The fact that Jesus of Nazareth was executed on the cross is one of the most securely established historical facts in the story of Jesus."[1] The historical and biographical components of the history of salvation in Jesus Christ find particularly pointed expression here in the reference to the crucifixion. As we saw already in the previous chapter, the Creed's affirmation of the full humanity of Jesus does not first become visible in the word "crucified." His humanity is attested already from his birth onwards, in opposition to all Docetic attempts to water down the reality of God's incarnation. What is revealed in the crucifixion and death of Jesus, however, is the full and unqualified seriousness of this act of becoming human. In going to the cross, Jesus Christ demonstrates his ultimate solidarity with us; he surmounts the final barrier to human solidarity, namely, death itself, the accursed death of the cross.

But the cross is in no sense a chance "boulder" that just happens to crop up in the Creed, a lonely outstanding peak. This peak clearly emerges from a whole mountain range of events. In other words, the cross appears as one inseparable episode in a single vast and turbulent history. It has its historical antecedents and its historical consequences. The New Testament witness clearly allows for no doubt on this score. For Paul, what is important is mainly the connection between the cross and the resurrection. For him, as for the apostolic witness generally, there is no cross without the resurrection and no resurrection without the cross. In the Gospels, it is the other connection—the historical antecedents—that is given special emphasis: the cross is seen as the culmination of Jesus' life and ministry.

If we are to avoid turning the cross of Christ into an ideology, by making it the isolated "cornerstone" of a world view centered on Good Friday and on suffering, it is essential to keep in view this twofold connection of the cross as attested in the Creed and in its biblical foundation. The danger of turning the cross into an ideology is a very real one, especially in Protestant circles. We touched on it in the previous chapter in connection with Calvin's exegesis of the clause "suffered under Pontius Pilate," though in fairness to Calvin it must be acknowledged that in his case the danger is neutralized by his strong emphasis on the "glory of God" and the resurrection of Jesus Christ. The danger is much greater in Luther and in Lutheran theology, especially where Luther's protest, historically justified, against a false "theology of glory" was developed into an almost metaphysical "theology of the cross." Where this kind of development occurs it usually has a paralyzing effect on Christian commitment to the transformation of the world. An example of such an abstract ideological theology of the cross is found in Luther's polemical battle cry against the rebellious peasants: "Suffering, suffering, cross, cross—this is the Christian's part!" What is needed here is reflection on the indissoluble connections of the cross in the biblical witness. In this first section, where we are considering the historical and biographical dimension of the cross, the connection I want to stress is that between the cross and the concrete life story of Jesus as narrated in the Gospels.

It is remarkable how closely the evangelists connect their accounts of the passion of Jesus and of his active ministry. To employ Marti's language, the "takeoff point" of the "flight" of Jesus is the cross. Clearly the passion and action are connected, and this is no accident—it is a matter of "strict necessity," to put it in a way that is almost sure to scandalize and is certainly open to misinterpretation.

131

"And he began to teach them that the Son of man *must* suffer many things . . . and be killed, and after three days rise again" (Mark 8:31f.). Again and again in the Gospels we encounter this "must" and usually with specific reference to the suffering and cross of Jesus: the Son of man must suffer (for example, Mark 9:31; 10:32–34; Luke 18:31–34). This expression of necessity is open to misinterpretation; it can be taken to mean a deterministic fatalism. In the history of Christian doctrine there have been arguments and theories of salvation that tended in this direction, interpreting Jesus' death on the cross as a necessary fulfillment of a divine objective. But this is certainly not what is meant in the Gospels, or in the Creed. What is involved here is not some predetermined external compulsion, but an inner logic in the way of Jesus itself. Ratzinger hits the nail on the head when he says:

> The cross does not appear in the Bible as an event in a due process of offended criminal justice. Quite the contrary; it appears there as an expression of the lengths to which love—a love that gives itself completely—will go, as an event in which someone whose being and action are indivisible *is* what he does and *does* what he is, as the expression of a life that exists totally for others.[2]

This is the necessity of which the Gospels speak, this inner logic of love. We see it most explicitly in the Fourth Gospel, in such general affirmations as: "Greater love has no man than this, that a man lay down his life for his friends" (John 15:13), or again when it is said directly of Jesus that his love for his disciples was a love that goes to the very limit and beyond ("to the end," John 13:1).

We see yet another aspect to this inner logic of Jesus' way, however, if we look now not at Jesus himself but at the reaction of his contemporaries. The words and works of Jesus, to be sure, awakened a good deal of interest and won approval of many people. From the very beginning, however, Jesus also aroused increasing hostility. The man from Nazareth increasingly became an object of suspicion for many people, for the "scribes and pharisees" in particular. His way of life, his special interest in outcasts and in people on the margins of society, and his message with its trenchant offer of forgiveness and its radical demand on behalf of his heavenly Father—all this provoked opposition and appeared to strike at the very roots of sacred traditions. So the custodians of law and order were called in. The established authorities, first the religious leaders and then the political rulers, took countermeasures. This unusual and unholy alliance between these religious and political authorities, represented by Caiaphas and Pilate, who in all other matters were at complete loggerheads, is an indication of just how seriously they reckoned the danger to be. From their standpoint, certainly, they had cause for alarm and they acted appropriately.

> In all his teachings and his actions, Jesus constituted a continuing scandal which either inspired a spontaneous response of trust and love or else invited deadly attacks. The "scandal of the cross" was already anticipated by the "scandal of Jesus of Nazareth."[3]

It is important to respect this historical and biographical background of the cross and to keep steadily in view the precise contours of the life and death of Jesus. The cross is no vague and elastic symbol, the passion no accidental or incidental suffering, the scandal of the cross no arbitrary offense. What we encounter in the cross, in the message of the cross, in the theology of the cross is the persistently expressed love of Jesus of Nazareth, together with the offense it occasioned and the consequences to which it led.

Its consequences were bitter and terrible: brutal torture and a particularly cruel execution—cruel not just because of the protracted agony involved in death by crucifixion but also because of what for a Jew was the special curse attached to such a death. "Cursed be every one who hangs on a tree" (Gal. 3:13), declares the apostle Paul, citing the regulations of the Jewish law (Deut. 21:23). To be "cursed" meant to be excluded from the community of the people of God and even from God's covenant—removed from both God and human society to an abandonment that can only be called "hell."

This aspect of Jesus' passion is also attested in the Gospel narratives. In the throes of appalling physical torment he suffers at a deeper level the "cross within the cross," the inward calvary, the shaking and even shattering of all faith and hope—as the logical consequence of love. I am thinking here, above all, of Jesus' cry of dereliction: *Eloi, Eloi, lama sabachthani?*—which means, "My God, my God, why hast thou forsaken me?"—according to Mark (15:34) the last words uttered by Jesus on the cross. If we are to begin to understand the depths of Jesus' agony we have to stress, once again, the indissoluble connection between the cross on the one hand and his life and message on the other. In both ministry and teaching, the life of Jesus was one of the deepest intimacy with God, his Father. But now, in these obviously final moments of his life, what has become of his Father?

> In the words "My God, my God, why hast thou forsaken me?" it is not only Jesus' personal existence which is at stake, but very precisely his theological existence, his whole message of God. In the last analysis, therefore, what is also at stake here is the deity of his God and the paternity of his Father.[4]

It is not only the Son but also the Father who hangs here in agony. These are the depths into which we must descend if we are even to begin to do justice to the meaning "crucified," not to speak of the credal words that follow all the way down to the "descended into hell." As Heinrich Vogel puts it:

> Someone may ask the idle question: What is the most hopeless place on earth? He may be thinking of a hospital for incurables, the punishment stake in a concentration camp, the gas oven in an extermination camp, a cell on death row, the life of one of those blinded victims of Hiroshima, or any other of the places of deepest torment and despair. In truth, however, the most hopeless place on earth is there where the person who never abandoned God hangs dying, abandoned by God Himself.[5]

Remembering this, we shall resist any temptation to soften the message of the cross, to tone down its offense. Indeed, we shall find ourselves endorsing the words of Hans Iwand, who thought constantly about the meaning of the cross.

> We have garlanded the offense of the cross with roses and turned it into a theory of salvation. But this is not the cross. This is not its native severity, the harshness implanted in it by God himself. Hegel defined the cross by saying "God is dead"—and he was probably right in recognizing that what confronts us here in the cross is the power of God's remoteness, the real, ultimate, and inexplicable absence of God. . . . Our faith begins at the very point where the atheists think it must end. Our faith begins in that specific severity and power—the power of the cross, of abandonment, of radical temptation, where we lose hope in everything![6]

God's Compassion

Here the second dimension of the cross is revealed, the eschatological and soteriological dimension that is inseparable from the first. These dry technical theological terms simply mean that in the crucifixion we are invited not only to "Behold, the man!" but also, at the same time, to "Behold, God!" In at least two senses we are invited to behold the man. First we are to see the tortured, crucified human being—suffering humanity in the person of the suffering Jesus and in the persons of the least of his suffering brothers and sisters. But second, we are to see in the background the appalling depths of hatred, indifference, and cruelty to which we human beings can sink, the suffering we are capable of inflicting on others, even to the point of destroying them. It was specifically with the cross in mind that Anselm of Canterbury spoke of ultimate disclosure of the true dimensions of human sin: "You have not yet considered the full weight of sin." For the Creed, however, there is even more to it than that; here we are invited also to "behold God," to consider God's action and passion.

This is not simply a matter of the "doctrinal logic" implicit in the whole structure of the Creed, which when it speaks of Jesus Christ as "crucified, dead . . ." certainly remains within the overall context of his history, that is, the history of God's becoming human. It is also and above all the New Testament witness that invites us to see God at work and suffering here in the cross. To be sure, only on Easter morning do the involvement and commitment of God in the event of the cross become fully visible. In the darkness of Good Friday (and Holy Saturday) there was still no sign of the resurrection light, either for the world or for the disciples—or even for Jesus himself. Good Friday was the day of abandonment by God, the day when faith and hope were shattered—as the logical consequence of love. This is expressed by the evangelists in their references to the eclipse of the sun, the earthquake, and the rending of the veil of the Temple. But the very use of this almost cosmic and apocalyptic imagery (in Matt. 27:52 there is even talk of the "resurrected bodies of the saints who had fallen asleep") already gives to their Good Friday narratives an Easter morning perspective. From God's point of view the end of Jesus—inevitable, total, and consistent with the "flight path" of his historical and biographical destiny—is not the end. For all its un-diminished historicity, the cross proves at the same time—in the light of the resurrection—to be an eschatological happening, the place where *God* suffers and acts. God is not absent at Golgotha. He did not withdraw from the case of Jesus when the going got rough. This possible interpretation, by the way, was thoroughly explored by the Docetists and even in the Koran, the theory that it was not the Son of God who was crucified but someone else who stood in for him, perhaps the Simon who carried Jesus' cross, and that Jesus himself escaped unharmed. For the New Testament such an explanation is quite out of the question: God himself is present here at the cross—not as one looking down "from on high" or looking on "from the outside" like some hidden stage manager, but as one who is present "here below," "on the inside"—who is in and with Jesus himself in-volved in the struggle and suffering.

This alters for Christian faith the character of the cross and the significance of Good Friday. The cross signifies not the cancellation but the seal of God's covenant. It is *Good* Friday, a day not of frustra-tion but of fidelity—the supreme demonstration of God's covenant fidelity, a fidelity that knows no "limits of liability" but abides "to the bitter end." Accordingly the disastrous day of dissolution becomes the wondrous day of revolution, when the faith is given a new lease on life. Jesus' cry of dereliction does not echo unheard in the endless and indifferent interstellar spaces. It pierces the very "heart of God"—a mystery on which later trinitarian theology would reflect. Jesus' desperate cry is heard and answered. God is not indif-ferent to the fate of his Son, nor—in him—to our fate, the fate of all creation. We are not forsaken in the hour of our death. Even our dereliction, our sense of being abandoned by God, is "crossed out," canceled by the cross of Christ, taken up with Christ into God. To put it in the simple words of Paul's confession of faith: "I am sure that neither death, nor life, nor angels, nor principalities, nor things pres-ent, nor things to come, nor powers . . . will be able to separate us from the love of God in Christ Jesus our Lord" (Rom. 8:38f.).

What we said earlier with respect to the historical and biographical dimension of the cross can and must now be dialectically extended and even surpassed: the inner logic of love leads, in the presence of God, not to the shaking and even shattering of Christian faith and hope but to their establishment and confirmation.

Earlier I cited Heinrich Vogel's words about "the most hopeless place on earth." Let me now complete that quotation. Vogel ends with the following affirmation of faith which we can only endorse:

> In a thousand and one ways we pursued our religious quest of God and ended up only with reflexions of ourselves. But God sought and found us where we were completely lost and at the end of our resources. To him, Jesus, God spoke his approving "Amen" by raising him from the dead. But because Jesus wanted to be one with us in life and in death, we too are one with him. Thus he is our open door to God's future. He himself is the future of humanity, our future.[7]

To draw out the implications of this eschatological dimension of the cross and make them intelligible to Christians and other contemporaries in their practical daily life has been one of the most important tasks of Christian theology. It has provided soteriology in particular, the doctrine of reconciliation and redemption, with its main theme. For, from the standpoint of the apostolic faith, the cross is *the* saving event. This comes out more clearly in the Nicene Creed than in the Apostles' Creed. Not only do we find at the very beginning of the Nicene recital of the history of Christ the explicit reference to its motive—"for us human beings and for our salvation"—but when we come to the word "crucified" we also find the additional explanatory phrase "for us." This "for us," "for me," is vitally important for faith and for theology. However shocking and strange the fact of the cross may be, it is not simply a brute fact that in the last analysis has nothing whatever to do with us. Because it is a matter of God's passion and action it is part of the personal history of every one of us. We live and die no longer for ourselves alone but "to the Lord" (Rom. 14:8), "in Christ." We and all our little crosses have become part of this event of Christ's cross; we are no longer strangers to but sharers in the love of God. Our own destiny is involved in what happened at Golgotha; wrapped up in that eschatological history is the history of our salvation, our reconciliation and liberation.

This is not the place to offer a survey of the history of Christian soteriology, as the reticence of the Apostles' Creed itself on this score suggests. (The interested reader is referred to my book *Reconciliation and Liberation*, which provides a survey of the classic soteriologies.)[8] Christian soteriology took many different forms in accordance with the various ecclesiastical and cultural traditions in which it took shape. There was, for example, the classic "Christus Victor" so-teriology of the Greek church fathers, who saw the cross as the victorious campaign of the love of God against the satanic powers of enslavement and alienation. There was Anselm's impressive "satisfaction theory," according to which the sacrifice of Christ restored the order of justice and law. And there was the Abelardian doctrine of salvation, very modern in tone, in which emphasis is placed on the "infectious love of Jesus" as demonstrated supremely in his suffering and death. The only point I would make here—and it is a striking and important one—is that in all these very different interpretations the cross has a central place. In all of them, the cross is the foundation and inspiration of faith. In the polyphony of ecumenical voices, there is a remarkable unanimity—a clearly audible melody which is the heartbeat of the Christian faith.

In a large church in the center of Prague, there is a Latin inscription still clearly legible. The very fact that it is in Latin is a significant indication that the inscription has survived undamaged a whole succession of eras and regimes. *Ave crux—spes unica* ("Hail, cross—our only hope") is a doxological explanation derived from the rich tradition of Catholic piety, an "arrow prayer" in which all Christians can wholeheartedly join. We are struck by its brevity; the foundation of the Christian faith could hardly be formulated more succinctly or with deeper commitment. The cross is regarded here as "the one thing needful" and, at the same time, as the one thing which really meets our need because it establishes our only real hope. What is confessed here is distinctively Christian—the cross as the basis of hope—God with us not only beyond history, beyond our life and death, but already here and now, in the midst of the sinful and alienated situation in which we find ourselves at all times both good and bad.

The hope of the cross is a narrow way between utopian illusion on the one side and nihilistic defeatism on the other. Because it is not based on conditions in the world, it does not glorify them either; but, for precisely the same reason, neither does it despair of them or those who figure in them. To the optimists a stumbling block, to the pessimists foolishness, this narrow way of the cross is to faith "the power of God and the wisdom of God," to recall Paul's words once more.

"In this sign conquer!" These are words of promise that the Emperor Constantine was said to have seen written below the vision of

138

a fiery cross in the sky. They were true words, but in a different sense than the emperor imagined. The hope of the cross lies not in the love of power but in the power of love, that love which overcomes the world.

The Dangerous Remembrance of the Passion

We come now to the third dimension of the cross, its ethical and political aspect. What the words "crucified, dead" at the very heart of the Creed primarily establish is a firm confidence based on God's solidarity with us in our life, our dying, and our death. At the same time, however, they alert the church both theoretically and practically to the dimension of danger in any "remembrance of the passion," a phrase that in contemporary theology is associated primarily with Johann Baptist Metz and Jürgen Moltmann. The emphasis here is on the dangers of such remembering. We are reminded that the consequence of accepting the cross of Christ is not simply a passive assurance of life but an active imitation of Jesus of Nazareth in his sacrificial service for others—a basic attitude that was manifested from the very beginning of the life of Jesus and not simply at its end. Once again the connection between the cross and the whole of Jesus' previous life is emphasized.

Remembrance of his passion is dangerous because following Jesus in his sacrificial concern for people who are suffering necessarily entails becoming identified with those who are oppressed and disfranchised; indeed it often leads to conflict with the oppressors and the powerful. A realistic theology or spirituality of the cross, therefore, does not mean a naive glorification of human suffering or a facile and tolerant acceptance of evil, postponing all hope of redress; on the contrary, it means challenging evil situations and conditions, protesting hopefully on God's behalf against the tyranny (and enslavement) of suffering. This is something that has not been given sufficient emphasis in the history of the church or in Christian theology, even though it has inescapable ethical and political implications for our theory and our practice.

1. Remembering the cross has important implications for theory, for our view of the world. In encourages a certain interpretation of humanity and the world. Take, for example, the interpretation of history. To the present day, even in Christian historiography, the prevailing

tendency has been to view history as the saga of the successful, the victorious, the survivors. To a very large extent, the victims, disinherited, and ordinary people are ignored. In our pictures of history and of life, suffering tends to be suppressed, whether consciously or unconsciously. Only too readily is "the cross of history" glossed over and the "contemporary cross"—to use Hegel's image—overlaid with ideological or theological roses.

All such attempts to suppress this dimension of suffering are resisted by a christologically interpreted remembrance of the cross. Such remembrance does not conceal the gaps that accompany every history; it does not keep quiet about the wounds and gloss over the tears. In its struggle to understand the past, it inquires into the fate of the pariahs of each period. The dangerous remembrance of Jesus' passion excludes all theories that seek to transform suffering either by denying its reality or by exaggerating its status. By their alert remembering of the cross, Christians can already render a service to their times intellectually, at the theoretical level.

2. Still more important, of course, Christians should remember the cross in their lives and practices. Remembrance of the cross in a New Testament sense means developing an eye for God's involvement in political affairs. The scenes enacted around the cross of Jesus of Nazareth take place in the political context. Remembrance of the cross, since it has to do with the history of Jesus' passion, points clearly in a certain direction: Acting in the name of Jesus of Nazareth, it points to his suffering brothers and sisters and inquires into the lot of those who share his suffering. It asks about the fate of oppressed human beings in all the concrete forms of their suffering and distress. In doing so, it recognizes the diversity of this suffering and distress, just as Jesus does in his Beatitudes (Matt. 5:1–12) or in his "parable" of the Last Judgment (Matt. 25:31–46)—the poor, the bereaved, those who hunger for food and justice, the persecuted, the sick, prisoners . . . What we have here, of course, is not a final and complete program for "Christian" politics, but certainly, once and for all, the direction, motivation, and goal for initiatives and advances.

To the present day various ways have been found in the history of the church to tone down and even deny altogether this dangerous dimension of remembering the cross, but its complete suppression has never proved possible. The "crucified" that stands at the heart of all the creeds has never been erased from Christian memory. Think, for example, of the faithful ministry to the sick and the weak, persistently pursued throughout the history of the church in spite of all its forgetfulness. The church's varied ministries of mercy and, above all, the fundamental recognition that the weak and defenseless cannot simply be left to their fate, have been a perennial contribution to the history of humankind and part of the historical distinctiveness of Christianity, unparalleled in the religions of antiquity. Without this practical remembrance of the cross, many social aspects of our cultural history, and even of the history of the world, would have been quite inconceivable.

All too often, however, such initiatives have been too narrowly conceived. For the most part, they were developed exclusively along the lines of charitable service and too seldom in a really comprehensive way as political programs. While we must never cease to cherish the permanently positive aspects of loving personal *diaconia*, there are many corrections and improvements to be made and much lost ground to be made up—without delay. Ecumenical Christianity has been gradually coming to realize this—with some halting first steps and some setbacks. The antiracism and antimilitarism initiatives of the World Council of Churches could be of fundamental significance in this respect, whatever their occasionally controversial aspects. In no sense are such programs a substitute for the diaconal and philanthropic work of the ecumenical movement and of the churches, but they are pointers to the structural consequences inherent in any "remembrance of the passion." They remind us that we must work not only to assuage the consequences of evil by our deeds of charity but also to counteract the structural roots and effects of the demons of racism and militarism. To put the matter in rather sloganistic terms: we need not only a "philanthropy" but also a "pedagogy" and even a "politics of the oppressed" (Paulo Freire). To champion this concern with society is one of the authentic tasks of the church under the cross of Christ. It is an indispensable aspect of the church's communication of the central message of the cross, and of its confession of the one crucified.

To the Bitter End

In our exposition of the credal words "crucified, dead and buried, descended to hell" we have so far concentrated on the cross, and rightly so since the cross is the central point in this credal passage. The other statements buttress the affirmation of the crucifixion and bring out its full significance. They are nevertheless not superfluous.

The first two buttresses—"dead" and "buried"—are closely connected with the preceding "crucified." They attest the finality of the crucifixion and therefore in an emphatic and eloquent way emphasize the true and complete humanity of Jesus.

Two points are particularly important here. The first concerns the contemporary Docetic temptation to which reference has already been made. The Son of God not only suffered on the cross—for the Docetists this was scandal enough—but actually died there. This affirmation about death is the final rejection of all notions of a happy ending to the history of Jesus, a notion that was still entertained at the time when the Creed was in the process of formation. The death of Jesus, it was said, was only a stratagem, a semblance, a trick, by which the preeminent son of God outwitted his enemies. Even in modern times rationalist theologians, for a variety of different reasons, have advanced the theory that the death of Jesus was not a real death but only a "semblance." For the Docetists, the idea of any possible connection between God and physical suffering and death was anathema; the problem for the rationalists, on the contrary, was to find an intellectually respectable explanation of the resurrection. In opposition to all such theories, the Creed was emphatic with its "dead and buried": the earthly life of Jesus came to an irrevocable end in history with his death on the cross. The complete humanity of Jesus Christ includes also his death and, in accordance with human custom, a grave, a burial, the final act in death and dying.

This emphasis on death and burial is important not only from the standpoint of the history of ideas but also doctrinally. The identification and solidarity of the Son of God with us goes right to the final limit of the inescapable historical destiny of a human being.

The word "dead" in the Creed clearly marks this final limit in the physical sense: death is the *terminus ad quem* of finite—and sinful —human existence. As far as nature and history are concerned, there is nothing more beyond. "It is finished" (John 19:30). What the word "buried" adds over and above this, is to describe this final end from the standpoint of the dead person's environment, in terms of the historical and cultural accompaniment of death. Burial is the last thing one human being can do for another. Interment means a final leave-taking, a last departure. The dead person achieves final rest even with respect to the environment; the book of his or her life reaches its final full stop and passes into history.

In view of the two words "dead" and "buried," therefore, we can say that Jesus was spared none of these human "last things," that nothing is excluded from his life story. Above all, and stated in the positive terms already mentioned in connection with the incarnation but now radically intensified and deepened in virtue of this ending: nothing human is alien to the Son of God. In Jesus Christ, the love of God also has this final and conclusive dimension: dead and buried. It is not just pious rhetoric, therefore, when Paul ventures to affirm that not only suffering and distress but even death itself cannot separate us from *this* love of God in Christ Jesus our Lord. This is the direction in which I look for the abiding theological significance of the credal words "dead and buried."

Hope's Descent to Hell

But what are we to make of the next words: "he descended to hell" (into "the realm of death," as the ecumenical version of the Creed translates it)? Here is certainly one of the most obscure clauses in the Apostles' Creed. It does not occur in the Roman and Nicene Creeds and is therefore a distinctive feature of the Apostles' Creed. But the Apostles' Creed did not invent the clause, but here endorses an ancient tradition of the fathers, a tradition that despite its mythological overtones has remained vital to the present day.

> The belief that Christ spent the interval between his expiry on the cross and his resurrection in the underworld was a commonplace of Christian teaching from the earliest times. Apart from the possibility of its having been in the minds of New Testament writers, the Descent was explicitly mentioned by St. Ignatius, Polycarp, Irenaeus, Tertullian, and others.[9]

There is indeed some New Testament basis for this theological affirmation. The main New Testament passage to be noted in this connection is 1 Pet. 3:18f. where we are told that Christ "preached to the spirits in prison, who formerly did not obey." Further precision is given a few verses later when it is stated that "the gospel was preached even to the dead" (1 Pet. 4:6). Ephesians also seems to point in the same direction: Christ "also descended into the lower parts of the earth" (Eph. 4:6). The reasoning that ultimately led to the affirmation of the descent to hell was also nourished by the statement in Revelation that Jesus Christ has "the keys of Death and Hades" (Rev. 1:18). When it came to details, however, the precise meaning of the credal statement continued to be a matter of dispute among the early Christian theologians. Despite all the differences of interpretation, though, the intention behind the mythological language was clear. The work of Christ concerns the whole of humanity and is not to be artificially and parochially restricted, either in the sense of a cultural, racial, or geographical parochialism or in the historical sense. It is not only Jesus' contemporaries who benefit by his death, nor even only those who live and have lived since his birth, but also those who died before Christ was born. It is to endorse this legitimate and authentically "ecumenical" concern that the Apostles' Creed ventures to speak of the descent to hell.

Even after its inclusion in the Creed, of course, this article continued to be a matter of controversy and has remained a disputed point ever since. The two great Reformers, Luther and Calvin, have interesting explanations to offer.

Luther continued the patristic tradition, seeing the descent to hell as the beginning of Christ's triumphal procession, his victory over the powers of sin and death. In accordance with this dramatic view of Christ's battle for our salvation, Luther interprets this credal clause as a summary of Christ's offensive against Satan and all his forces, against the dominion of death, and also—this above all—as a reference to the deliverance of the saints of the old covenant from their imprisonment in that realm of death. What we have here is a "soteriology of liberation" which played an important part in traditional Lutheran thinking, though for the most part, unfortunately, only in reference to the individual and metaphysical context, not to the historical and social context. The soteriology is expressed, for example, in the concluding words of Bach's Christmas oratorio:

Sin, Death, and Hell, and Satan
The mighty Victim own;
And Man doth stand forgiven
Before His Father's throne.[10]

Calvin—and most Reformed theologians—found this interpretation too mythological and offered a different explanation of the descent of Christ to hell. What, asked Calvin, does the Bible mean by "hell"? Surely not a locatable underworld with its hierarchical order of powers. It means, primarily, separation from God, abandonment by God. Quite legitimately, Calvin interprets the words "descended to hell" in the light of Jesus' cry of dereliction on the cross: "My God, my God, why hast thou forsaken me?" (Mark 15:34). Hell is the experience of the crucified Christ that lies behind these words. Calvin's Catechism states, therefore:

> He not only suffered natural death, which is the separation of the body from the soul, but also . . . his soul was pierced with amazing anguish, which St. Peter calls the pains of death (Acts 2:24).[11]

Not only physically but also and above all spiritually, the Son of God was mortally wounded by the sting of death, that is, by the sin he bore on our behalf. Here in this descent to hell Anselm's dictum finds its most poignant expression: "You have not yet considered the full weight of sin."

Later specialists in Christian doctrine found it significant for the history of confessional differences that whereas the descent to hell is already linked in Luther's interpretation with the exaltation of Christ attested in the next credal clause, "rose again from the dead," in Calvin it is regarded as the deepest point of the humiliation of the Son of God. The spiritual heirs of the two Reformers then conducted their doctrinal skirmishes on the corresponding battlefronts.

In view of the ambiguity of the biblical evidence for the descent to hell, I see no compelling reason to insist on either one of these interpretations rather than the other. Both bring out themes and concerns that are important christologically and should be accepted, if not at this time then at some other point. In the case of Luther, who certainly approximates more closely to the ancient church's understanding of the Creed, it is his emphasis on the importance of the descent to hell for a theological understanding of liberation that requires assent, though greater emphasis is needed, of course, on the historical and social-ethical aspects of the liberation achieved by Christ. In the case of Calvin, it is his deep understanding of the terrible estrangement of hell that is important. It speaks to the condition of many of our contemporaries—even those who have distanced themselves from the church—in face of the distresses of the present time. We think, for example, of the oft-quoted final words of Sartre's *No Exit*: "Hell is other people"—but also of T. S. Eliot's reply: "I myself am hell."

The fundamental theological insight contained in this dark clause is common to both the Luther and the Calvin interpretations. What is here affirmed is how broadly and deeply Christ's work of liberation is connected with reality. Its scope is such that no human being is hopelessly excluded from, much less cast beyond, the pale of his salvation. Nor is any person so remote from God as to be utterly "hopeless," irredeemable. Christ descended into the "deepest dungeons" of our godlessness and hopelessness. Nowhere in heaven or earth, or even in what is called "hell," are we "without Christ." "For," as Paul notes, "to this end Christ died and lived again, that he might be Lord both of the dead and of the living" (Rom. 14:9). Although these words of the apostle were framed in a different context, they are a good summary of the essential significance of the credal clause: "He descended to hell."

12

On the Third Day He Rose Again from the Dead

"I know that my Redeemer liveth"

Let me begin here with a personal reminiscence. It was as a young student in Scotland that I first heard a performance of Georg Friedrich Handel's oratorio *Messiah*. In accordance with an almost universal tradition in the United Kingdom, this oratorio, first performed in Dublin in 1742, is often played and sung shortly before Christmas, not only by professional but also by nonprofessional musicians and singers. I heard it performed by the students of the University of St. Andrews in Scotland. For me this first encounter with Handel's great work was an unforgettable experience both aesthetically and theologically. I was particularly impressed by the two successive parts: the full chorus "Hallelujah, for the Lord God Omnipotent reigneth . . ." (No. 44) and the soprano aria: "I know that my Redeemer liveth and that he shall stand at the latter day upon the earth . . ." (No. 45). What impressed me, certainly, was not simply the beauty of Handel's music but also the response of the audience. It is the custom in Britain for the audience to rise to its feet when the choir sings the Hallelujah Chorus. Tradition has it that this custom dates back to the first London performance of the oratorio in 1745 in the presence of King George II. During the singing of the now famous chorus, the king stood up and his example has been followed to this day. Seated again for the following soprano solo, the audience listens all the more quietly and intently and takes the message in words and music deeply to heart: "I know that my Redeemer liveth . . ."

How, I asked myself, was this response of the audience—including myself—to be explained? Was it the music? So moving, almost over-

147

powering, so undeniably impressive. Perhaps, too, in the case of the Hallelujah Chorus, it was Handel's typical reverberation! That was certainly part of the answer, but not the whole, I believe. The words themselves play an important part here. The chorus and the solo are both concerned with a single event in the messianic destiny of Jesus—his resurrection. Was it mere chance that precisely here Handel's music should have reached a peak of majesty and impressiveness? Does it not suggest, rather, that Handel, whose libretto is itself a remarkable achievement even from the theological standpoint, here quite unconsciously—and appropriately—brings the deepest resources of his musical talent into play? And as for the audience, is not its obvious emotion due in part at least to the fact that even in a largely secularized Western society it is still not entirely forgotten that precisely here, in the credal "rose again" beats the very heart of Christianity—and perhaps of our own hearts too? However that may be, this experience gave me a much more direct access to the message of the resurrection of Jesus Christ than all the theological reflections that at the time engaged me in my studies.

It needs to be remembered that at that time (the end of World War II) theologians were in the throes of the demythologizing debate, which affected even faith in the resurrection. The resurrection seemed to pale into insignificance in comparison with the cross of Jesus. Bultmann's question was symptomatic: "Can talk of the resurrection be anything other than an affirmation of the significance of the cross?" His own answer pointed in the same direction: "Faith in the resurrection is simply faith in the cross as the saving event."[1] Here the resurrection is in danger of becoming no more than an adjunct to the cross. Its historicity as an event seems to be abandoned: "The resurrection itself is not an event of past history; only the Easter faith of the disciples can be understood as an historical event."[2]

Quite different views were also being expressed at that time by other theologians, views which were always much more attractive to me than those of Bultmann. I am thinking in particular of Karl Barth, who vigorously dissociated himself from his Marburg friend precisely on this matter of the historicity of the resurrection. For Barth, where the resurrection of Christ is concerned God's action takes priority over our faith. The resurrection is never to be understood and grounded on faith; on the contrary: faith is always to be understood and grounded on the resurrection of Christ. The on-

148

tological basis and the ontological consequences of the resurrection were extremely important for Barth. He employed dynamic images and statements to describe this ontological basis:

> The Easter message is the proclamation of a victory already won. The war is at an end—even though here and there troops are still shooting because they have not heard anything yet about the capitulation. The game is won, even though the player can still play a few further moves. Actually he is already mated. The clock has run down, even though the pendulum still swings a few times this way and that. It is in this interim space that we are living; the old is past, behold it has all become new.[3]

Fine! Fine! — But is it really so.

Statements of this sort impressed us. At a time when the sense of a new beginning after the war was still fresh, they had a vivid quality and a note of realism. But Bultmann's questions would not go away. In fact, even those of us who, far from sharing Bultmann's existentialist reduction of the concept of faith, were interested in the social and historical dimensions of theology became increasingly aware of the explosive nature of his questions. This was true in my own case, standing as I did in the Prague theological tradition and being strongly influenced by theologians like J. L. Hromadka and J. B. Soucek. How was the resurrection related to history—to world history and not just to the historicity of faith? With the cross, it was different; the cross is almost tangibly historical. The resurrection, on the contrary, eludes our grasp and has the aura of an intangible mystery. In the 1940s, living as we were in the midst of such momentous historical happenings, we asked ourselves whether in this matter of the resurrection we had firm theological ground on which to stand. We were confronted here with a fundamental theological question— and many of us are still faced with the same question today. At all events, I find the experience of Handel's *Messiah* a constant help and stimulus even if it remains for the present somewhat inexplicable. The witness to the resurrection while it may not be historically verifiable nevertheless has about it an indisputable connection with and reference to historical reality. We should not be in too great a hurry to demythologize it.

It should be stressed, of course, that a stimulus of this kind is only a temporary aid in our theological endeavors. It has to be followed up by efforts of thought (and of course action). In the fifties and sixties, theologians made strenuous intellectual efforts and with some success. I am thinking here not only of Karl Barth, who in this period produced the great volumes of his church dogmatics on the doctrine of reconciliation, but also his disciples—such as Gollwitzer, Moltmann, Ott, and Pannenberg. For Pannenberg in particular the resurrection's ontological anchorage in history became the dominant concern. Some account of this is called for at this point.

The Historicity of the Resurrection

Pannenberg is nothing if not a theologian of the resurrection: "In the resurrection of Jesus we . . . have to do with the sustaining foundation of the Christian faith. If this collapses, so does everything else which the Christian faith confesses."[4] It is only in faith that the solidity of this foundation is verified, but the question of the credibility of the resurrection message opens up ontological connections. Pannenberg develops this argument in two directions—anthropologically and historically.

The anthropological setting for the theme of the resurrection has been given in and with the fundamental situation of human life. Of all the creatures, we human beings alone are aware of the inescapable sentence of death that hangs over us. At the same time, however, knowing this to be our destiny, we also raise, just as inescapably, the question of what awaits us beyond death. The fact that we inevitably ask this question is no guarantee, of course, that there really is a life that overcomes death; it does, however, "keep the mind alive to the idea that the secret of life surpasses all our present knowledge."[5]

Bearing in mind this anthropological datum helps us to approach with a more open mind the question of the historicity of Jesus' resurrection. In other words, this question can be described a priori as meaningless only if we decide from the outset that the dead remain dead, that death is the absolute end, and that the human habit of going beyond all limits and crossing every boundary is therefore an illusion. But such an assumption is really a prejudgment that has nothing to do with a scientific approach to historical enquiry. It is hardly responsible to argue that a historian who takes into account the possibility of the resurrection is bound to run into conflict with the findings of natural science. Objections of this kind are seldom encountered among scientists nowadays, least of all among physicists. It is for the most part among theologians that such objections are still to be found!

Pannenberg, to put the record straight, is not seeing a "historical proof" of the resurrection of Jesus. No such proof is possible here, any more than in the case of other historical judgments. No one can be spared a critical struggle with the tradition. "Consequently, Christianity will have to get used to the fact that this basic assertion of its faith will remain a matter of dispute in this world. But it is neither confuted nor does it lack for evidence."[6] The reality of the resurrection cannot be proved by our reflections upon it, but they can perhaps open up a meaningful way of thinking about faith and its connection with reality.

Even if it is not everyone's cup of tea and will certainly not convince everyone, this argument of Pannenberg seems worthy of serious consideration. In my own theological efforts to understand the connection of the resurrection with reality and to find access to the Easter event, I have been helped by another encounter and another context, namely, the dialogue between Christians and Marxists. This may, indeed must, seem an unlikely setting for discoveries about the resurrection. One would hardly expect Christians and Marxists to find common ground in the theme of "resurrection." One would expect, indeed, that Marxist thinkers would steer clear of such a mythological theologoumenon. Is it not, in their view, precisely here in the message of the resurrection that Christianity proves itself to be "opium of the people?" Would not secular-minded and historically oriented contemporaries find more convincing and fruitful themes in the life and death of Jesus than in his resurrection? This was in fact the case— when the dialogue first began. The situation soon changed, however. It was precisely the resurrection theme that soon came to fascinate the Marxist thinkers—and not despite their historical orientation but because of it! Some Marxist partners in the dialogue realized more quickly than many bourgeois theologians that it was not the "historical" but the "kerygmatic" Jesus Christ who became a force in history, an insight for which Martin Kähler and the religious socialists among the Christian theologians rightly contended. Had not Christ's resurrection been understood and attested in practice by many Christians, especially at the beginning, and subsequently in left-wing "radical Christian" circles, as an authorization to rebel against the forces of death? For obvious reasons, the Marxists pricked up their ears at this. There was more to the resurrection kerygma than vestiges of obsolete mythology.

These Marxist emphases seem to me of fundamental importance.

151

In the main stream of German theology, in particular, we have tended to get bogged down in a one-sided interest in the cosmological aspects of the questions raised by the resurrection. Discussion has focused primarily on cosmology and world views, on the problem of reconciling faith and science, on the question of myth. The "demythologizing" debate is just one example of this. This cosmological concern is not in itself wrong, for these questions about world view are serious questions that need to be tackled if the message is to be communicated in a credible way in our world today. If other dimensions are ignored, however, concentration on these cosmological questions leads us to a dead end. The reality reference of the resurrection is by no means exhausted in our attending to questions of cosmology and world view. This reference to reality has many aspects. As my experience with Handel's *Messiah* shows, it even has an aesthetic dimension. Above all, it also has a historical and world-transforming dimension, as the Marxists now quite rightly remind us, and these dimensions are not less important, but if anything more important, than the others. At any rate, there is a good deal of lost ground to be made up here. At the same time and more important still, we have here an opportunity to discover a new and more-convincing approach to the resurrection of Jesus. What we are being challenged to do at this point in our contemporary theological endeavors is to break out of the intellectualist ghetto in which the debate on the resurrection has been pursued and to face the question resurrection poses with the context of our personal and social existence.

In this direction, too, there is also a great deal to be learned from Marxist thinkers—not only in the formal sense but also substantively. To give just one or two examples from my own experience: Ernst Bloch reminds us that the biblical concept of resurrection has its roots primarily not in a concern for individual salvation but in the promise of and demand for greater social justice; Vitezslav Gardavsky points out that the meaning of the resurrection is to be found in the awakening of love between human beings in the form of a passion for life in all its fullness; Roger Garaudy regards the resurrection of Jesus as the initial impetus, the "detonator," for an epoch-making transition (still not fully understood today by either Christians or Marxists) in the direction of a humanity committed to transforming the world—with all the positive but also the destructive consequences such a change entails.

The Three Days

Against that background and in that context, we return to the credal "rose again." We will look first at the event itself and then in the final section of this chapter at its consequences.

A brief comment, first of all, on the words: "on the third day." This remarkable phrase is found not only in the Apostles' Creed but also in the Roman and Nicene Creeds—which is surprising in view of the strict economy of the creeds—especially the Roman and Apostles' Creeds—in relating the saving aspects of the history of Jesus Christ. The inclusion of these words must have been the result of careful consideration. What were they meant to affirm? When we examine the biblical background, it becomes clear that the Creeds are here reproducing a stereotyped formula, one that is quoted, for example, by the apostle Paul in his important "resurrection chapter": Jesus was raised from the dead "on the third day according to the Scriptures" (1 Cor. 15:4; cf. Acts 10:40). The supplemental phrase "according to the Scriptures"—which is specifically included in the Nicene Creed—also deserves attention, for here the ancient creeds establish a connection with the biblical tradition of both testaments. It is worth noting that frequently when it speaks of Christ's death and resurrection the New Testament makes mention of the "three days," particularly with reference to Old Testament themes. For example, in Matt. 12:40, we read: "For as Jonah was three days and three nights in the belly of the whale, so will the Son of man be three days and three nights in the heart of the earth." This is a motif that also leaves its mark on ancient Christian art and is frequently found on Christian tombstones. Another example would be the use of Hos. 6:2: "After two days he will revive us; on the third day he will raise us up, that we may live before him." These associations are theologically important: the crucified Messiah is understood in the light of the hope of the Old Covenant; his cross and resurrection are seen not as isolated events but within the context of the whole history of salvation.

This use of preestablished motifs as a "scriptural proof" certainly does not mean that the statement about the three days is pure invention, lacking any historical foundation. The time interval between Good Friday and Easter, or rather, between the events connected with these two days in the Christian tradition, can certainly represent a historical caesura as well. For the theologians of the ancient church, this historical pause was important both pastorally and doctrinally.

153

Time intervenes between the cross and the resurrection—as a comfort and a warning to Christians who themselves live "between the times," between the first and the second coming of Christ, Christians who live in hope having not yet reached the goal, and who are hence aware of the ambiguity of time. In this sense too, this bitter sense of the shaken and even destroyed hope of those who followed him, Jesus bore the cross of history. The bitter and wretched time of shattered dreams does not end immediately on Good Friday but lingers on into the succeeding days. This fact is also doctrinally important and still has implications even for our christological discussions today. As Heinrich Vogel puts it, with an oblique reference to Bultmann's view of the resurrection merely as a key to the interpretation of the cross:

> These "three days" that are so offensive to our thinking . . . make it impossible to interpret cross and resurrection, death and life, grace and judgement merely as two aspects of one and the same dialectical principle. Without the act of the divine omnipotence, the cross remains cross, death remains death, and judgement remains judgement.[7]

Vogel is surely right. The "three days" save us from succumbing to the temptation to rob the event of the resurrection of its reality, or even to explain it away altogether in a symbolic or dialectical sense. The words "on the third day he rose again" in the Apostles' Creed are not a metaphorical code term for spiritual, historical, or even natural phenomena. They refer to the concrete and unique Easter event. How are we to understand this event?

Risen Indeed

"Christ is risen! He is risen indeed!" The witness of the resurrection could hardly be expressed more succinctly than in this well-known Easter greeting of the Russian Orthodox Church. The emphatic "indeed" vouches for the reality, the down-to-earth character of the resurrection faith. There is nothing fraudulent or sham about the rising of Jesus Christ from death; deception or self-deception, dreams and hallucinations are excluded. This is the assumption shared by all the New Testament witnesses. Their accounts differ, to be sure. In fact there is an almost confusing diversity of statements that cannot easily be reconciled. From the standpoint of a narrative historian wanting to provide a clear, intelligible, and coherent account of what really happened, the first Easter day is a most unsatisfactory and incomprehensible day—bound to be suspect.

Not surprisingly, therefore, many attempts have been made—particularly by modern theologians with apologetic interests—to bring some order into this confusing diversity. They harmonize the accounts in order to provide a more satisfactory picture of the actual course of events. They do so with the best of intentions, hoping to vindicate the biblical witness to the resurrection. But such an enterprise is foolhardy. Not only can it not succeed—given the textual evidence—without a draconian twisting of the New Testament text itself, but it is also misguided for biblical and theological reasons. The biblical witnesses themselves were obviously not troubled by the "confusion" of motifs. This can hardly be put down to a naive carelessness on the part of the ancient writers. It is to be explained, rather, as we shall see, by their recognition that it was the inconceivable event itself that really mattered, not its reflection in the faith and words of the various witnesses.

At this central and decisive point, moreover, there is complete unanimity among all these different witnesses: Something quite inconceivable had happened. The history of Jesus did not come to an irrevocable end with his appalling death on Good Friday. Something happened that radically transformed the situation. The response of faith to this happening—a rather timid, hesitant response at first, as frankly portrayed by the New Testament, but one that became increasingly clear and unambiguous in the kerygma—was: Christ is risen! He is risen indeed! So earnest were the apostles in this confession of the risen Christ that they put their lives on the line in order to proclaim it. They set on their confession of faith the seal of radically changed lives, a willingness in most cases to accept even a martyr's death. It was preeminently the apostle Paul who stated in the most direct and pointed way the seriousness of this question concerning the truth and reality of Christ's resurrection: "If Christ has not been raised, then our preaching is in vain and your faith is in vain" (1 Cor. 15:14).

The resurrection of Christ, therefore, was an event, an incomparable event that constituted the basis of the apostles' understanding of themselves and of the world. But what sort of event? The words of Paul just quoted indicate one possible way of answering this

155

question. The apostle mentions two specific things: "preaching" and "faith." He points here to the context in which the event of the resurrection is to be understood. This event does not simply stand on its own in stony objectivity; it becomes reality within a specific frame of reference, a framework of reality and knowledge that is concretely referred to by the terms "preaching" and "faith." It is impossible, therefore, to understand the event of the resurrection in just any terms we please—in the categories of natural science or history, for example. It is an event that calls for faith and is communicated in witness. It is an event of revelation and of salvation. Any ontology of the resurrection must do justice to the specific character of the event.

Roger Garaudy has shown an astonishing perceptiveness to this aspect of the resurrection. He examines the question of the "givenness," the "factuality" of the resurrection of Jesus, but in so doing he fully respects the distinctive character of the event. It is impossible to get at the heart of this event by using the intellectual methods of scientific positivism. What confronts us here is not a tangible scientific fact. Nor, says Garaudy, is the resurrection "a historical fact in the sense that it can be clearly understood and proved by tangible traces or witnesses, for Jesus appeared only to those who believed in him. . . . That Jesus is risen can be grasped only by faith, not by the senses."[8] Precisely in this mode, however, the resurrection is indeed operative and real. To transpose these events into symbols would be to vaporize the reality of the Easter event: "A Mozart devotee can say that in a way Mozart lives in him whenever he hears his music, but that is not how Christ lives in us."[9]

To define the specific character of the resurrection event, and to get beyond the false option between the interpretative methods of historical positivism on the one hand and those of existentialist symbolism on the other, one might speak of the resurrection as "eschatological event"—a theological formula which I first used in the fifties to try to define the specific nature of the resurrection reality.[10] The term "eschatological" is meant here in its strict sense. In the view of the New Testament, the resurrection concerns the "ultimate One" and the "ultimate reality"—the ultimate One being God. In the view of the evangelists and apostles, the resurrection of Jesus is the ultimate revelation of God, comparable only with the revelation of the divine Name in the context of the Exodus event in the Old Testament. When the New Testament speaks of God (and also of Jesus, of course) it does so on this basis. It is no accident that the clearest confession of faith in God occurs in encounter with the risen Jesus Christ: "My Lord and my God" (John 20:28). It is also significant that one of the shortest "definitions" of God—as I mentioned in the last section of chapter 5—is "him that raised from the dead Jesus our Lord" (Rom. 4:24). But this means that if the resurrection is ascribed essentially to God, then clearly the unique and sovereign subject of this event is God himself.

At this point a comment on terminology, our own and that of the New Testament, may be helpful. So far, I have mainly used the word "resurrection," keeping in this respect to the language of the Creeds. When they say "he rose again from the dead," they are reflecting a very firm New Testament tradition. But it is impossible to ignore the fact that there is another, possibly even stronger, New Testament tradition that prefers the passive form of the verb and speaks of Jesus as the one who "was raised" from the dead by the Father. There is no need for us to posit a mutually exclusive alternative here where none exists, indeed where on the contrary the New Testament resurrection narratives and the whole apostolic witness characteristically use the two forms interchangeably, affirming in fact the "two-dimensional" character of New Testament Christology. Thus one can say with Ratzinger:

> These two ways of speaking of the resurrection come together at the point where the total love of Jesus for human beings—which brings him to the cross—is fulfilled in his total crossing over to the Father, wherein it becomes stronger than death because it is at the same time totally sustained by the Father.[11]

But from the other, the complementary standpoint, we have also to say with Vogel:

> Only as God's act of love, only in consequence of the spontaneity and freedom of the eternal God, can it be understood that the Son could become incarnate and "empty" himself, "humble" himself, and hence become "passive." The activity throughout, through death and hell,[12] is exclusively that of the Merciful One.

The raising of Jesus from the dead is the work of the "ultimate One," namely, God.

But it is an eschatological event also in the sense that it points to the "ultimate things." In the New Testament testimonies to the resurrection, there is hardly room for doubt on this score: the event is not seen as a miraculous continuation of Jesus' earthly career. There is no return to the former conditions, no resuscitation of the corpse, no prolongation of the penultimate things but the arrival of the ultimate things. I am not referring here to the last things in the sense of the general anthropological question of our postmortal destiny. That is a dimension that also needs to be emphasized, since in the New Testament the Easter destiny of Jesus is indissolubly connected with the destiny of all humanity, with our human questions about death and the victory over death. The light of Easter also illuminates this dimension. To give just one example, this frame of reference, of concern to all human beings, has a central place in Paul's central "resurrection chapter" (1 Corinthians 15). What is meant by the "ultimate things" in the New Testament, however, is something far more inclusive. The raising of Jesus from death already inaugurates the new age of the future. "The old has passed away; behold the new has come" (2 Cor. 5:17b). It is not that the new is in some general sense a possibility; the new has in fact been *made* possible. It has been made possible, moreover, not merely as a variation of the old, still marked by sin and death, but as God's radically new world. The resurrection must be seen against the background of this "new creation" that brings liberation and reconciliation to completion.

When we perceive this eschatological horizon of the resurrection it is easier for us to grasp the specific character of the resurrection and also to answer the difficult question of how this event can be grasped and communicated in the conditions of the penultimate in which, according to the New Testament, we continue to live our lives. We *believe* in the God who raised Jesus from the dead but we do not *see* him. With the instrumentalities of the old, it is impossible to grasp clearly the new. This is why the diverse forms and emphases of the resurrection narratives in the New Testament are not really seen as a stumbling block. There is no need to harmonize them artificially. They are to be accepted with all their tensions because they accord with the realities of the situation. To demand conceptual unambiguity here would, indeed, be to misunderstand the eschatological mystery in a positivistic way. Garaudy is right: we cannot get at the heart of the resurrection event by scientific or historical methods. To put it theologically, the medium here, the means of communication, is preaching and faith—and of course the practice of the resurrection as well.

Resistance Movement Against Fatalism

This brings us to the second stage of our reflections on the resurrection, namely with respect to its consequences. What mainly concerns us here is the historical, world-transforming dimension of the Easter experience—the way the raising of Jesus from the dead becomes visible. To avoid any misunderstanding, it should be emphasized right away that not *all* the consequences of the resurrection become visible by any means, and even fewer of them can be *made* visible. We must not forget that when we deal with the resurrection we are dealing with an eschatological mystery. "Lo! I tell you a mystery," says Paul in his "resurrection chapter," (1 Cor. 15:51), using a very solemn form of address and pointing in a quite different direction. He is pointing to inaccessible and inexpressible aspects of our participation in Christ's death and resurrection, and hence to our hope in the face of death and in what lies beyond it. It is impossible, thank God, to erase this dimension of ultimate mystery from the biblical accounts of the resurrection. For even in a secularized culture, the question of the power of death and the question of our human destiny beyond the bounds of death are the unsettled fundamental questions of human existence. The resurrection message meets this set of questions head on; it would be foolish of us to forget this, or seek to replace it by other emphases—for example by a feverish activism. "Foolish" if only because, if this dimension were abandoned, even Christian activity itself would be condemned to the twilight of meaninglessness. Paul leaves us no room for doubt on this score when he says: "If for this life only we have hoped in Christ, we are of all people most to be pitied" (1 Cor. 15:19).

We have no right, therefore, to leave these eschatological consequences of the resurrection out of account. They are also given an explicit central place in the Creed itself—implicitly in all the succeeding credal affirmations, but above all explicitly and unmistakably in the conclusion: "I believe in the resurrection of the flesh and eternal life." At the present stage in our exposition, however, we wish to focus particularly on the *historical* consequences of Christ's resurrection. There are good biblical and theological grounds for doing so inasmuch as the eschatological mystery of the raising of Christ from the dead is no unhistorical miracle. As attested in the New Testament the event has definite historical dimensions. It has its historical antecedents and its historical consequences. What precedes is the historical ministry of Jesus of Nazareth. The one who is raised from death is not an unhistorical faceless ghost; undeniably, even if inconceivably, he has the lineaments of Jesus. In other words, this prior history of Jesus—his message, ministry, and suffering—is not dissolved into metaphysics or mythology, but is confirmed eschatologically, that is, with a final legitimacy. The resurrection not only has its historical antecedents; it also has its historical consequences. What follows is the confident venture of response to the event, that is, the historical practice of the resurrection.

The disciples interpreted their experience with Jesus as an invitation to freedom—freedom of a kind otherwise unknown in a period so fraught with oppressive powers and belief in fate. It was for them proof and promise that the power had been removed from fate and death and all their satellites. Hard on the heels of this knowledge came the practical response, the incomparable missionary venture of the infant church. Knowing what they knew, the apostles could not simply leave the world to stew in its own juice. In the light of the resurrection, they knew that the world and its history were now open—a realm that had been forced open, and in principle remains open, and in the course of their mission would be transformed. To be sure, principalities and powers still possess their oppressive power, but they are no longer able to separate us from the love of God, confirmed in the raising of Christ from death (Rom. 8:38). The human being is no longer a slave, but the child of this love. We have no reason, therefore, to be fatalistic or resigned. The ventures of hope are not a final desperate gamble. They are consistent with the Easter perspective. It is on this basis and with this goal in view that faith lives.

These consequences of the resurrection have lost none of their relevance today—of that I am convinced. They match the undeniable need of our time. One of the most disabling and oppressive forms this need can take is the temptation to fatalism. Depressing experiences in church and society, in both East and West, come to mind here. The demonic power of fatalism is contagious. It spreads easily. I have seen it in the attitudes not only of many apathetic and indifferent people

160

but also of many committed persons who have endured bitter experiences, especially—in my homeland—since 1968. Social initiatives that seem so desperately needed fail to survive. Our world seems to be caught firmly in the grip of the powerful, whether great or small. The result is resignation—or addiction to fits of defiant violence.

Under such circumstances faith in the resurrection takes on a new relevance for both church and society. It rallies us to resist fatalism and resignation in all its forms. As at the beginning, the message of Easter awakens us to patient and persistent struggle against fatalism, against abandoning life—both individual and social—to its fate. We carry on the struggle without any optimistic illusions, operating simply "under the cross"—aware of the dangerous tendencies and mechanisms that threaten to overwhelm us, but refusing to capitulate to them. In a world of sinful human beings it is not easy for the new to gain a foothold, but as faith sees it—in consequence of the birth, crucifixion, and resurrection of Jesus Christ—that possibility is never foreclosed.

I conclude this chapter with two questions, from two Christians who were outstanding witnesses to the resurrection—and its consequences! First, Dietrich Bonhoeffer, who was totally committed himself and aware of the fatalistic tendencies of his day, protested against the gruesome but subtle obsession with death in the "myth of the twentieth century" and summoned people to the sobriety of the resurrection faith:

> The miracle of Christ's resurrection shakes to its foundations the idolization of death current among us today. When death is the final thing, earthly life is everything or nothing. The defiant gamble on earthly eternities then goes hand in hand with a frivolous toying with life, the desperate affirmation of life with indifference to or contempt for life. Nothing more plainly betrays this idolization of death than when a generation claims to be building for eternity while simultaneously treating life as worthless, when there is grandiose talk of a new humanity, a new world, a new society which is to be ushered in, yet the only novelty is the destruction of life as we know it. . . . When it is recognized, however, that the power of death has been shattered, when the light of the miracle of the resurrection and the new life shines into the depths of the world of death, we do not demand of life any eternities but take from life what life has to offer, which is not everything or nothing but good and evil, important things and trivial things, joy and sorrow . . .[13]

161

The second voice, complementary to the first, is that of Leonhard Ragaz, who makes it clear that the sobriety of the resurrection hope does not mean any lowering of human expectations but rather an overarching horizon of hope that casts its rays of hope into every sector of life. On the basis of the resurrection of Jesus Christ:

> we believe in the resurrection of everything that has been trodden under foot and slain, whether it be things or persons, individuals or nations. Through the breach of the open grave of the crucified Christ an endless stream of resurrection and life courses into the world. That is Easter, that is the Easter faith.[14]

Ragaz

A notable survey.

162

13

Ascended to Heaven,
Sits at the Right Hand
of God the Father Almighty,
Thence He Will Come to Judge
the Living and the Dead

Jesus Christ—Yesterday, Today, Tomorrow

If asked to cite a biblical passage to explain why I deal with these three short credal statements together in this chapter at the end of the Second Article—the "christological" article of the Apostles' Creed—I would choose the familiar New Testament words: "Jesus Christ is the same yesterday, today, and for ever" (Heb. 13:8, NEB). This is one of the central christological affirmations of the New Testament. The author of Hebrews here declares his faith in the eternal identity of Jesus Christ—yesterday, today, and to all eternity. The Creed confesses the very same faith; not only in these final three clauses but in the whole of this Second Article. Here, however, right at the end, the identity of the person and saving work of the Son of God is affirmed in a particularly vivid way. We need only note the grammar of these three clauses and the verbs they use: "ascended," "sits," and "will come." Three different tenses are employed here: past, present, and future. All three clearly refer to the same agent: Jesus Christ—yesterday, today, and tomorrow.

With this transition from the past tense to the present and future tenses, a turning point is reached in the Creed. A whole series of statements about the past comes to an end. The grammatical aspects must not be pushed too far, of course. In the context of the Apostles' Creed, the perfect tense does not denote a dead past. Because the central figure in all cases is one and the same, a rigid insistence on any one of the three time dimensions of his history would be open

163

to question from the very beginning. The same applies to the baptismal setting of the Creed, to which repeated reference has already been made. In the act of confession and baptism, Christians not only remember Jesus, but also at the same time confess their faith in him as Lord of the present and the future—which has practical implications for life now and for all time to come. The divisions between past, present, and future thus become transparent. They do not, however, disappear. This dialectical situation is clearly reflected in the credal clauses that now concern us.

It is surely no accident that in the New Testament this question concerning the different times is raised explicitly in the ascension narrative. The disciples question the risen Christ: "Lord, will you at this time restore the kingdom to Israel?" His answer is a sobering one: "It is not for you to know times or seasons which the Father has fixed by his own authority" (Acts 1:6f.). The community of Jesus has no room on the agenda for speculations about the divine plan of salvation; its agenda is completely taken up with the activities of witness and mission in the new age.

The ascension of Jesus to heaven marks the transition to this new age. It brings to a final conclusion the earthly history of Jesus Christ. At the same time, however, the new stage in salvation history begins—the time of the Spirit, the time of the church. It could almost be said that the ascension signalizes the departure of Christ and the coming of the church. To say this, however, would all too easily invite misunderstanding—what Emil Brunner calls *"the misunderstanding of the church"*[1]—namely, the idea that the church could now ensconce itself in the place of Christ. How often, indeed, has the church thus presented itself—whether as institution or through its hierarchy! Clearly this is not the meaning of the ascension. It hardly needs to be pointed out that, on reaching the last of its perfect tenses in the Second Article, the Creed does not immediately pass to the confession of the church's present and future (as it will properly and emphatically do in the Third Article); it first of all confesses the present and future of Jesus Christ. We shall do well to keep this fundamental theological fact in view as we proceed with our dogmatic reflections. Even in the concluding three affirmations at the end of this central article of the Creed, the one and only subject is still clearly and unmistakably Jesus Christ. He is the theme. We shall now look in turn at each of the three assertions about him.

164

Were the Gods Astronauts?

The credal affirmation that Jesus Christ "ascended to heaven" is almost as controversial as the related affirmation that he "descended to hell." To be sure, it has strong liturgical support—witness the Feast of the Ascension, which has had a more or less important place as part of the Christian year in all Christian traditions since the fourth century. It also has a broader biblical basis than does the "descent to hell." There is not only the ascension narrative (Acts 1:4–12), to which we have already referred, but also a number of other passages in the New Testament, especially Hebrews, where Jesus is several times referred to as the High Priest "who has passed through the heavens" (Heb. 4:14; 9:11f.). But the silence of the Gospels on the subject of the ascension, plus the fact that the ascension has a close affinity to the resurrection and—for Paul, for example—is almost identical with it, has led many New Testament scholars to have reservations about the theme and even to reject it altogether. In Rudolf Bultmann's demythologizing, for example, the ascension was used as a supreme example of New Testament mythology, with its "three-storey" universe of heaven, earth, and hell. This view is accurately summarized by W. G. Kümmel as follows:

> Compared with the original faith in Christ's resurrection, the narrative of Christ's ascension is a secondary "late legend" (Grass) that stands in tension with the central primitive Christian faith in Christ's resurrection and exaltation. As a materialization of the earlier faith it has to be regarded critically as a later mythology.[2]

This critical view of the ascension cannot be ignored. It puts its finger on disconcerting features that have often been associated with the theme of the ascension in the history of the church, features that still cause Christian preachers certain difficulties and not a little embarrassment. Yet I find Kümmel's (and Bultmann's) criticism far too sweeping and inflexible. It ignores certain essential aspects, as well as the central intention, of both the Lukan narrative and the credal statement (which is equally important in the Roman and Nicene Creeds as well). It will be helpful, therefore, to look more closely at both these objections, that the ascension represents a "mythologizing" and a "materializing" of the original faith.

The Lukan narrative undeniably has features that to us seem

definitely mythological and for which mythological parallels can undoubtedly be found. Before the very eyes of the apostles, Jesus was "lifted up and a cloud took him out of their sight," while "two men in white robes" inform them of the significance of what was happening. Listening to these words and allowing our imaginations to roam a little, we could easily echo Erich von Däniken's comment: "The gods were astronauts!" For German-speaking Christians, verbal associations may play an additional role here. The German word for the ascension, *Himmelfahrt,* includes the notion of a "journey" (*Fahrt*) and means, literally, a "journey to heaven." This, in an age of "journeys in space" (*Raumfahrten*), suggests a tendentious parallel. Certainly criticism of mythology is in place here. It must also be discriminating criticism, however. These mythical elements and ideas by no means exhaust the main purpose and scope of the Lukan narrative—or of the credal statement. Indeed, both have an anti-mythological purpose. Far from offering secret information, they are a summons to sobriety. Notice how the Lukan narrative ends. It is the men in white robes in fact who counsel the disciples not to mistake the ascension of Jesus for a "spectacle": "Men of Galilee, why do you stand gazing into heaven?" There's nothing more for you to see there. The show is over! There is nothing here for television spectators, only for witnesses! Instead of myth, there is history. Instead of a world-viewing attitude, a world-changing one!

We turn next to the objection that the ascension theme represents a materializing of the original faith. This observation is true, though, in a quite different sense than that intended by the existentialist theologians. It is true in a quite positive sense. Rightly understood, the ascension insists that faith be "materialized"—effectively demonstrated in history. What is important here is not simply that our *existence* should be authentic and liberating (though that too is a fundamental concern) but that our *practice* should be authentic and liberating. It is significant that the ascension narrative is in fact the introduction to the New Testament book that bears the title "The *Acts* of the Apostles." Is that purely accidental or rather is it meant to show that from the very outset the ascension reveals a specific understanding of Christian practice (as well as a concrete practice of Christian understanding)? This, at any rate, is the direction in which the central words of Jesus to his disciples seem to point: "You shall receive power when the Holy Spirit has come upon you; and you shall be my witnesses in Jerusalem and in all Judea and Samaria and to the end of the earth" (Acts 1:8).

In the New Testament this commission and equipping for practice is of course connected also with the resurrection and the outpouring of the Holy Spirit. Carrying the same emphasis as the ascension words of Jesus just quoted, the missionary mandate in Matthew's Gospel is also an inseparable part of the legacy of the risen Christ. And in Luke, the decisive breakthrough to the practical commitment of faith is inseparable from the events of Pentecost. Easter and Pentecost are the foundations of the praxis of the apostles. But does this not make Christ's ascension to heaven, this minor festival between the two great festivals, superfluous? Not quite! And one reason why it is not superfluous could well be precisely this "materializing" tendency of the ascension. The ascension makes it clear (clearer perhaps than do the major events of Easter and Pentecost) that Christ is not raised from the dead simply in the heart of the believer, that his Spirit is not just the enthusiasm of a religious movement. It is precisely because of his *heavenly* connection that Christ also has an *earthly* connection. We are reminded of the biblical view of creation as the creation of heaven *and* earth! Salvation history works itself out in world history. Christ's ascension to heaven becomes his disciples' "descent" to earth; his "journey to heaven" becomes their "journey to the ends of the earth." It is with this completely eschatological and wholly historical horizon of faith, this "holy materialism," this inseparable connection of faith with reality, that the credal affirmation "he ascended to heaven" is concerned. Is it not conceivable that the difficulties we encounter with this theme and this festival have to do not so much with our modern ways of perceiving the universe as with the problems we experience in our practical witness and service? In that case, however, the first thing we need to do in theology and church is not to demythologize the ascension but to rediscover its significance.

Citizenship in Heaven

After these introductory clarifications of the ascension theme, we now turn to the christological substance of the statement "ascended to heaven." Here our best approach is by way of the second of our three credal clauses: "sits at the right hand of God the Father almighty." These first two clauses are closely connected. In all the creeds of the ancient church they are recited "in one breath." This prevents us from misunderstanding the ascension to mean the "removal" of Jesus, his absence or evacuation from history; as if the final occurrence of the perfect tense in the Creed ("ascended") signalized the conclusion of the Christ event, calling only for the final responsive "Amen!" This is not the case; in the Creed the ascension to heaven is not self-contained; it is not an end in itself, a final full stop. It is a purposive event. The christological perfect tense passes into the present tense: "sits at the right hand of God the Father almighty." What does that tell us about the "purpose" of Christ's ascension to heaven? I shall try to answer this question in three sections: one christological, one soteriological, and one anthropological.

To interpret the image used in the clause "sits at the right hand of God" as topographical specification of the present whereabouts of Jesus Christ would be a complete misunderstanding (as also in the case of the term "heaven"). The image denotes not the place of Jesus Christ but his role and function. It is important here to keep the Old Testament background in view, especially the first verse of Psalm 110, so often cited in the New Testament: "The Lord says to my lord: 'Sit at my right hand, till I make your enemies your footstool'" (Ps. 110:1; cf. Mark 14:62 parr.; Acts 2:23; Heb. 1:3, 13; 10:12f.). The psalm in question is a coronation liturgy. In the ancient Near East the place at the right hand of God (or of the ruler) was reserved for the person who exercised authority on his behalf. From the standpoint of the Creeds, it is in this sense that Christ's ascension to heaven and his session at God's right hand are to be understood. They affirm the installation of the Son of God into his divine dignity and authority. This reflects a clear note in the New Testament witness—the confession of Jesus as the exalted Lord. The risen and ascended Jesus is given his part in the power of God (Rom. 1:3f.; 1 Cor. 5:4; 2 Cor. 12:9; Phil. 3:10; Eph. 1:20f.; 1 Pet. 3:22) and the glory of God (Phil. 3:21; 2 Cor. 4:4; 1 Pet. 1:21). In short:

> Raising up to the right hand of God does not therefore imply being spirited away to an other-worldly empyrean, but Jesus' being with God, his being in the dimension of God, of His power and glory. It does not mean distance from the world, but a new way of being with us; Jesus is now with us from God and in God's way; expressed in imagery, he is with God as our advocate: always making intercession for us (Heb. 7:25).[3]

168

The history of Jesus Christ, therefore, does not end with the perfect tenses of the Second Article; on the contrary, it is taken up into the present tense and presence of the living God; in faith, his history orders and determines our living present.

That brings us to the second dimension of the three credal clauses under consideration, the soteriological aspect. My reason for mentioning it here is that it is not explicitly mentioned in the Apostles' Creed and is therefore easily overlooked. The "subject" of the ascension and of the session at God's right hand is not some vague or general anthropological symbol but quite unmistakably Jesus Christ, named specifically at the beginning of the Second Article. It must never be forgotten, however, that the way of the Son attested in the Creed, and hence the whole way of the Triune God, is not that of exclusive self-glorification but that of inclusive salvation. This is unambiguously affirmed in the Nicene Creed where it defines the direction and purpose of the coming of Jesus: "Who for us human beings and for our salvation, came down from heaven." What the Nicene Creed says about the descent from heaven can be equally affirmed when speaking of the ascension to heaven: "Who for us human beings and for our salvation, ascended to heaven and sits at the right hand of God the Father almighty." Jesus' faithfulness to us human beings did not end on the cross. On the contrary it was there confirmed in the most radically possible way. But that means that the ascension and the session at God's right hand concern *us*. Our cause, our humanity, which Jesus Christ made completely his own, was not abandoned at the gate of heaven or at the heavenly throne but is still the central concern in the exaltation of Christ: "What is at stake in the resurrection of Jesus Christ is the exaltation of humankind . . . As a result of his work we are with him above, with him in God."[4]

Developing this soteriological line further—it plays a central role in recent theology, especially in Barth's doctrine of reconciliation—let me turn now to the third, the anthropological dimension of these three credal clauses. "We are with him above, with him in God"—the soteriological dimension has anthropological consequences. The human being is immeasurably more than can be grasped in earthly categories, in the categories within our reach. In the light of Christ's ascension to heaven and his session at the right hand of God, the human being is a "heavenly being." *Not*, of course, in any idealistic or Gnostic sense—timeless, abstract, dualistic—but in the terms of the ultimate goal of Christ's concrete history, our participation in

169

Christ's destiny, as embodied in but at the same time transcending all earthly realities. Josef Ratzinger, who has made a special study of the ascension theme, writes as follows: "By its very essence, heaven is what is not man-made or makeable by man."[5] It is so, not merely in the sense of something "existent" which we do not make and are incapable of making, but in the sense that it is a presence and future of God that comes not from us but *upon us*.

> Heaven, therefore, is that future of the human individual and of the human race which we cannot secure for ourselves, which indeed is sealed off from us as long as we expect it only from ourselves, and which was only opened up to us fundamentally and for the first time in the human being whose basis and place of existence was God and through whom God entered into the being of humanity.[6]

If all this sounds far too speculative and difficult to grasp, I can only reply that the ancient church, too, often employed a massive metaphysical language in its efforts to bear witness to this truth. I am thinking, for example, of the oft-quoted dictum of Athanasius: "He became human that we might become divine." But the biblical witness permits us to understand our "heavenly condition and destiny" in much more concrete and dynamic terms. Paul for example uses the vivid image of our "citizenship in heaven" (Phil. 3:20). He speaks of the heavenly "city of God," the Jerusalem that is "above." The reference here is to the epitome of the Christian hope, which resides not just in comfort for the individual but also in a reality that liberates us and commits us to the transformation of the world. What is involved here is a dimension of human existence which cannot be "produced" within this world, and which for that very reason can never be wholly taken from us either—by other human beings or by circumstances—and is therefore the magna charta of inalienable freedom. It is of this radical right of citizenship and humanity, this gift and promise of the freedom of the children of God, amid all the imaginable and actual constraints and tyrannical conditions of our life, that we are reminded when we confess that Jesus Christ "ascended to heaven and sits at the right hand of God the Father almighty."

Deliverance in the Judgment

"Thence he will come to judge the living and the dead." This third credal clause points in the same direction. Here it is the third dimension of the history of Jesus Christ that comes into prominence—the future. He who was and he who is will also be present in the future; or, to put it even better and in language more in accord with that of the New Testament language: he is coming. The expectation of Christ's return, his "coming again," was, of course, a fundamental tenet of the apostolic faith. *Maranatha!*—"Our Lord, come!"—is one of the oldest prayers of the Christian church. This orientation toward the future is a distinctive feature, an inherent dynamic, of practically all the New Testament writings and of a large part of ancient Christian literature. To recall the ascension narrative once more: the watching disciples are pointed peremptorily to the future of Christ. "This Jesus, who was taken up from you into heaven, will come in the same way as you saw him go into heaven" (Acts 1:11). As a result of the "delay" in the Parousia, of course, the horizon of expectations was pushed back, but although this raised many questions and brought special trials and temptations for the disciples, it never led to a collapse of faith. Hope in the future of Christ remained unshaken. This is attested by all three creeds in almost identical words.

At this point, however, the Apostles' Creed does not speak of some universal future, nor of the coming of Jesus Christ in general terms. It speaks plainly of the coming of Jesus Christ as judge: "Thence he will come to judge the living and the dead." Here is sounded the theme of the last judgment. As traditionally understood, this is a somber and gloomy theme. We need only recall medieval theology, the medieval world view, medieval art. Here the doctrine of the last judgment played a major part. To a large extent, Christian piety was dominated by contemplation of "that day, that day of wrath." It was an alarming, even terrifying prospect, as the dramatic opening words of Thomas of Celano's impressive sequence clearly show, words that have become familiar to us from countless requiems:

> Oh, what fear man's bosom rendeth
> When from heaven the Judge descendeth
> On whose sentence all dependeth![7]

Similar gloomy portrayals are also found in other art forms. The last judgment is vividly depicted as a final reckoning and separation, the artistic imagination usually dwelling with particular care on the well-deserved torments of those whom the world's Judge sets on his left hand.

I prefer not to adopt the rationalist critique and simply to dissociate myself from the medieval mood, which clearly reflects one aspect of the biblical theme of the last judgment. Nevertheless, I want to interpret the credal text in a different, more-nuanced way. The creeds themselves point the way. Without exception, they place this clause into a context that helps in its clarification and interpretation, namely, at the end of the Second Article in the context of the saving history of Jesus Christ. The last judgment, that is to say, is not an isolated and independent theme. It is the final culmination of a quite definite movement and way. The idea of judgment is to be interpreted accordingly. It does not mean an independent mechanism for ensuring cosmic equilibrium—as for example the idea of *samsara* in India—nor an inflexible law that operates inexorably. On the contrary, judgment here is a personal transaction taking place within the history of Christ as summarized in the Second Article. The theme of judgment must be interpreted in concrete christological terms.[8] What does this mean in practical terms? The answer has at least five aspects:

1. When the last judgment is given its full christological content, that removes the note of fatalism from the dark and gloomy atmosphere in which the traditional church picture of the last judgment is so often shrouded. The "day of wrath" is the day of the Lord Jesus Christ. It is the goal of his way with us and for us. It includes judgment of course: the apostolic faith embraces the Judge. In human life there are decisions and divisions, standards and distinctions. "God is not mocked" (Gal. 6:7). At the same time, Christians know that this judge is none other than their Lord. What interests *this* Judge is not some kind of abstract justice to be executed "come what may"—"Let justice be done, though the world perish." As the life, death, and resurrection of Jesus Christ show, his justice has at its purpose the restoration of the rights of his creatures. It is his declared will that sinners should not perish but be delivered—in the judgment. As faith sees it, therefore, the judgment of the world does not mean some incalculable endless horror but the restoration of justice, with everything put to right. Those who confess this faith, therefore, face the prospect of this judgment, if not with a "quiet conscience," at least with "quiet confidence" and positive hope.

This attitude to the last judgment is memorably expressed in the *Heidelberg Catechism*:

Question 52: What comfort is it to you that Christ shall come again to judge the living and the dead?

Answer: That in all afflictions and persecution, with uplifted head, I may wait for the Judge from heaven, who has already offered himself to the judgement of God for me, and has taken away from me all curse.[9]

Parenthetically it may be noted that the Calvinist Reformation, in striking contrast to the somber tones of medieval and baroque piety, clearly sounded the note of a christologically founded confidence at this point (see for example Calvin's *Geneva Catechism*, QQ 86 and 87).[10]

2. Seen in this perspective, the traditional picture of the last judgment is also purified of another questionable element, namely, the rigid dualism reflected in the "symmetry" of artistic representations of the last judgment—with the saved on the right and the damned on the left—but reflected also in doctrinal disquisitions on this theme. In both cases, the presentation is so constructed as to secure a symmetrical correspondence between the "two sides"—heaven and hell, the just and the unjust. But the effect of this is a very questionable "stabilization" of the drama and movement of New Testament eschatology and the sayings of Jesus about the judgment.

> The fundamental intention of the Word of Jesus is utterly asymmetrical and anti-static. It is a dynamic Word, a Word implying God's movement towards us with the aim of determining our movement towards him. The meaning is not: these *are* the two realities. Rather it is: come forth from perdition into salvation.[11]

Given its fundamental thrust and purpose, the last day is part of the history of salvation, not the history of damnation.

3. The teaching of Jesus reveals the criterion of the last judgment, most clearly in the well-known passage Matt. 25:31–46. Our destiny is decided in God's sight by our responsiveness or our indifference to the concrete needs of our fellow human beings—the hungry, thirsty, strangers, naked, sick, prisoners. What is presented here is certainly not an ideology in praise of the achievements of the self-righteous; in fact the "righteous" do not even know that it is Jesus they were helping when they helped the "least" of these his brothers and sisters. Obviously, therefore, they were not investing in their own merits, collecting good marks in order to pass the final examination. The righteous live by grace, letting grace also govern their lives. They refuse to become hardened to the gracelessness of human hearts and

173

conditions. They do not fritter their freedom away in selfishness and indifference, but exercise it in the same spirit as Jesus and in the same direction, namely, by sharing the lot of his—and their—brothers and sisters in practical demonstrations of solidarity.

4. In the context of the Christ event, the last day is the day of final deliverance, the day when Christ's saving history is completed and fulfilled. Not in any cheap and obvious sense, of course, and certainly not in the sense that the pious are here vindicated and given a pat on the back! Jesus' words in the Matthean passage that it is the self-confident ones who are disconcerted and put to shame, and the diffident ones who are reassured. The point is simply that the last day is the day of deliverance for the oppressed and the vulnerable. In the terms used by Jesus in the Beatitudes, it is the day of deliverance for the poor, the mourners, the meek, those who hunger and thirst for justice, the merciful, the pure in heart, the peacemakers, and those who are persecuted because of their stand for justice. For all these, the last day is the day of the final exodus, the day of deliverance. And the liberating momentum of this prospect is visible not only at the end of time but already here in the midst of time. It helps us already here and now, in the impenetrable jungle of all the subjective and objective conditions that make up our never wholly transparent human life, to take our bearings and to direct our steps toward the fundamental and final goal, to begin already today to learn the way of justice. It is a summons to commitment, to ethical and political responsibility, in some circumstances also to discipline and asceticism, for the sake of God's justice and judgment. But, precisely because it is all that, it is also a call to freedom.

> The expectation of Christ's coming again to judgement is the foundation of that certainty of the standard whereby the Christian withstands the pressure of ruling circumstances and the tendencies of the spirit of any given age.[12]

5. This focus on him who "will come to judge the living and the dead" also has a personal and individual reference. It helps us to extricate ourselves from our entanglement in false human judgments and to discover and experience the liberty of the sons and daughters of God. "Who shall bring any charge against God's elect?" asks Paul, in reference to the last judgment. He answers: "It is God who justifies" (Rom. 8:33). But this same promise also has a transpersonal

dimension. It has to do with both the living and the dead. Affecting us all, it has to do with the history of the whole human race—above all, that strand of human history that is so often ignored and forgotten by human courts of justice and by conventional historians.

In our interpretation of the cross of Christ and remembering the passion, reference was made to the consequences of the cross both for the way we view history and for the way we view and shape our lives. We have to pick up this point again here. How often are our accounts of the past—and the present—focused almost exclusively on the successful, the survivors, the people who made good. This viewpoint seems to determine the criteria whereby we live and evaluate our lives, individually, communally, and even in the church. But if Jesus is the coming judge, this fact paves the way for a transvaluation of all values. The meaning of life and the meaning of history do not depend primarily on what happens to the successful people. The history of Jesus takes up into itself the history of those who suffer—promising for them a justice beyond any they have ever known in human history. In this sense too it can be said with emphasis and with gratitude not that the world's history is the world's judgment but that *salvation* history is the *world's* judgment. Max Horkheimer once formulated his deepest philosophical and human desire as a longing "that the murderer should not triumph over the innocent victim." That yearning finds here for the first time a realistic grounding and a promising goal—in face of the crucified and exalted One "who is and who was and who is to come" (Rev. 1:8).

The Kingdom Without End

We conclude with a side-glance at the Nicene Creed. It has already been noted that the three main creeds are largely in agreement in these three concluding clauses of the Second Article. Only at the very end does the Nicene Creed offer an additional clause—"of whose kingdom there will be no end." This is clearly a doxological addition (signaled already by the *doxa* addition in the Nicene to the previous clause—"come again *with glory* to judge"). This addition is no mere rhetorical flourish, however; it is important theologically and is refreshingly relevant for our own times. The central theme of Jesus' own preaching was the kingdom of God, and here this crucial theme is now taken up into the Christian Creed—as the kingdom of Christ.

The way of the Son of God—and with it the faith of the Christian—is not just a private enterprise, or even a church enterprise. What is at stake here is God's own kingdom, that kingdom which has no ending. (Is it pure chance that this emphasis should be found in the Creed of the Eastern church?)

The effect of this additional clause is to set the Second Article in an "infinite horizon" and at the same time, by the use of the political term "kingdom," to relate it to world history in the sense of political history. This has both polemical and constructive implications.

Polemically, it means that the faith must be applied critically to all systems and ideologies in order to expose as spurious the absolute claims of all political imperialisms. How many kingdoms have been spawned by world history—regrettably even by church history—kingdoms that were planned to last for a thousand years, to be final, indeed totalitarian, and then were concretely tested in actual operation, with all sorts of grim and brutal consequences. The sober and encouraging knowledge that Christ's kingdom alone is really enduring helps Christians in the political field.

But this additional clause also has constructive implications—as a criterion and signpost. Kingdom of God also has to do with the transient kingdoms of this world. For all their transience, these earthly kingdoms are to be launched and shaped in keeping with the standards of this coming judge and the trajectories of his kingdom. World history may not be the world's judgment, but it is nonetheless to be shaped in the light of that judgment. In great things as in small, this too is part of the mission and task of those who are privileged to confess their faith in the One who "ascended to heaven, sits at the right hand of God the Father almighty" from whence "he will come to judge the living and the dead."

14

I Believe in the Holy Spirit

Neglect of the Spirit in Christian Theology?

Christian theology is suffering from an acute mental blackout where the Holy Spirit is concerned. . . . For centuries we have been so attached to a christocentric theology of the Second Article that we never reached the Third Article, the continuation of the salvation history in the form of an independent, post-pentecostal christological theology. The consequence of this mental blackout is a failure to realize the basic truth that it is only through confession of faith in the Holy Spirit that we have any access at all to a theology of the First and Second Articles.[1]

In these forthright terms Otto Dilschneider voices his disquiet over modern ecumenical—and especially Protestant—theology. His complaint and accusation are not entirely unfounded. If we consider only the history of the interpretation of the creeds, we are struck at once by the way the pace quickens as expositors pass from the Second Article to the Third; the exposition gathers speed and races almost breathlessly ("spiritlessly"?) to the end. Even today we find textbooks on dogmatics that do not allocate as much as a single chapter to the Holy Spirit.[2] There is a real danger here of a mental blackout. There are good reasons for Dilschneider's question and, more important, for the insistent questions addressed to our Western churches and theology from other parts of the world—from Africa, for example. Indeed the questions come as well from increasingly articulate groups in the growing charismatic movement within our own churches. In this whole area we have a good deal of ground to make up.

In the quotation from Dilschneider, however, there is one important point on which I cannot agree. He attributes this development to "a christocentric theology of the Second Article," and he thus, so to speak, plays the Third and Second Articles off against each other. Dilschneider is not alone in doing this. Rudolf Bohren appears to do the same thing in the field of practical theology, even offering a concrete justification for the procedure. Whereas a christological theology tends, he says, to encourage "an authoritarian structure in our preaching," pneumatology, on the contrary, with its "theonomous reciprocity of the Spirit" "as a divinely established mutuality and bilaterial relationship," promotes a "characteristic partnership" that removes "the element of intolerance inherent in christology."[3]

These judgments seem to me questionable. In the light of the New Testament, it is hardly permissible to describe Christ's person and work as potentially "authoritarian" and to contrast it with the Holy Spirit, characterized as promoting partnership. Not only that, but it also seems to me dubious in the extreme to treat the three articles of the Creed as if they were in competition with each other. Such a view is certainly alien to the spirit of the Creed itself. What the Creed sets forth is *one* faith, formulated in three indivisible, coherent, and mutually interconnected acts and declarations of faith, all of them inseparably related to the one Triune God—Father, Son, and Holy Spirit. The sequence here is not to be mistaken for an order of precedence. In later trinitarian theology the term "perichoresis" was used of the divine Persons—meaning that the divine Persons were not to be assigned special "departments" but that their relationship to each other is to be understood as one of the mutual circumincession and reciprocal partnership.

We have to bear this in mind when we think of the Creed and its three articles. These articles are not sealed off from one another but mutually interpenetrate and reciprocally interpret and explicate each other. Dilschneider says that "it is only through confession of faith in the Holy Spirit that we have any access at all to a theology of the First and Second Articles." That is true—but only if at the same time we are equally insistent that there is no confession of faith in the Holy Spirit that is not itself filled with the content of the Second and First Articles. Pneumatology without Christology is fully as dubious an enterprise as Christology without pneumatology. The neglect of the Holy Spirit in our theology cannot be made good by a one-sided or even abstract theology of the Third Article.

Such theologies of the Holy Spirit, moreover, have not exactly been in short supply, even in the period to which Dilschneider refers, and especially among Protestants. Adopting the interpretative terminology of Karl Barth, could not the mainstream of modern Protestant theology, especially in its supreme exemplar Schleiermacher, be described as a "theology of the Third Article"?[4] It is in this direction, at least, that we should have to look for the theological legitimacy of its special interest in the world of human experience. The only problem is that it was their concept of the Spirit that induced these theologians to concentrate on the mysteries of the human spirit, on human feelings, intelligence, and moral capacities, and not at all, either primarily or exclusively, on the mysteries of the biblical Holy Spirit. The Second Article—and soon the First Article as well—paled into insignificance in comparison with this powerful modern current. To a large extent, the Holy Spirit of the Creed was a stranger to this religion of the spirit. In other words, we cannot make up for modern neglect of the Spirit in theology by developing some abstract theology of the Third Article, one which is not a fulfillment of the Second and First Articles.

Subject to this qualification, the positive emphasis on the Holy Spirit in Dilschneider and Bohren and, it must be emphasized once again, the contemporary witness to the Holy Spirit in the worldwide church must be welcomed wholeheartedly and unreservedly. Theology has no more important task than a "theology of the Spirit," and in view of all the ground that has to be made up this task certainly has priority today. What this means in an exposition of the Creed is that as we come now to the Third Article there can be no "sudden descent." We are not yet at the exit, listening only to an echo. We are in fact playing the third movement of a single sonata, indispensable because it completes and fulfills all that has gone before. If we should happen to find ourselves out of breath here, the fault is certainly not in the musical score but in ourselves.

Renewing Power

After the First and Second Articles, what does the confession of faith in the Holy Spirit offer us that is new? Why was the candidate for baptism in the early church asked not only the other two questions but also this question: Do you believe in the Holy Spirit? The question as to the new element introduced at this point in the Creed is one that is often asked, but this is really a mistaken or at least a misleading question, as Karl Barth has pointed out:

> Time and again, people fall into the error of supposing that the Holy Spirit is necessarily something new and distinctive alongside the simple truth of faith and the life of faith. On the one hand, some have thought they had, in the name of the Holy Spirit, to add human reasoning to the truth of Christ. . . . The result was a little blending of the Holy Spirit with our various intellectual discoveries. On the other hand, there were the Christian sects, which believed that the Holy Spirit, on the contrary, is something irrational, something to do with mysticism and extra-sensory life, something with astonishing possibilities compared with what we see in the person of Christ. In short, they said to themselves: Poor Jesus, not to have had all these lovely things the Holy Spirit has given to *us*![5]

Barth was surely right. According to the New Testament, the role of the Holy Spirit is not to innovate in a hitherto unparalleled way, in the sense of adding to and rounding off the saving work of Christ—whether from the spiritual resources of nature or those of the supernatural. Whenever the church or its theologians look in this direction, they miss seeing the Holy Spirit. And they have in fact tried both the approaches referred to by Barth, sometimes with truly impressive efforts. Think, for example, of the deep spirituality characteristic of the modern theologians of reason and feeling; or again, of the vigor and force of the mystics and spiritual enthusiasts who have again and again appeared on the scene throughout history. Both these phenomena represent an enrichment of our cultural history. But they can hardly be said to have served well the Holy Spirit attested in the Creed.

For the novelty brought by the Holy Spirit is not located in the economy of nature nor in that of the supernatural. As is clear from the very structure of the Creed, this novelty belongs within the economy of the Triune God, in terms of which it is certainly legitimate to speak of something new. In fact it is remarkable how frequently and emphatically the Bible speaks of the concept and work of the Spirit as a force for renewal and new life. The promise and the reality of the new are associated especially with the Spirit, and not just in the New Testament but already in the Old, as we shall discover at every step in our exposition. The new proclaimed in the Bible, however, is not something vague and ill-defined, not just any newness. The Bible does not introduce some abstract category of "the new," although the biblical message helped to alert philosophy to the possibilities of the new (as is particularly clear in the ontology of the contemporary Marxist philosopher Ernst Bloch). The "new thing" is always anchored in the "old"—the Third Article in the two preceding ones.

How then are we to understand this "new" dimension of the Third Article in relation to the Second and First Articles? Provisionally, as a first approach to an answer, as a sort of keynote for the more concrete reflections that are to follow, let me propose two concepts as an aid to comprehension—first "contemporization," in the sense of making present and contemporary, and second "participation."

I understand the Holy Spirit, in the first place, as the power whereby, in Jesus Christ, God himself becomes present and contemporary. The Holy Spirit is God in his intimate nearness. Already in the Old Testament, the "Spirit of God" denotes the unexpected and blessed presence of God. That is to say: God is not only Lord of the beginning and Lord of the end but also the God who is present. He is not only the God of the heights and the depths but also the God of the soul; not only the God of creation but also the personal God, the God who is closer to me than I am to myself, the God of my inexchangeable present.

It is this particular aspect of our faith in God that comes to the fore in the Third Article. When in addition to the first two questions the baptismal candidate was also asked this third question, an affirmative response clearly meant: In my faith in God the Father and in Jesus Christ, I am not tying in to events now gone and receding ever further into the past; I am not just finding solace in nostalgic memory. I am here and now, in my present time—which is thereby affected and changed—coming into the very presence of God. I live in the presence of my salvation, rooted in and revealed to me in the name of God and of Christ. This dimension of the divine presence was already there, of course, in the two preceding articles, for God the Father is not just "the ancient one," and the Christ event too, though anchored in history and attested by a series of witnesses as historically completed, has its emphatic present and future dimensions. (We have only to recall the change of tenses in the Second Article.) But this dimension of presence, already reflected in the retrospect of faith,

181

now becomes central and emphatic, unmistakably the main focus of attention. Being a question of the Holy Spirit, it is therefore a question of the power of contemporization, of the presence of the Spirit. When I recite the Creed, it is my "today" (and my "tomorrow") that are in question.

But there is more to it even than that. This contemporization is understood, at the same time, as participation. The Holy Spirit is the power of participation. In the Holy Spirit, God becomes indissolubly identified with humanity, and humanity with God. In this Third Article, it may be said, the Creed puts the spotlight on humanity. Not only here, of course; humanity is already present in the First and Second Articles, as the Creator's creation and above all as God's covenant partner in the destiny of Jesus Christ, right down into the depths of historical sufferings and metaphysical death. Could anything more essential be said about humanity than had already been said in the First and Second Articles? There not only the foundation but also the abyss and, above all, the destiny of our humanity were affirmed in a way that left nothing more to be said. But now, in the Third Article, once again and to our relief, the completed work is taken up, only now from the standpoint of its appropriation by us and our participation in it. We are not merely the "objects" of God's work of salvation; we are addressed as "subjects," as persons. God does not simply treat us as objects; he seeks our response. He wants us to appropriate his work, to participate in it—not just from the outside, as it were, but in the inner depths of our humanity. He involves us and empowers us to become involved; he, the present God wants us also to be present, as contemporaries of his salvation, subjects of his history, real partners in his covenant history whose goal is our participation.

In what follows, let me try to define more precisely this power of contemporization and participation and, at the same time, to grasp the main dimensions of pneumatological renewal in more specific terms. The exposition here will be in three stages: the present Christ; the inner witness; the renewal of creation.

The Present Christ

That the primary role of the Holy Spirit is to make Jesus Christ present and to enable us to participate in his destiny is not merely a formal conclusion based on the direct proximity of the Second and

Third Articles in the Creed. It is in keeping with the substance of the New Testament message. For the evangelists and apostles, the Spirit is undeniably and unmistakably the Spirit of Jesus Christ. Paul's statement "The Lord is the Spirit" (2 Cor. 3:17) is really equivalent to an axiom.

In this identification of the work of the Spirit with the work of Christ, both sides of the statement "The Lord is the Spirit" must be kept in mind. Within the framework of this basic equation, the New Testament witnesses differ, of course, as to where the emphasis lies.

Speaking in rather general terms, it may be said that, for the evangelists, the equation primarily stresses the fact that Jesus is the true bearer of the Spirit. He is the heir of the Old Testament promises concerning the Spirit; in him the Spirit enters human history with final authority. "The Spirit of the Lord is upon me"—according to Luke (4:18f.), this text from Isaiah was the text of Jesus' first sermon, preached in Nazareth. It is not only in the message of Jesus, however, but also in his practical ministry that the Spirit plays a decisive role. It is by the power of the Holy Spirit that Jesus performs his works of healing and mercy; they bring God's coming kingdom into the present (Matt. 12:28). The decisive stages of Jesus' ministry, therefore— his baptism, for example (Mark 1:10f.), or his return to Galilee (Luke 4:14)—are always connected by the evangelists with the creative presence of the Holy Spirit. Matthew and Luke, when they reflect on the nativity of Jesus, see none other than the Holy Spirit at work (cf. Matt. 1:18 and Luke 1:35)—which is where the Creed, as we have seen, also locates the beginnings of Jesus: "conceived by the Holy Spirit."

In view of this New Testament witness, therefore, we could say that the concept of Jesus and the concept of the Holy Spirit are identical. The Holy Spirit is set forth, exhibited, explained, in the history of Jesus of Nazareth, and takes concrete shape and basic direction from this history. This "anchorage" of the Holy Spirit was of tremendous importance for the apostolic church. After the resurrection of Jesus, the church had experienced the presence of the Spirit in a turbulent charismatic happening. The main feature of this Pentecostal event was the outpouring of the Holy Spirit. The experience of the Holy Spirit in the first Christian communities was also a turbulent and chaotic business, therefore, as can be gathered from Paul's account of the effects and gifts of the Spirit in Corinth, for example, with the prophesyings, healings by prayer, and speaking in tongues. Certainly

Paul did not underestimate the power of the Spirit. The Holy Spirit cannot be measured by the standards of normal "bourgeois" culture: what happens "in the Spirit" is something extraordinary, abnormal, and inconceivable. But it is made emphatically clear, precisely in reference to the authoritative presence of the Spirit in the history of Jesus that the extraordinary, the abnormal, the inconceivable do not in themselves add up to the presence of the Holy Spirit. There are also demonic and fanatical spirits, and these appear often enough with white-heat intensity. It is necessary, therefore, to "test the spirits" (1 John 4:1), to examine them soberly to see what is here being offered, and this testing too is a gift of the Spirit. The spirits have to be identified. It is in this identification process that the axiom "The Lord is the Spirit" acquires its binding theological and ethical force: the Spirit of Jesus becomes the criterion for testing the spirits. This is why the love inspired by Christ is defined emphatically in 1 Corinthians 13 as the ultimate and decisive gift and evidence of the Spirit.

At the same time, however, the axiom "The Lord is the Spirit" must also be understood from the other side. It is not only a pneumatological but also a christological clarification. It answers the question: How is the crucified and risen Christ present among us? The primitive Christian community was deeply concerned with this question, and it is a question that concerns the disciples of Jesus and their assailed community in every age. The faith that the Lord had not simply vanished from the scene since his crucifixion and resurrection (or, more precisely, since his ascension) had already been confessed in the concluding clauses of the Second Article: "ascended to heaven, sits at the right hand of God the Father almighty, thence he will come." Yet these confident affirmations of faith could not silence the question: What does this mean for us? The Creed speaks of heaven, but we are here on earth. It speaks of Christ's return at the end of time, but we are still living today in the time before the end. Between us and Christ, is there not a "nasty gulf" in every sense, both temporally and spatially? Are not the lives of Christians since the crucifixion and ascension marked by Christ's absence from us, or at least by a distance between him and us—by "the absent Christ"?

The New Testament does not hide the anguish and pain of these questions, or the consequent trial of faith for Jesus' disciples—and all succeeding generations of Christians. There are painful farewell scenes in the New Testament. The parting from their brutally tortured and crucified master brought his followers at the foot of the cross to almost total despair. But there is also the parting from the risen Lord at the very beginning of the Acts of the Apostles (and the title of this book should be taken literally—we have here the beginning of the praxis of the apostles!). Although there is no despair or collapse, even here there is an experience of deprivation and abandonment, of being "left behind." This is not concealed, glossed over, or glorified. We are deprived and needy Christians in straitened circumstances. In the lives of most of us—including Paul himself, the most energetic and "successful" of the New Testament witnesses to Christ's presence—there are moments when this condition almost drives us to despair, and we would prefer to finish with it in order to "be with Christ" (Phil. 1:23).

That is only one aspect of the situation, however. There is another. Paul shows us the direction in which this "other side" points. His desire is "to depart and be with Christ" but "to remain in the flesh is more necessary *on your account*," that is, for the sake of others. Clearly, therefore, in the "absence" of Christ, the Christian does not simply live in a void, abandoned by God; Christ's cause is not left in a vacuum but continues; it is now committed to his disciples, who become the authorized agents of the history of Christ. This is why the moment of Christ's parting does not become funereal; it becomes the moment when the disciples go forth into all the world. But what motive inspires them? Is it simply the stubborn determination to see things through, to carry on in a last ditch mood of defiance? That would have been an understandable human reaction. But the New Testament tells a very different story. The departure of the disciples into all the world is inspired by the promise of the Holy Spirit and by the power of the Holy Spirit. This truth is reflected in John's Gospel in the farewell discourses, in which the situation of the disciples after the ascension is anticipated and prophetically interpreted. These farewell discourses of Jesus are not funeral orations; they are filled with the promise of the Spirit—the Paraclete, the Comforter, the Advocate (John 14:26; 15:26; 16:7). The absence of Jesus is interpreted not as plunging the disciples into the void but as translating them into the presence of the Spirit. For the apostolic communities, moreover, this is not something purely theoretical but a reality that concretely affects the way they live. As even the professional historians have noticed, their life style is not one of passive resignation but one marked by dynamic fresh beginnings. Existence in discouragement and despair becomes existence under promise; not abandoned and left in the lurch but alive to the presence of the Spirit.

This overwhelming presence of the Spirit is automatically assumed by the New Testament to be the presence of the Lord Jesus. In this sense, too, the axiom "The Lord is the Spirit" is to be interpreted as a confession of faith in the presence of Christ. In the Spirit, the One who has been taken away is brought near; in the Spirit, the One who is in heaven is present on earth; in the Spirit, the One who came and will come again is already present in the midst of his church. In the Spirit, not in the flesh. But the loss in visibility is more than compensated by the gain in dynamic thereby revealed. The "absent" Jesus is cancelled out by the "present Christ" who is present in the gift and mission of the Spirit. And this indeed—to emphasize the point once more—not in some dying echo of Jesus' cause but in its breaking out "into all the world," in the "crescendo" of the Spirit. This is the way in which the crucified and coming Lord is present for his church.

Identity and Fulfillment of the Free Human Being

The presence of Christ in the Spirit is realized in human history, to begin with in the inner life of human beings. As I have already pointed out, the Holy Spirit is, in a special sense, God coming close to us and entering into us. In the trinitarian confession of the Christian faith, the Third Article takes in hand our human appropriation of the First and Second Articles. The Father's act of creation and the Son's act of salvation are focused on humanity; on humanity, moreover, in its individual subjectivity, namely, on the knowledge, faith, and love of individuals. That is their goal. This is what theologians have referred to as the inner witness or testimony of the Holy Spirit. To employ the classic definitions developed in the history of doctrine in obedience to the biblical witness, the Holy Spirit is the "Spirit of truth," "the bond of love" (Augustine), and "the Spirit of freedom." The fact that the Spirit is regarded in the trinitarian tradition of the church as the Third Person of the Holy Trinity underlines the incomparable and fundamental importance of our human appropriation of salvation. For God, the final thing is not the way to Calvary and the objectively consummated sacrifice of Jesus Christ, not the destiny of the risen Christ on earth and in heaven; the Triune God attains his goal only in the freedom and love of the human heart conquered by the truth. What sounds forth, therefore, in this third dimension of the trinitarian concept of God is a clear and binding emphasis on the theological importance of human freedom. In opposition to all forms of mechanical religious objectivism and doctrinal fundamentalism, to all forms of church sacramentalism and institutionalism, but also—in its ethical and political implications—in opposition to the manipulative pressures of economic and political structures and systems, the confession of faith "in the Holy Spirit" champions the cause of the subjective liberation of human beings. "Where the Spirit of the Lord is, there is freedom" (2 Cor. 3:17).

Oddly enough, it is Karl Barth, so often accused of dogmatic objectivism and a "positivist view of revelation," who impresses on us this significance of faith in the Holy Spirit for the liberation of the human subject. "It would be cold comfort if everything were to remain objective."[6]

> God is Spirit and therefore he truly awakens the human being to freedom. That he lets us experience his divine power does not mean that he crushes and overwhelms us, steamrollers us and forces us to be what he wants us to be. . . . He sets us on our own feet as partners. He wants us to stand up and walk on our own legs as his partners; in other words, he wants *us* to believe, to love, to hope.[7]

The Holy Spirit creates not slaves but free children (Rom. 8:17; Gal. 4:5), who are not treated by God (and are therefore not to be regarded and treated by others or by themselves) as "worthless" human beings. On the contrary, the declared intention of the Spirit of Jesus is that I should not lose my life but find it, that I should come to myself (as the parable of the prodigal son puts it), that I should be, and be permitted to become, myself.

This brings us to one of the fundamental questions posed by the human mind, one that is properly the subject of intense discussion today among students of the human sciences and contemporaries generally who seek to understand the meaning of life—the question of personal human identity amid all the external social pressures and forms of social alienation. None of us can remain indifferent to this question. Does faith in the Holy Spirit point to an answer, or at least an approach to an answer?

Contemporary theologians are exploring this possibility. To some extent, of course, an answer based on pneumatology runs in a direction counter to that which is usually given or expected here. More often than not those in quest of individual identity are advised to focus attention directly on the individual self: Attend to yourself, be your own best friend and neighbor, cultivate independence and freedom from the threatening proximity of others. But the biblical motif of the Holy Spirit points in a different direction.

Eberhard Jüngel shows us this direction in his major work on the Cartesian *cogito* ("I think"). Dealing with the question of individual identity and human fulfillment, he formulates this "anthropological principle":

> Only in abandonment of the self do we really discover the self. . . . In seeking to achieve our own individual fulfilment, we lose that salutary closeness to our individual selves for which the Holy Spirit of God equips us.[8]

It is important not to misunderstand these words. They are not inspired by any resentment of the human longing for self-discovery and authentic selfhood, for real individual identity and close familiarity with the self. Indeed, in the light of the Holy Spirit, the God of intimate presence, we are permitted and even required to take this longing seriously, for it is also the longing of the Holy Spirit. At the same time, however, the reference to the Holy Spirit means that this longing is not fulfilled if we settle down on our own, revolve around the self, and destroy the bridge to transcendence that is found in other human beings and in God. Experience of the self is not redemption of the self or even discovery of the self. Self-fulfillment, moreover, if it is nothing but the ego's own power play, is simply counterproductive. Real freedom is achieved only in the Spirit, and the Spirit is the Lord, the Lord present in the love of Jesus. Only in this Spirit, in love, do we truly discover the self and fulfill the self. Jesus' own "anthropological principle" is axiomatic: "Whoever would save his life will lose it; and whoever loses his life for my sake and the gospel's will save it" (Mark 8:35).

Wolfhart Pannenberg also looks in this direction for a new approach to "the essence of the spiritual" in the light of the Holy Spirit. This problem has been to the fore previously in this history of the Third Article and plays an important role above all in idealist thought. Pannenberg suggests:

> Spirit would have to be understood here not in terms of consciousness and the subjective character of the conscious self but, on the contrary, the conscious self would be seen as a special stage in a living being's participation in the spiritual reality which operates in the self-transcendence of all living things.[9]

I take this to mean that the way to a new and better understanding of the anthropological mystery of the spirit could be pointed out by precisely this pneumatological axiom that the Holy Spirit is not an anthropological predicate, not a potential or existing human resource, but the presence of God in our human hearts, that is, a theological and christological "predicate." The spirit is to be understood not as a possession of the self-absorbed thinking self, sovereignly positing the nonself, but rather as a participation in the spiritual reality, as a communicative self-transcendence, as an "I-Thou" movement. I consider this proposal to be the permanent and very pertinent contribution of theological pneumatology to the struggle of philosophy and the human sciences for the identity and fulfillment of individual persons.

For in the last analysis—and, here I summarize the two previous sections—the coming of the Holy Spirit means on the one hand the presence of the God who loves in freedom and champions the freedom and love of human beings, and on the other hand, correspondingly and in indissoluble connection with this, the free and loving human being who responds to this God who loves in freedom.

Theology of the Spirit:
The Church and the New Creation

The movement of the Holy Spirit is outwards and its goal is renewal. It begins in the deepest and most inward reaches of our human existence but does not remain lodged in the inner world of human beings; it reaches out, encouraging and equipping people to move outwards "into all the world," including the outward and visible world of human society. The God who is "closer to us than breathing" is not only a God of the inner depths but also the Lord of all creation. The prophet of Israel reminds us of this in his question: "Am I a God at hand, says the Lord, and not a God afar off?" (Jer. 23:23). In the well-known passages on the Spirit in the Old and New Testaments we are repeatedly confronted with this movement and dynamic of the Holy Spirit. God's creator Spirit is already present and at work in the creation of the world. Eschatologically too, it is not only individual believers and not only the people of God but all the peoples of the earth who are included under the promise that the Spirit will be "poured out upon all flesh" (Joel 2:28ff.). This promise is taken up again in the New Testament and, according to Acts 2, fulfilled in the coming of the Spirit at Pentecost. This fulfillment, moreover, means not only the gathering of the community but also its mission, the sending, across all the boundaries, "into all the world." The horizon of the Spirit evidently embraces not only the "new heart" but also the "new world."

This dimension, too, is taken into account in the Creed. In the Third Article, as I have already pointed out, the spotlight is on humanity. However, we must now be more precise: the focus of attention here is not just on the individual human being but on the human being as member of the new community and within the eschatological horizon of God's new world. While the Third Article opens with the affirmation "I believe in the Holy Spirit," it follows this up immediately with other affirmations, first concerning the church and then concerning the "resurrection of the flesh." In theological terms: pneumatology has a teleological thrust in the direction of ecclesiology and eschatology. This thrust merits full attention in two respects: First, it is necessary to understand the church and the hope of everlasting life in terms of the Holy Spirit—a point we dare not forget in the succeeding chapters. At this stage in our exposition, however, the main emphasis must be on the other point, namely, that the Holy Spirit is to be seen and attested in terms of the movement toward renewal of the faith community and of creation.

A distinction—but no separation—must be made between these two dimensions, these two steps outward—church and (new) world. The Holy Spirit is no free-floating world soul, no shapeless universal. As the present Christ, the Spirit is in the first place the Spirit of Christ's church. This is clearly brought out in the Pentecostal event: Pentecost is the birthday of the Christian church, a particular and unique fellowship, the community of faith. In somewhat the same way as the human being is understood in biblical as over against idealistic anthropology, not as a formless spirit (in which case he would not be a human being but a ghost) but as the soul of this particular body, so too in biblical pneumatology the Holy Spirit is not a formless ghost but a Creator Spirit bent on incarnation, who creates for himself a "body."

A parenthetical remark is required here in order to guard against a misunderstanding that has cropped up all too often in the history of the church. In one of the best-known New Testament passages on the Spirit, Paul contrasts "walking in the Spirit" with following "the desires of the flesh" (Galatians 5). Paul lists here as works of the flesh: "fornication, impurity, licentiousness, idolatry, sorcery, enmity, strife, jealousy, anger, selfishness, dissension, party spirit, envy, drunkenness, carousing, and the like" (Gal. 5:19f.). But the fruit or harvest of the Spirit, he says, is "love, joy, peace, patience, kindness, goodness, faithfulness, gentleness, self-control" (Gal. 5:22f.). Mesmerized by a dualistic and idealistic anthropology, people within the church and outside it have repeatedly been tempted to interpret this sharp opposition as a struggle between the two aspects of human nature—body and spirit. In consequence, the two were seen strictly in terms of black and white, the human spirit as all good and the body as evil. Concretely, there was discrimination against the body, and the Holy Spirit was assigned exclusively to the spiritual realm.

But this anthropological preconception is a theological misconception that has tragic consequences for Christian ethics. Carefully studied and correctly understood, this Pauline passage provides no grounds whatever for such a distinction. It is perhaps true that, in the list of vices especially, there is a rather one-sided emphasis on what are traditionally known as "sins of the flesh." In principle and even concretely, however, this bias is cancelled out: strife, jealousy, party spirit, and envy, for example, can hardly be attributed exclusively to the body. The contrast between spirit and flesh has to be understood in a different way. What is involved here is the tension between the spirit of Christ and the "spiritless" life of the human being caught in the grip of sin, the decision that in *both* directions, whether positive or negative, engages and affects the *whole* human being. At all events, the Holy Spirit is not to be contrasted with or played off against the body. So much for the parenthetical remark. I come back now to the "em-*bodi*-ment" of the Spirit.

The body of the Holy Spirit is the church. The image of the church

191

as "the body of Christ" is one of the most vivid and seminal themes of New Testament ecclesiology. It depicts in an impressive way the organic cohesion and unity of the people of God. We shall have occasion to return to this image at the appropriate point in our exposition. What is not so often noticed is the way in which the image of the body establishes at the same time the connection with the Spirit: "For by *one* Spirit we were all baptized into *one* body—Jews or Greeks, slaves or free—and were all made to drink of the *one* Spirit" (1 Cor. 12:13). These words are enormously helpful in illuminating the special connection between Spirit and church, and in particular the two dialectical aspects of this connection.

In the first place, the Spirit directs us into this concrete community. We cannot, indeed we are forbidden simply to bypass the church. It can, and more often than not certainly will, cause us pain. That was frequently Paul's own experience. We are not to be under any illusions about the church! It is not the elite of the human race, the cream of the crop. It is not composed of outstandingly gifted people, people who intellectually and culturally are patently superior. "Not many of you were wise according to worldly standards, not many were powerful, not many were of noble birth . . ." (1 Cor. 1:26). Yet it is obviously this human, all too human, community of faith that is the object of the Holy's Spirit's working. The church is the place to which the Spirit ushers us. In faith, moved by the Spirit, we are not at liberty to despise or even ignore it in elitist fashion.

But there is also the other dialectical aspect of this connection between the Spirit and the church. The fact that the Spirit ushers us to this place does not mean that we have simply to accept this concrete community of faith exactly as it is, silently and docilely resigning ourselves to its human weakness. The Spirit of Christ is not the prisoner of his body, does not simply vanish into and merge with its existing characteristics; on the contrary, the Spirit means to mold and fashion the body. But in what direction? Paul tells us: the one Spirit with whom we have all been imbued unites us with other human beings across all existing barriers and divisions. It is certainly no accident that the passage quoted mentions some of the most deep and divisive barriers between human beings—cultural, religious, and social cleavages. Yet it is precisely these walls of division that the Spirit assails. While it is true that the Spirit blows where he wills, it is clearly in this direction that he wills to blow, namely, in the direction of over-

192

coming divisions, removing the barriers that not only separate people from one another but sooner or later inevitably generate hostility and conflict between them. Every form of apartheid or separation is sin— indeed, in this concrete sense, sin against the Holy Spirit. The mission of the church, as the first step of the Holy Spirit, is to move against such barriers wherever they exist in the concrete circumstances and conditions of history and human society.

But we cannot emphasize this first step without at the same time insisting that it is inseparable from the second. The step whereby the Spirit moves us into the church necessarily leads us—*with* the church—beyond it. Another prominent New Testament passage on the Holy Spirit here claims our attention, Romans 8. Here the two essential dimensions of the biblical witness to the Spirit—the "vertical" and the "horizontal"—are inseparably combined. There is the "inner witness" of the Holy Spirit, interceding for us in our most individual spiritual needs. The Spirit comes to the aid of our weakness, takes our part even and especially when "we do not know how to pray as we ought" (Rom. 8:26). Rooted as it is in the work of the Spirit on our behalf, this inner freedom (a freedom which is obviously also freedom over against our own inner condition, however important the struggle in prayer for our personal relationship to God and to ourselves may be) also sets us free for other human beings, indeed for all other creatures, and it does so in a way that transcends everything specifically churchly or even Christian. The prize here is not just the new humanity of Christians but the new creation. The final goal of the Holy Spirit is not reached in the church—not even in a genuinely ecumenical and catholic church. Paul uses a striking image to describe this open-ended character of the Spirit entrusted to Christians: he speaks of the "first fruits of the Spirit" that have been given to us (Rom. 8:23). This clearly implies that Christians have no monopoly on the Spirit; the Spirit is not an exclusive predicate of Christian existence. We are not at liberty, therefore, to commandeer and misuse these "first fruits of the Spirit" to satisfy our own self-centered needs. Indeed the opposite is the case: The characteristic effect of this gift of the Spirit is to open our eyes to see and our hands to do something about the "groaning" of the whole creation and whatever threatens to destroy it, and to constrain us to suffering solidarity with all other creatures, including those outside the church (Rom. 8:19ff.).

Eduard Schweizer's comment is to the point:

The new creation of humanity by the Spirit is not a flight of faith into heaven or an abandonment of this imperfect world. We are not supposed to become "religious" in our thinking and no longer groan with the world's groaning or watch its futility and destruction. On the contrary, the new creation means beginning to see the world as it is, suffering with it and taking its suffering to heart. . . . When a human being recognizes his or her solidarity with the world, this above all is the work of the Spirit.[10]

The Holy Spirit ushers us into a solidarity of destiny and hope with all creation. The only logical and consistent response to the movement of the Spirit is an all-inclusive ecumenical attitude to and practical solidarity with the whole world (including the ecological consequences of such an attitude).

This centrifugal witness of the Holy Spirit (in distinction from but also in combination with what classic dogmatics referred to as the inner witness or testimony, one could also speak here of an external witness or testimony) down through the history of doctrine and of the church has received less attention than it deserves. The open horizon of biblical pneumatology has often been obscured and narrowed—in Roman Catholicism by binding the Spirit in principle to the organized church and even to its ministry; in Protestant orthodoxy by a one-sided shift of interest to the intellectual question of "pure doctrine"; and in liberal Protestantism by an equally one-sided interest in the more general problem of human self-knowledge and spirituality. In consequence, the Holy Spirit tended to become domesticated and diluted in the mainline churches, and important aspects of the biblical pneumatology, especially the dynamic prophetic and charismatic themes, were left to the "enthusiasts."

What is needed today is a countermovement away from this tendency to turn the Holy Spirit into a dogmatic or private—or even bourgeois—property. Traditions that have repeatedly been suppressed in church history need to be critically and creatively reassessed, traditions that despite the predominance of the established church championed again and again the dynamic of open-ended hope based on the Holy Spirit. I am thinking here, for example, of the tradition associated with the name of Joachim of Fiore. This exceptionally stimulating and, in the last analysis, truly realistic thinker kept astonishingly close to the biblical witness, not least in his combination of the historical and eschatological dimensions of pneumatology.

It is interesting that Henri Bett wrote about a Methodist took an interest in Joachim.

These are the three states of the world . . . attested to us by the mysteries of Holy Scripture: the first, in which we were under the law; the second, in which we were under grace; the third, which we expect will arrive soon, in which we shall enjoy a still more perfect grace. . . . The first, in servile dependence; the second, in filial dependence; the third, in freedom. . . . In succession: fear, faith, and love. The first, as slaves; the second, as free human beings; the third, as friends.[11]

In other words, world history is moving toward the goal of the Holy Spirit, while at the same time the kingdom of the Holy Spirit, which is understood as being in its essential features the kingdom of brotherly and sisterly love and perfect freedom, recruits and gathers its faithful ones here on earth. Affirmations of this sort in the course of the Czech Reformation had social consequences that transformed the whole world. I think especially of the Hussites and of the efforts of the Czech Brethren, Comenius in particular, for a general reformation in church and culture. Looking back on all these efforts, we may, indeed we certainly will find much that was time-conditioned and utopian. Yet the heart of their theological concern deserves to be taken up and seriously considered if we wish to do justice to the powerful dynamic of the affirmation: "I believe in the Holy Spirit"—and to correct and make good our neglect of the Holy Spirit in theology and church.

195

15

The Holy
Catholic Church

The First Step of the Spirit

It is somewhat surprising to find the Apostles' Creed, after having affirmed its faith in the Holy Spirit, going on immediately to speak, in almost the same breath and in the same Third Article, of the church. The three articles are clearly concerned with the being and work of the Triune God. It is solely to the glory of this Triune God that the faith is confessed. The theme of the church and the themes that follow are simply not on the same level. It is easy to understand why some of the oldest Christian creeds preferred to adopt a fivefold division. They wanted to distinguish clearly between the first three trinitarian articles and the ecclesiological and eschatological affirmations that followed.

Like the Roman Creed before it and most of the Christian creeds after it, the Apostles' Creed did not adopt this fivefold pattern. The church and the other topics that follow are included directly in the Third Article itself. Not that the Apostles' Creed ignored the theological problems raised by this procedure. It uses a subtle stylistic device to mark the fact that at this point we arrive at a certain threshold, that in speaking of the church in the same breath as the Spirit the Creed is well aware of what it is doing. The little preposition "in" used where the Creed speaks of faith in God ("I believe *in* God . . . and *in* Jesus Christ . . . I believe *in* the Holy Spirit") is *not* used where the Creed comes to speak of the church and the last things. The confession of God and the reference to the church involve a difference in the act of faith. God and the church are not comparable entities. We do not believe *in* the church; but believing in God the Father, in Jesus Christ, and in the Holy Spirit, we also believe *the* church.

Even in the case of the church, however, it is still a matter of belief.

197

Or—in order to avoid the impersonal construction which would be inappropriate here—it is still a matter of *my* believing the church: "I believe . . . the holy catholic church." The holy catholic church belongs in the Creed. Indeed, it has its rightful place at the precise place where it is actually mentioned in the Apostles' Creed, that is, in the Third Article—as the continuation of (or, more precisely in fulfillment of) faith in the Holy Spirit. We must not forget this stylistic threshold: The church is not in any unqualified sense a prolongation of the Holy Spirit. The sequence followed here, the "procession of the Holy Spirit," has a definite inclination that is irreversible. Yet this procession does take place; the Holy Spirit reaches out, processes, proceeds, moves in this definite direction. The *first* step is in the direction of the church.

The close connection between the first two clauses of the Third Article is very important theologically, above all for the two theological disciplines concerned, namely, ecclesiology and pneumatology. Church history offers ample warning that whenever a dividing wall has been erected in doctrine or in practice between Spirit and church, between pneumatology and ecclesiology, distortions have resulted. These have endangered the different confessions of Christendom in different ways: in Roman Catholicism mostly by the domestication of the pneumatological themes in a rigid ecclesiology; in Protestantism by underestimating the value of a concretely committed ecclesiology. The weak point in both tendencies is the same: they both divorce the first two statements of the Third Article.

One of the most heartening features of the contemporary ecumenical movement is that these dangers are being overcome. Modern expositions of the Creed, at any rate, are unanimous on this point. I give two examples. First, Karl Barth:

> We cannot speak of the Holy Spirit . . . without continuing: *credo ecclesiam*, I believe the existence of the church. And, conversely, woe betide us if we think we can speak of the church without establishing it wholly on the work of the Holy Spirit.[1]

But this interrelationship between Trinity and salvation history is no less emphatically championed by the Catholic theologian, Josef Ratzinger, who describes as "disastrous" the loosening of the bond between pneumatology and ecclesiology:

> Both the doctrine of the church and the doctrine of the Holy Spirit have suffered damage as a result of this development. The church came

to be understood not pneumatically and charismatically but exclusively in terms of the incarnation, all too earthbound and, in the last analysis, wholly in the categories of secular power. But in this way the doctrine of the Holy Spirit also lost its place, except where it eked out a meager existence in the service of edification and uplift.[2]

A Composite Entity:
Invisible and Visible

The reminder that the two adjacent credal clauses are intimately interconnected takes us at once to the heart of the problem raised by faith's affirmation concerning the church, namely, the meaning of the word "church." The Greek word *ekklesia*—which surprisingly enough was left untranslated even in the Latin church (*ecclesia*) and so became the universal technical term for "church" in both East and West—is a translation of the Hebrew word *kahal*, meaning the assembly of God's people. It denotes, therefore, the "elect community" assembled in the world in response to the call of God. In the New Testament it can denote quite specific groups of Christians in particular places. Within the specifically christological and pneumatological framework, however, its ultimate reference is to the charismatic mystery of the "body of Christ" (Rom. 12:4f.; 1 Cor. 12:12ff.), to the new people of God established by, in, and with Christ. In the concept "church" the sociological and theological dimensions intersect as two distinct yet indivisible ecclesiological dimensions or aspects of one and the same reality.

The distinction between the visible and the invisible church, which has been so marked a feature of many discussions of the church in the past and even today, is really rooted here, in this two-dimensional character of the concept and reality of the church. The distinction is a safeguard against precipitate equating of the established institutional church with the eschatological event of the Holy Spirit.

From the very beginning, the temptation to make this equation was strong. The tendency in this direction can be traced in detail even in the early church fathers. Ignatius could still define the relationship between Christ and the church (or between the Holy Spirit and the church) in authentically biblical terms: "For where Christ is, there is the catholic church."[3] But the irreversible character of this sequence was soon challenged. As early as Irenaeus, we find the affirmation: "For where the church is, there too is the Spirit of God.[4] From then on, the tendency in the direction of ecclesial hubris accelerates, and the church tempted to absolutize itself in its actual organized form. Cyprian may serve here as illustration, with his well-known argument:

> Anyone who separates from the church and unites with an adulteress, excludes himself from the promises of the church, and no one who abandons the church of Christ will obtain Christ's rewards, but is a stranger, a profane person, an enemy. No one can have God for his Father who does not have the church as his mother. If escape was impossible for anyone outside the ark of Noah, so too is it impossible for anyone outside the church of Christ.[5]

Evidence of a disastrous failure to remember the Holy Spirit when thinking about the church, this claim dominated the ecclesiology of the exultant and triumphant church over wide areas, and not only in that of the Roman Catholic Church. There, indeed, it has been particularly influential—until the Second Vatican Council. It is found as recently as 1943 in the papal encyclical *Mystici corporis*, in the following self-portrait of the church:

> Certainly our holy Mother shows herself without stain in the sacraments with which she begets and nourishes her children; in the faith which she preserves ever inviolate; in the holy laws which she imposes on all and in the evangelical counsels by which she admonishes; and, finally, in the heavenly gifts and miraculous powers by which, out of her inexhaustible fecundity, she begets countless hosts of martyrs, virgins, and confessors. But she cannot be blamed if some of her members are sick or wounded.[6]

The distinction between a visible and an invisible church is found already in Augustine. It proved valuable ecclesiologically as a safeguard against any temptation on the part of the church to boast of its own power and glory. It was enthusiastically adopted in the medieval reform movements, by John Wycliffe for example, and above all by Jan Hus. It helped those who suffered because of the spiritual and moral decadence of the established church to see that church in perspective and to look for the renewal of the people of God. The true church is also invisible. It is subject to the sovereign economy of the Holy Spirit and not to the sole management of church institutions. The existing visible church is not permitted to equate itself triumphalistically with the invisible church. It is given the go-ahead for movements of reform and renewal.

However, we must not let ourselves be carried to the other extreme by this talk of visible and invisible, which is meaningful only up to a certain point. We must not succumb to the temptation that was to haunt the Protestant camp, that of thinking that because the true church is also invisible, *we* are given the go-ahead to make ourselves invisible ecclesiastically! Here the traditional talk of visibility and invisibility becomes dangerously misleading and needs to be examined critically. What lies behind it, consciously or unconsciously, is a specific assumption—that of classical Platonism and medieval realism. Given this assumption, the further projections are already in principle established: what is visible, objective, earthly, and material is inferior; authentic being is invisible, nonobjective, heavenly, and spiritual. This assumption, which encourages the traditional prejudices of religious idealism, seriously distorts the biblical view and can have unfortunate consequences for church theory and practice.

For church theory the problem is that lurking behind the distinction in question there may be a very real danger of ecclesial Docetism. We can have a very high view of the church—we can even develop a "high church" ecclesiology—but in the last analysis this essential church, this "high church," lies beyond the actual Christian community; it is a platonic community. Then, consonant with this theory, there is a danger for church practice: if the real home of the people of God is heavenly and spiritual, then our ultimate loyalty too will be to the heavenly and spiritual realm; the earth's agenda, the questions of social ethics and politics, will no longer be of central concern for the church but at most only a marginal, secondary, derivative concern—only its strange work. The general attitude of theoretical and practical indifference to involvement in history is thereby reinforced.

Biblical thinking challenges the validity of this attitude and its ideological scaffolding, that is, the idealistic and dualistic divorce between the two ecclesial dimensions of visibility and invisibility. In the New Testament the concept of the church is not Docetic. The earthiness of the Christian community is not denied or played down. The glorious promises avail for it too, for this community that is only too plainly visible, and often painfully so. They avail for the Twelve, and for the local apostolic communities. The apostle Paul wrestles with these communities but does not abandon them. *"Here* is Rhodes! Let us see the jump *here!"* (Aesop's Fables 181).[7] The church is made up of human beings and human beings are not invisible! The argument is reinforced christologically: in Jesus Christ the invisible identified itself with, bound itself to, the visible—God with humanity. The mystery of the church founded on this union cannot, therefore, be defined in the unconsciously assumed categories of Platonism. The struggle for the true church takes place here and now, not in the world to come but here on earth, in the earthly Christian communities with all their human weaknesses and disappointments.

For theologians, this means: "Here is the Church! Let us see you jump here!" In other words, don't just sit there or lie there—get moving! Jump! "Fight the good fight of the faith" (1 Tim. 6:12)! For the Creed connects the church with faith (*credo*) and faith rightly understood combines two dimensions: on the one hand, life on the basis of the promise, and hence movement in the direction of something extra, including critique and reform of the church; on the other hand, the realization that we walk by faith and not by sight, that we live not in heaven but on earth, and hence amidst conditions such as they are here on earth among our contemporaries.

Marks of the True Church

The tension between these two aspects of the single reality of the church, this dialectic of the invisible in the visible, raises the question: if the church is a composite entity, where are we to look for the criterion that can point us in the right direction theologically and in practice? What direction is our commitment to the church to take? Here we come upon the frequently debated question about the marks of the true Church. The Apostles' Creed is somewhat sparing on this point. It names only two marks of the true church—it is holy, and it is catholic.

Holiness is not a demonstrable characteristic of the church. To take this biblically minted concept as denoting the quality of life of members of the church would be to misunderstand it completely. The term "holy," which we shall have to consider more fully later, emphasizes on the contrary that the church is the people "sanctified" by God, called and commissioned by him for special service. Knowledge of this special summons, call, and commission, however, knowledge of this the church's "holiness," inspires at once a commensurate effort to move in the direction indicated by Christ's work of salvation—in other words—an effort to sanctify our lives as individual Christians and as the church.

Catholicity, the other mark of the church named here—which in many Protestant churches is rendered by the pallid word "universal"—denotes what we should call today the "ecumenicity" of the church, its all-inclusive range. This is a quality of undoubted significance and import. But here again it has to be soberly acknowledged that none of the visible churches, not even the Roman Catholic Church, has any monopoly on catholicity, though it is certainly true that the Roman Catholic Church has pioneered further in this direction than others. The basis of catholicity, like that of holiness, lies not within us but outside ourselves—in the foundation which is Christ, in his Holy Spirit, who crosses all frontiers and divisions and sets them all in motion, who is the hope of all human beings. On this foundation we are called to oppose every kind of selfish isolation and to make visible true catholicity and ecumenicity.

It should be noted that both these marks of the church point beyond the empirical state of existing ecclesial institutions. Neither holiness nor catholicity is a possession; they represent rather the church's mission and task. How is this task to be defined? As the two terms themselves indicate—comprehensively: multi-faceted and all-inclusive. The two terms relate to the whole of human life sanctified by the triune God; they are aimed at the whole of the people of God and every aspect of its life. They therefore reject any singling out of certain areas as "holy," any selection of certain groups as "elites."

One reality, however, one concept, must be set very firmly in the center, namely, the service of God. And this means first of all the service of God in the sense of the church service—worship, the liturgical assembly of the Christian community gathered for praise and proclamation, for intercession and edification. In his Gifford Lectures on "The Knowledge of God and the Service of God" Karl Barth had this to say about the church service:

> The church service is the most important, momentous, and majestic thing that can possibly take place on earth, because its primary content is not the work of man but the work of the Holy Spirit and, consequently, the work of faith.[8]

So lofty a claim may seem somewhat of an exaggeration when we remember the poverty of our liturgical life and our church services. Yet it accords with the view of the ancient church for which the Creed also speaks. For the ancient church, the liturgy was the real contemporization of Christ, the making present and contemporary of Christ's history, the particularization in time and space of the presence of the Holy Spirit. This can be seen most impressively even today in the great liturgies of the Eastern church. Nor was it entirely forgotten even at the time of the Reformation. The definition of the church given in Article VII of the Augsburg Confession, for example, points unmistakably to the church service: the church is "the assembly of saints in which the gospel is taught purely and the sacraments are administered rightly."[9]

It is here, at this specific point—the church service—that the heartbeat of the church is to be found and heard even today. We must never forget that. Here, in this action, this event, the church is really in its own element, doing its own thing. Here the church truly comes into its own. If it were to abandon this "point," it would abandon itself. Here in particular the warning about having the rose and having its thorns must be heeded—especially by the theologians. Even today we have no more important and pertinent service to perform than this struggle for a living Christian liturgy, an authentic church service.

But the Reformation view of the service of God cannot be restricted to this central point alone. From this center, the lines radiate outwards. This center becomes the focal point for the whole of life. Indeed it is our *whole* life—in the widest sense—that constitutes the service of God.

It was primarily the Swiss and Czech Reformers who championed this comprehensive view of the service of God, as can be seen from their expansion of the marks of the true church. To the two main Lutheran marks of the church—proclamation of God's Word in its purity and the right administration of the sacraments—the Reformed churches added a third, the godly discipline, that is, the duty of the individual Christian and of the Christian community to live according to the gospel. The Czech Reformers went even further. From the beginning the Czech Reformation put great emphasis on the normative character of apostolic practice, and hence on the life style of the poor Christian community as over against the Constantinian church's lust for power. Five sure and infallible marks of the true church are listed in the Bohemian Confession of 1575. In addition to the two classic Reformation marks, it mentions: (3) obedience to Christ's gospel and law, with special emphasis on love between Christians; (4) suffering (cross) and persecution for the truth and kingdom of God; and (5) a disciplined ordering of church life (church discipline).[10]

An important aspect is underscored by "these additions." In the Christian life, in the struggle for the church, it is not just "orthodoxy" (correct doctrine) that matters but also a related "orthopraxy," (correct practice), that is, the maintenance of the Christian faith in all aspects of life, in all our dealings with other human beings; the willingness to act and to suffer for God's kingdom and justice; a disciplined discipleship. The church is the company of those who are gathered around this service of God and for this service of God. As Calvin would say, it is "the company of the faithful." Only in union with this company of the faithful, only as we share in its spiritual struggle does our confession of the church ring true. The church has never been a gathering of neutrals and mere spectators. It is no accident that in the "Letters to the Seven Churches" in the Book of Revelation it is "lukewarm" Christians rather than avowed opponents of the church who are identified as its real source of danger: "Would that you were cold or hot! So, because you are lukewarm and neither cold nor hot, I will spew you out of my mouth" (Rev. 3:15f.). In Christ's army a noncombatant is a dubious Christian!

These emphases point to a fundamental ecclesiological truth: the church, in the sense intended in the Creed, is not an end in itself. It exists in the active service of God, meaning both God's service to the world and the Christian's service of God and the world. In both senses, the church is assigned an all-embracing horizon which cannot possibly be called "ecclesiocentric." On the contrary, the church is essentially an "ex-centric" community or it is not the church.

All the terms employed in this credal clause—church, holy, catholic—point in this same direction. Understood in their biblical sense, all three terms make audible a summons to service within the horizon of the whole world, a call to cross our own frontiers and to go into all the world. This was how the Old Testament people of God was understood by its own prophets: Israel is an elect people, a holy nation. It is so, however, in a quite precise sense. It had been chosen and sanctified not in and for itself but in the midst of all the other

205

nations and for their sake. This comes out even more forcefully and with extremely practical and tangible effects in the apostolic church. Its members do not remain in a huddle behind closed doors; in the power of the risen Christ and the Holy Spirit they move out into the world, there to take up their world-transforming venture of missionary witness and compassionate service.

The Horizon of the Kingdom of God

The best New Testament term for this open horizon of the church is the term "kingdom of God," which is the central theme of the message and ministry of Jesus himself. Jesus proclaimed the coming, saving, and judging reality of God; he has also made it present and contemporary. The comforting and binding directive given by Jesus to his disciples was that, amid all the circumstances and pressures of their time, they should take their bearings and set their course by this reality. It was a comforting and liberating directive: it gave them a perspective from which to view those pressures and to find real possibilities for changing human hearts and human conditions. It was a binding directive: the vision of God's kingdom and God's justice were to be understood as a call to corresponding obedience and discipleship. For the disciples, therefore, the kingdom of God became the fundamental reality that shaped their lives as Jesus' followers; indeed, it became the very cause of Jesus himself.

How does the church see itself in relation to the coming kingdom of God? This is the decisive question for the church's understanding—or misunderstanding—of itself. In Jesus' own view, the kingdom of God is absolutely sovereign over every human community. The disciples have a special relationship to this kingdom, of course: their calling is to serve this kingdom and bear witness to it. They are working for the kingdom. But this does not make the coming kingdom *their* cause, their exclusive preserve. The coming kingdom is the hope of the whole human race. It is possible, of course, to make mistakes here. There were misunderstandings even among Jesus' first disciples. The special mission entrusted to them was quickly transformed into a special claim. Some of them wanted privileges and places of honor in the kingdom of God (cf. Matt. 20:21). Despite Jesus' forthright rejection of this attitude, misunderstandings continued to arise in apostolic and postapostolic times.

206

The Holy Catholic Church

[handwritten margin note: Loisy was concerned also with the fact of the delay of the Parousia.]

"What Jesus proclaimed was the kingdom of God, but what came was the church"—this was how Alfred Loisy epitomized his devastating critique of developments in early Christianity. Stated in such bald and categoric fashion, of course, the verdict is unquestionably one-sided. Yet it illuminates in a flash what may well be the preeminent temptation in the entire history of the church. The church tries to force its way into the kingdom, not by its discipleship but by seeking to identify itself with the kingdom. It tries to take over the management of the kingdom of God, to put itself forward as the realization of that kingdom. Constantinian Christianity in particular was plagued by such attempts.

In the light of the New Testament, all such attempts must be rejected. The kingdom of God is not a kingdom of Christians. Christians can and should even now live, act, and suffer in hope of this kingdom—this is the special, the "distinctively Christian" dimension of Christian existence. But precisely because this is the hope by which they live, they cannot overlook the fact that the kingdom of God is not for them only; the kingdom is the future not just of the church but of the whole world. What appears in the horizon of the kingdom of God is not a church devoid of world, but a new heaven and a new earth—the new creation. Indeed we in the church need to be aware that, from the standpoint of Revelation 21, which speaks of this new heaven and new earth, there will be in the new Jerusalem, the new city of God, no temple. As the ultimate reality, the kingdom of God makes the church a penultimate reality.

Does this diminish the significance of the church and its service? Does it encourage us to ignore and forget the humdrum details of actual church life in the blaze of a euphoric eschatological universalism? The New Testament provides no grounds for such hasty and false conclusions. When we remember the central message that God became incarnate in Jesus Christ, it is impossible to treat the ultimate and penultimate consequences of that message as rivals to be played off against each other. The kingdom of God which is our future does not annihilate the church which is our present. It relativizes it, unseals it, opens it to the kingdom of God and to the world which this kingdom has in view. In this relativity, however, in this awareness of its own limits and servanthood, the church is and remains the indispensable field of operation for the kingdom of God. We repeat: not the only one! It is also possible to work for and serve the kingdom of God in

207

society, in the struggle for greater social justice and better human relationship. A friend of mine once told me that, precisely in light of the kingdom of God, he felt his membership in the Social Democratic Party to be of more immediate importance than his membership in the cantonal church. I can appreciate what he is saying. For my own part, however, I would want to warn not only against pseudo-alternatives but also against misleading orders of priority. Normally, however, the church takes priority. Precisely in the light of the kingdom of God the "stony ground" of our empirical congregations is a sphere of operation that has admittedly not an exclusive or even a universal priority but surely a relative priority.

This, at any rate, is the conclusion to which the Creed leads me. I would be chary of including a political party in the Christian Creed—even though I obviously have no hesitation about making my own political decisions. But faith's affirmation of the church *is* there in the Creed. This gives the church—for all its relativity and for all our sober awareness of its provisional character and its frailty—its human and theological dignity. In the light of the kingdom of God there can be no justification for devaluing the church. On the contrary, precisely in the light of the kingdom, we are encouraged to persevere with the church and not to abandon it.

> If we really hope for the kingdom of God, then we can also endure the church in all its wretchedness.[11]

I believe . . . the holy catholic church.

16

The Communion
of Saints

Holy Things to the Holy Ones

To faith's affirmation of the church the Apostles' Creed adds a definition of the church as "the communion of saints." In this respect the Apostles' Creed differs from the *Symbolum Romanum* and the Nicene Creed. In the Reformation tradition this addition is usually regarded as a clarification of the previous clause, "the holy catholic church," emphasizing the bond of mutual solidarity between Christians as members of the church. This is undoubtedly an important aspect of the New Testament view of faith and the church. It will also have a central place in this exposition of the Creed. Given the present situation in church and society, it is a particularly pertinent aspect. There are, however, other possible interpretations of the *communio sanctorum* that approximate even more closely the original significance of the clause in the Creed. To these we turn by way of introduction.

In both the Greek and Latin versions the clause is ambiguous. The word *sanctorum*, because it can be construed as either masculine or neuter, may be the genitive plural of *sancti* (Gk. *hagioi*, meaning "holy persons"—"saints") or the genetive plural of *sancta* (Gk. *ta hagia*, meaning "holy things").

In the terminology of the Greek liturgy, the latter understanding is preferred as having reference to the eucharistic elements. Here the credal clause means "communion in the holy things," that is, the partaking of the Holy Sacraments. "Holy things to the holy ones!" is the call of the celebrant in the eucharistic liturgy. This sacramental understanding, however, can also be extended beyond the Eucharist: the church, being anchored in the mysteries of Christ, is not exhausted in the "horizontal" dimension; its ultimate mystery is con-

209

ceivable only in "vertical" terms, that is, in terms of its participation in the destiny of Christ and as an event of the Holy Spirit. This meaning of "communion in the holy things" is emphasized particularly in the Roman Catholic and Eastern Orthodox churches, with their emphatic sacramental orientation, but it is one that should not be ignored by Protestants. When this vision of the church is obscured, our understanding of the church is impoverished and our church life trivialized. According to the Creed, it is impossible to understand the church exclusively in sociological or even in purely social human terms. In the church we partake of the "holy things" given to us all together—the "benefits of Christ," the gift of the Holy Spirit. Awareness of that fact belongs to the very essence of the church.

Communion Beyond Time and Death

Parallel to this interpretation of the clause in terms of "holy things," and probably even earlier in origin, is yet another interpretation—the communion of holy persons, that is, the mutual relationship between holy beings. What this means is illustrated by one of the oldest commentaries on this credal clause:

> What is the church but the congregation of all saints? From the beginning of the world, patriarchs, prophets, martyrs, and all other righteous persons who have lived or are now alive, comprise the church, since they have been sanctified on one faith and manner of life and sealed by one Spirit and so made one body of which Christ is declared to be the head, as the Scripture says. Moreover, the angels, and the heavenly virtues and powers, too, are banded together in this church. . . . So you believe that in this church you will attain to the communion of saints.[1]

This is clearly a reference to the communion of Christians that embraces space and time, heaven and earth—to their mutual participation in the common faith and its fruits.

In the ancient and medieval church, however, this emphasis soon acquired a quite specific reference. It was taken to refer primarily to communion with the *departed* saints, to the fundamental bond between the church militant and the church triumphant. The veneration of departed saints initially pointed in the same direction. This development is certainly a questionable one, especially when it involves the addition of a certain soteriological dimension to the com-

210

munion of saints; where the merits of the saints are thought to ground our own hope of salvation, there is clearly a departure from the biblical basis of the idea. The Reformation brought a radical rejection of all such notions and a rediscovery of the Pauline emphases on "faith alone," "grace alone," and above all "Christ alone"—in accordance with the biblical understanding of the holy. Even today, there can be no going back on that.

But a warning is in place here. This Reformation rediscovery must not be made an excuse for completely rejecting this second possible interpretation of the "communion of saints." An interpretation in terms of the *departed* saints need not necessarily mean their veneration. The basic meaning is not the veneration of saints but the communion of saints—an extremely important idea, even if the focus is primarily on departed saints. We need to reflect again today, perhaps, on this inclusive vision of church communion, this vision of the church as a fellowship not only in space but also in time. Ecumenicity is historical as well as geographical. When we seal ourselves off from any of the faithful, either in time or in space, we impoverish ourselves spiritually and theologically. Historical provincialism and parochialism are just as dangerous as their geographical counterparts. From a cultural and theological standpoint, this may well be the special danger in our present intellectual and spiritual situation. In a fast-moving age, we are in danger of running out of steam, and in the West particularly we do live in a fast-moving and ephemeral society. It is in the interests of the church—and of its culture—to take the communion of saints seriously. How important and emancipating this understanding can be is illustrated unforgettably for me by the experience of Christians in Eastern Europe. In a relatively closed and ideologically isolated society, there is always the liberating and heartening possibility of attending reflectively to the heritage of the past, and engaging in dialogue with those who have gone before us.

In this context communion even with the departed can assume significance. This qualification is indispensable, for I am not speaking of spiritualist attempts to establish contact with the dead. A theology that takes its bearings from the biblical witness can only distance itself from such attempts. But in view of the cross and resurrection of Christ, we must affirm emphatically that the communion of saints also includes the "departed." In recent years, J. B. Metz has been to the fore in impressing this idea on ecumenical Christianity—not of

211

course as an escape from our contemporaries into a religious cult of the dead but as a dimension of the struggle for justice. Justice is not to be taken to mean justice for our contemporaries alone; although it certainly means justice for them primarily, it also means justice for the departed—in the sense of remembering those who down through history have been ignored and left by the wayside, victims on the victors' paths of conquest.

That this aspect of justice gets short shrift can hardly be denied when we consider Western historiography and our current life style. Consider, too, the laborious efforts of ideological officialdom in totalitarian systems not only to silence contemporary dissenters and wherever possible to consign them to oblivion in society and also constantly to "correct" the history of the past, even to the point of doctoring historical photographs in order to erase all memory of officially unpopular persons from the public record. A quite different attitude is expected of the Christian church. Knowing as it does that the communion of saints is inclusive, it is required also to practice a retrospective solidarity. In the communion of saints, all apathy and indifference even to the departed are to be rejected.

Christian Solidarity

The main testing ground of the communion of saints comes into view in a third possible interpretation of this credal clause, namely, as a reference to the communion of *contemporary* saints. This reference is also supported by New Testament usage, where the term "saints" denotes ordinary Christians—living members of actual congregations. In the New Testament sense, therefore, saints are not outstanding brilliant Christians, still less religious virtuosi, but simply the Christian brothers and sisters in Corinth, Ephesus, Rome, or anywhere else. When the churches are defined in terms of communion, what is in view is their unity and solidarity, their relationship to one another.

This focuses attention on a vital element in the early Christian understanding of faith and the church—faith as communion and as love. More concretely, communion here denotes the solidarity that binds Christians to one another in love as brothers and sisters. Quite manifestly, the primitive Christian movement is a closely knit fellowship, a family of brothers and sisters who pray together and for one another, and order their lives accordingly. While we must be careful not to exaggerate the ideological significance of the accounts in Acts (2:42ff. and 4:32ff.) of a primitive Christian communism of love in which the first Christians "had all things in common" and "as many as were possessors of lands or houses sold them . . . and distribution was made to each as any had need . . . [and] there was not a needy person among them," it is quite clear that some of the consequences—indeed something quintessentially characteristic—of the "communion of saints" here became visible in an exemplary way and with undeniable repercussions for the society in which the primitive Christian community lived. Here was initiated a process of knowledge and living that emphasized forms of community solidarity, a movement that would never be utterly forgotten in the subsequent history of the church.

To illustrate the influence of this aspect of the communion of saints, the conflicts which accompanied its spread, and the direction in which it began to leaven the values of society, I would refer to an incident that purportedly occurred at about the time the Creed was beginning to take shape, and which may therefore throw historical light on this credal clause—the ancient Christian legend of St. Laurence. Laurence was a deacon who looked after the poor in Rome. During the persecution of Christians in 258, Laurence was arrested and imprisoned. Rumor had it that the prisoner had charge of the secret treasures of the church. The emperor demanded that he turn them in. Whereupon Laurence went and assembled those of his charges who were willing to risk appearing before the emperor. The blind, the cripples, the sick, the epileptics, and the lepers then accompanied Laurence to the emperor, and Laurence told him: "The gold for which you hunger is the cause of many crimes; its gleam is deceptive. The true gold is Jesus Christ, the light of the world. But these"—and here Laurence pointed to the crowds of poor and needy people—"are the children of the light and the true treasure of the church, its gold, its pearls, its precious gems." The emperor ordered that the deacon be strapped to an iron grill and slowly broiled over a charcoal fire. But the Lord relieved Laurence of all his torments.[2]

This legend shows the thrust of the communion of saints—its connection with reality. It expresses clearly and simply the meaning of loving solidarity among Christians. This was evidently what the life of the early Christian communities was like: they exist for all; they

213

have room for all—men and women, Jews and Gentiles, slaves and free, rich and poor. For primitive Christianity the church is a kind of melting pot, but that does not mean a mere hotchpotch. It is a committed fellowship in which attention is devoted particularly to those who in each concrete situation are the "poor"—the neglected, the overlooked, those who are marginalized. These constitute the true treasure of the church.

That being the case, inescapable questions arise as to the ways and conditions in which people live in church and society. Conflicts too arise with the dominant morality and with the morality of those in high places. There is a sharp cutting edge to the question: what does society regard as its treasure? Rulers in all ages, even democratic and technocratic rulers, and with them their faithful and obedient subjects inside as well as outside the church, tend to respond to this question with one key word and one key value: "Gold!" Not always, of course, with their sights so directly set on "filthy lucre" as was the case with the Emperor Valerian in the St. Laurence legend but usually in a more subtle, indirect, and concealed way. Yet the direction in which they look is the same: success and profit, production and power, what can be counted and priced—these are the guiding stars in the heavens of their societies. In these heavens, the sun shines only on the rich and the privileged, on the successful and the victorious. The rest—the poor and the aged, the weak and the losers, the unproductive and the failures—are left in the shade.

In the communion of saints a very different answer is given to the question of the church's treasure. What is central here is not gold and securities, representing money and Mammon, but—in remembrance of Jesus—the kingdom of God and his justice (Matt. 6:33) or, more concretely still, Jesus and the "least" of his brothers and sisters (Matt. 25:40). Here is the real treasure of the church of Jesus. Here are standards of humanity that are to be transplanted also into the conditions of today's fragmented societies. To ask about the treasure of societies is to inquire about the "least" of Jesus' brothers and sisters. The communion of saints focuses on human solidarity in society.

But stress here on the social implications of the communion of saints is quite deliberate, for these implications have largely been ignored in expositions of the Creed. But if it is true, as was suggested in the previous chapter, that the marks of the true church must be defined in terms not just of orthodoxy but also of orthopraxy, then in this respect we have much ground to make up. We are confronted with a task that could have particular relevance not only in the field of social ethics but also in the political realm. I want to make two comments on this.

First, there is the question of social policy in Western culture and society. Could it be our special need here to develop ways and conditions of life that are based on solidarity? The banner under which our political history has been pursued for generations has been the tricolor of "Liberty, Equality, and Fraternity," with some backslidings of course. I would certainly not wish to assert that the two most dominant notions, "Liberty and Equality," have reached complete maturity in the climate and structures of our society; they, too, have experienced setbacks and malfunctionings—in both East and West. But it is surely true that the third notion, "Fraternity," is the smallest, the most neglected, the least developed. It has a hard struggle in the equality system of the East; it also has a hard struggle in the freedom economy of the West. For "Fraternity" things are not going well anywhere in our industrialized societies today. Individually, culturally, and politically, there is an urgent need to make up lost ground in the matter of "Fraternity." Many of us, young people especially, are beginning to awaken to this need and hoping to see it met. Far from surprising us, this should rather make us ask ourselves as Christians: is it not our special opportunity and responsibility to make this radical heritage of our "communion of saints" more visible today?

Second, we need to consider our global domestic policy—the increasingly intolerable inequality between the economically rich and the economically poor, between the "North" and the "South." Questions of international justice are rightly becoming more and more the concern of ecumenical Christendom. Unless in a spirit of human solidarity we can narrow and eliminate the gap between first- and second-class passengers on spaceship Earth (to use the image and terminology that have become familiar in ecumenical circles since they were first used by the Australian biologist Charles Birch), the chances of any future at all for humanity—in all "three" worlds—are pretty dim. Our "Titanic" is on collision course. It is hardly an exaggeration to say that the vision and creation of a mutually caring community of solidarity among brothers and sisters everywhere is becoming the essential condition for our common human survival. It would be absurd and scandalous and quite inexcusable for Christians to obscure the vision and inherent dynamic of the communion of saints or to regard them merely as a private individual possession.

A Catholic theologian, D. Wiederkehr, has described the responsibility and contribution of Christians in this connection:

A number of futurologists have alarmed us with the shocking prospect of mutual destruction and starvation—otherwise we should never have awakened to the reality of our situation. Yet this prospect has a paralyzing effect—like that of the snake on the mouse. It could make us all the more resolved to hold on tightly and desperately to what we still possess or can still carve out for ourselves. But when we keep company with Jesus, another future becomes visible, the vision of human beings leading one another out into the sunshine, sharing their bread with one another, passing from hand to hand the cup of cold water. The church could be the community where this sharing, this mutual enrichment and encouragement, is already happening here and now, where in the name of the Lord all find their salvation and also—precisely in this way—their own identities.[3]

Wiederkehr expresses himself soberly and cautiously here: "The Church *could* be the community." He is right. The church is not yet that community; it still limps behind its potentialities, indeed, behind its authentic reality. Yet it can and is meant to become what it already is in the light of its origin and source, namely, the communion of saints.

The Lord's Supper—the Focal Point

There is one point in the life of the church where this promise and reality of the communion of saints find concentrated expression—in the Communion, the Eucharist, the Lord's Supper. In expositions of the Apostles' Creed, one constantly finds the view expressed, usually in the form of a complaint, that the sacraments are not mentioned in the text of the Creed. It is certainly true that there is no explicit reference to the sacraments in the Apostles' Creed. Implicitly, however, the whole Creed is imbued with a "sacramental spirit." I have repeatedly emphasized this with respect to baptism, and we shall have occasion to return to this again in the next chapter. The present credal clause, however, compels us to think of the sacrament of the Lord's Supper. On this point, surely, there is impressive agree-

ment between the three main confessional families of Christendom
—Eastern Orthodoxy, Roman Catholicism, and Protestantism—
namely, that the essence of the mystery of the "communion of saints"
is concentrated specifically in this sacrament. The three confessional
traditions may employ different terms and by doing so place the main
emphasis in different places in their understanding of the communion of saints—Eucharist, Communion, Lord's Supper—but all of
them point here in the same direction. All affirm that the gift and
the opportunity of the communion of saints are held out to us in an
exemplary way in this sacrament.

In the light of the exposition attempted here, this consensus can
be articulated even more firmly and concretely. All three strands of
this credal affirmation of faith in the communion of saints meet in
the focal point of the Lord's Supper:

1. The theme of participation in "the holy things," that is, in the
destiny of Christ and in the event of the Holy Spirit, is plainly embodied in the Lord's Supper as *Eucharist*. In this mystery of faith we
are visibly and tangibly taken up into the communion of the death
and resurrection of Christ; we give thanks for this in the liturgical
celebration and worship.

2. The communion with the saints, with the "cloud of witnesses"
surrounding and upholding us all, is likewise sealed in the *communion* of the Lord's Supper. The Supper is—as it already was in its
Old Testament roots in the Passover meal—the sacrament of the
pilgrim people of God, the covenant celebration, the provisions for
the long journey of faith.

3. But, above all, the loving solidarity and communion of Christian contemporaries is also visibly embodied in the *Lord's Supper*—
the "horizontal" consequence of the "vertical" participation in
Christ, and consequently the authority and command to demonstrate
practical solidarity with all other human beings. This third dimension
can be seen in the primitive Christian celebration of the Lord's Supper, where the sharing of bread and wine is a love feast that takes
place within the open-ended horizon of sharing in the daily needs of
other people and bringing "liberation for solidarity" (H. Gollwitzer).

In the celebration of the Lord's Supper, these three themes constitute a three-note chord. What Christians are called to do in their
mission in the world, therefore, is to live out the promise and command of the communion of saints.

217

17

The Remission of Sins

"I Have Been Baptized"

In the Third Article as I pointed out early on—already in chapter 14—it is humanity that comes under the spotlight. The Third Article's focus on humanity is especially intense in the clause about the "remission of sins." Here the Creed speaks directly of the concrete individual who has been called to bear the name of Christ. It speaks of the Christian's characteristic human condition in light of the person and work of Jesus Christ. The credal statement had its original setting concretely in the administration of baptism. In other words, it was related to a very special occasion in the Christian life—as it existed about the time the Creed emerged and came to be established in the church—namely the moment when faith was confessed on the occasion of baptism.

The probability of this conclusion is supported, at any rate, by the textual history of the Creed. In the final Textus Receptus, there is no explicit mention of baptism. But a glance at the Nicene Creed shows that we are on the right track here. The Nicene Creed speaks quite explicitly: "We confess one baptism to the remission of sins." This reference to baptism has a long tradition behind it, going right back to the New Testament. We recall Peter's first sermon in the Book of Acts, with its pregnant words: "Repent and be baptized every one of you in the name of Jesus Christ for the forgiveness of your sins" (Acts 2:38). This suggests that the connection of baptism with the remission of sins was deeply rooted in the consciousness of the ancient church. But it was more than a matter of consciousness; it also influenced baptismal practice—so much so that people tried to defer baptism as long as possible, even until late in life, in order to avoid postbaptismal sin and so ensure that the benefits of baptism would avail for all of life. Hermas writes: "We descended into the water and

219

obtained remission of our past sins," and other writers bear similar testimony. As Kelly says

> We are therefore justified in concluding that in practice, at the time it obtained entrance into the Old Roman Creed, the remission of sins must have conveyed the idea of the washing away of past offences and the opening up of a new life through the instrumentality of baptism.[1]

It is important to keep constantly in mind this original credal locus of the forgiveness of sins, which is still valid for us today. Baptism is the hallmark and keynote of the Christian life. It casts its shadow, or rather its light, not only backwards (in the sense of the baptismal practice of the ancient church just mentioned) but also forwards (as the practice of infant baptism makes particularly clear). Grasped in the concrete act of confession, the truth of baptism and its reference to reality embrace the entire life of Christians. It is said that for Luther the simple statement "I have been baptized" was a constant source of practical help throughout his life, especially in times of trial and temptation. The hallmark of Christ's fidelity, appropriated and sealed in the act of baptism, became the keynote of the whole course of the Christian's life.

The Common Denominator of the Christian Life

The truth of baptism, appropriated for the whole course of our human life, is not vague or arbitrary but specific and precise, namely, the forgiveness of sins. The formulation is notable for both its constancy and its richness of meaning. It is found in all the classic creeds and is the *only* formula there used to describe the human condition between the times. This is in marked contrast to subsequent developments in the history of doctrine, where other biblical concepts such as justification and sanctification, penitence and regeneration, soon came to play a major role. Certainly there is no rivalry between these other concepts and that of forgiveness. All of them point to the one basic theological reality—our life in Christ. Compared with these clear-cut concepts, however, the simple word "forgiveness" was almost lost from sight. In the Creed, however, forgiveness stands at the very center. Here a special significance is evidently attached to it. What is the explanation?

One important factor of course, as has already been pointed out, is a keen awareness of the baptismal setting of the Creed. In addition to this, however, the forgiveness of sins embodies a central element of the biblical message. It is impossible to overlook the fact that one of the strongest strands in the great hope of Israel converges precisely on this point. According to Isa. 27:9 and 59:20f., and especially Jer. 31:31, God's new covenant with his people is inseparably connected with the cancellation of sins. In the New Testament, this theme is related to the history of destiny of Jesus. It is in this sense, for example, that Paul interprets two passages from Isaiah (Rom. 11:26f.), summarizing the whole matter in the words: "And this will be my covenant with them when I take away their sins."

The remission of sins is central, however, not only for the prophets and apostles but also for Jesus himself—in his teaching and works as well as in his sufferings. Think for example of his parables. A surprising number of them are variations on the theme of the forgiveness of sins. The theme is especially prominent in the parable of the prodigal son (Luke 15:11–32), which has been called "the gospel within the gospel," but also in the Lord's Prayer with its emphatic petition: "Forgive us our debts [sins], As we also have forgiven our debtors" (Matt. 6:12). Think, too, of the works of Jesus. His healing acts are signs of the remission of sins. In fact this aspect of his ministry became an explosive source of contention, even rallying point for the opposition to Jesus, in view of his claim that "the Son of man has authority on earth to forgive sins" (Mark 2:10). Nor is it only specific deeds of Jesus that point in the direction of the forgiveness of sins. His whole way of life was truly an "alternative life style" compared with the behavior expected of religious people. Jesus accepted sinners, even keeping company with them and dining with them. Not, of course, in order to adapt his life to theirs, but in order to communicate to them the forgiveness of sins in a liberating and convincing way. This explains the tremendous joy people experienced in the company of Jesus: God comes to the sinner, not seeking to destroy but to impart a new life in freedom. The forgiveness of sins is the dawn of the full freedom of the people of God.

The good tidings of the forgiveness of sins is not contradicted by the passion and death of Jesus; on the contrary, it is reiterated here in a most profound way. Jesus' passion and death make it quite clear that the forgiveness of sins does not mean sin is taken lightly. Jesus' alternative life style, his forgiveness of sins, is poles apart, indeed light years removed from a happy-go-lucky kind of tolerance and permissiveness. Sin is to be taken seriously; not only does it often involve blood and tears, it must also be paid for in blood and tears. Christ's remission of sins is an act of solidarity with sinners, his service of them, his sacrifice for others. The new covenant of reconciliation and liberation is sealed with his own blood. "For at the very time we were still powerless, then Christ died for the wicked"—that is how Paul puts it (Rom. 5:6, NEB) in the very chapter of his letter in which he speaks of Christ and Adam and meditates on the central theme of the history of salvation, the theme of sin and its forgiveness.

Considering this multiform biblical witness to the forgiveness of sins, the ancient creeds were undoubtedly right on target in their choice of this particular biblical affirmation for defining the essence of the Christian life—in the light of baptism—as the remission of sins. We can also understand why biblically oriented theologians in the Reformation tradition praised the Creed highly for this choice. Luther, for example, declares:

> Even if heaven and earth should fall and nothing mortal remain, there can be no question of evading or surrendering this article.[2]

And Karl Barth describes this article as:

> the common denominator . . . upon which everything that can seriously be called Christian living must rest.[3]

Misunderstandings of Sin and Forgiveness

"The whole life of Christians is the forgiveness of sins." This is what the Creed, on good theological grounds, is clearly affirming. But what does this statement mean to *us*? For my own part, I readily subscribe to it. But at this particular point it is certainly not enough simply to subscribe to the Creed. We cannot ignore the fact that "the forgiveness of sins" is a phrase that for many of us today sounds incomprehensible and open to misunderstanding, especially if it is made the basic definition of the Christian life. Both the terms used in the credal clause—"sin" and "remission"—today present considerable difficulties. They invite misunderstandings and even suspicion both for the current outlook on life and for current linguistic usage.

The term "sin" has moralistic and misanthropic overtones today; it seems an implicit threat to honesty and love of life. But even the term "forgiveness" meets with distrust today; it seems disabling for a human being always to be wholly dependent on forgiveness, and forgiveness alone. To insist that people should practice forgiveness and reconciliation in the conflicts of a class society seems surely to trivialize ethical choice and action!

It was in the context of Christian-Marxist dialogue that I personally was confronted with these objections to the importance assigned to forgiveness of sins in the Christian understanding of human life. The objections came from my colleagues in the discussions. Most of the Marxists suspected the Christian doctrine of sin of being a demobilizing ideology encouraging a quietistic attitude to the world. Its stress on the universality of evil in human affairs discouraged any radical effort to change the world. An ethics of forgiveness was no less suspect in their sight. It improperly blurs the lines of division in the class struggle and leads to a sentimental concealment of the real clash of interests between the exploited and the exploiters, and to a premature reconciliation with unforgivable conditions.

Let there be no misunderstanding. I do not believe that these contemporary objections to the Christian doctrine of the remission of sins should lead theologians to leave in abeyance or even to abandon this central theme altogether. My experiences in the dialogue in an atheistic socialist society lead me, indeed, in precisely the opposite direction—to the realization that this message is more relevant than ever today. Marxists expect that a change of social structures will not only produce new living conditions but also the "new human being" who will overcome alienation. But such expectations are based on an unrealistic anthropology. Over against such a view the biblical reminder of the universality of sin in human society undeniably introduces a down-to-earth note of realism into the discussion. Moreover, in view of the persistent Stalinist drive to intensify the class struggle and ruthlessly pursue it in practice, the stubborn evangelical reminder of the creative power of forgiveness in human relationships also proved to be a profoundly human and active contribution. There was no reason, therefore, even to soft-pedal this central credal theme, much less withdraw it altogether.

This did not dispose of the Marxist objections, however, which were not pure invention. Indeed far from it, they pinpointed possible misinterpretations of the "remission of sins"—misinterpretations of both sin and forgiveness—that had actually cropped up in the history of the Christian tradition. The doctrine of sin has often been used by Christian theologians to defend a pessimistic and disabling ideology, one that timorously freezes the status quo. Christian preaching and practice too have not been without their superficial forgiving and premature reconciling. They have produced cheap broadsides against the Marxist analysis of the class struggle, by attackers who turn a blind eye themselves to the deep tensions in human society and whose response to the demands for greater social justice is no response at all because it seeks not to meet these demands but merely to mollify and appease them. Thoughtful contemporaries—not just the Marxists—have good reason to hesitate over this theological doctrine. If our confession of faith in the remission of sins is to carry conviction, we in theology and the church must examine and deal with these reasons. But the form and the content of this credal affirmation must be made more precise and concrete. We shall speak first of its form.

Only the Remission of Sins?

"The whole life of Christians is the forgiveness of sins." How is this statement to be interpreted? Does the Creed mean that the forgiveness of sins is the *only* thing that matters in our lives? Is the Christian life here reduced to a single dimension? Such a reductionist view would surely be a misunderstanding of the credal statement. It may be helpful here to recall our exposition of the earlier credal clause "suffered under Pontius Pilate." The whole life of Jesus is summed up there in the one word "suffered." We there adduced biblical reasons for not interpreting the shorthand of the Creed exclusively in terms of an ideology of suffering and indifference to other aspects of the life and work of Jesus. This suggests an analogous interpretation of the remission of sins. The remission of sins is the foundation of Christian existence but not in itself the whole building. It was in this sense that Karl Barth—quoted in the previous section—spoke of the forgiveness of sins as "the common denominator." What he means by this becomes clear in a later exposition of the Creed:

> The forgiveness of sins is the basis, the sum, the criterion of all that can be called Christian life or Christian faith.[4]

224

This foundation, or "basis," however, far from excluding further building or development, actually makes a richly diverse development possible:

> The Christian possibilities are many and there is no reason to be constantly quarreling on this score. *Faites vos jeux, messieurs!* Yes, gentlemen, place your bets! For there are games to be played and we are like children who have permission to play their games; whether with a little more secularism or a little more pietism matters little, if only their freedom game is permitted by and based upon the forgiveness of sins.[5]

That answers our question about the form of the credal affirmation, about the sense in which the forgiveness of sins is to be understood as defining the Christian life. Forgiveness provides not a diminution or obliteration of life's possibilities but a rooting and grounding for them. An image from Dietrich Bonhoeffer provides a particularly apt description of what is involved here. In an impressive passage in one of his letters from prison he speaks of the "polyphony of life."[6] The life of Christians is not a uniform and orderly life, cut to a single pattern and made to conform. It is not a preprogrammed, legalistic way of life. Faith, hope, and love are forms of freedom. They have a rich range of interests. Yet the diversity of these many living voices does not mean that they are haphazard or utterly chaotic. According to Bonhoeffer, the "polyphony of life" has its *cantus firmus*, its main theme, its fundamental, unifying key melody. The keynote of the Christian life is the remission of sins—nothing more, but also nothing less.

Breaking the Vicious Circle

We now turn to the second question, the question of "content": what is the substance of the forgiveness of sins? To put the question still more concretely, in view of the key position occupied by the forgiveness of sins in the Creed: what is the Creed saying about human existence when it views life specifically from this standpoint? On the human level, the credal affirmations in the Apostles' Creed—especially those dealing with Christ's way and work of salvation—obviously come to a focus on this specific point. What do they mean by "the remission of sins?"

I would suggest, to begin with, that what is at stake here is the question of human salvation or damnation. What we have here is the Christian answer to the age-old human question: what is the root of our distress and what is the root of our "hope against hope"? In our human world, evil has many faces. Human distress takes many forms. It has its physical and its metaphysical aspects, its material and its spiritual dangers. If our thinking is biblically oriented, we cannot be indifferent to or ignore any of these forms of human distress. In the view of the Creed, however, there is no room for doubt as to where the source of evil is to be located: evil has its origin in sinful conditions and in the acts of sin.

"Sin" means in the first place, from the formal standpoint, that our human world is a profoundly alienated world. It means also that we human beings are fallen creatures. Both these meanings are contained in the biblical concept of sin as condition *and* act—the downward pull of conditions and relationships in our environment that draws us toward evil, *and* the personal responsibility each one of us bears for our active participation in it.

This is the vicious circle in which we exist. We are repeatedly caught up and involved in it, not just as victims but also as seducers, not just as agents of betrayal but also as those who are betrayed. Ernst Käsemann has recently pointed out—in a very realistic and convincing way—how illuminating the obscure biblical term "possessed" can be in this connection.

> What word could better describe our present condition, even at the world level, than this word "possessed"? For everywhere we look today we find people, communities, nations, and continents living in a state of dread. Afraid of other people, afraid of the future, afraid of losing their possessions—material, spiritual, religious. Afraid of losing their power, their jobs, their freedom, their food for tomorrow. Afraid of tyrants, and of exploiters, and of demons.[7]

The biblical vision permits us no illusions here: "None is righteous, no not one; no one understands, no one seeks for God. All have turned aside; together they have gone wrong; no one does good, not even one" (Rom. 3:10ff.; cf. Ps. 14:1–3). In the ongoing debate about human distress and hope in our world today it is the privilege and duty of Christian faith to draw attention in season and out of season to this somber and generally unwelcome truth.

Christians also have a contribution to make as regards the substance of "sin." Materially they see the source and nature of sin in terms of the breaking of the covenant with God and neighbor. <u>Sin is the breach of community, the lovelessness of a human heart that is blatantly self-centered, turned in upon itself.</u>

But this is not yet the essential contribution and service to be rendered by Christian faith. What has so far been described is only the somber, negative aspect of the biblical message, not its core—a necessary counterpoint that is not to be concealed, but not yet the *real* point. The real point, the main point, finds expression in that other word, the main word, of the credal clause—the *remission*, or forgiveness, of sins. We must, and thank God we can, take the Creed quite literally here, noting that it speaks of sin in a very clearly defined setting. Its context is not damnation but the history of *salvation*. It is not sin that establishes the framework for the confession of Christ but the other way round: sin is seen in light of the destiny of Jesus. This does not reduce the seriousness of our situation as sinners. Nor does it glorify human culpability—in the sense of the well-known dictum *felix culpa* ("happy sin"), for example, or of Hegel's view that only through the fall did humanity come into its own historically. In the light of the cross of Christ, the profound degree to which we are individually and cosmically implicated and entangled in the conditions of alienation cannot possibly be treated lightly.

Yet the cross of Christ—together with its historical antecedents and consequences, already briefly sketched in the second section of this chapter—debars us from dwelling on our sinful situation and making a fetish of it, which in practice, means capitulating to it. For the cross is God's encounter with sin's power, God's suffering and struggling in solidarity with us, God's sacrifice on our behalf. And, for the New Testament, that means the resurrection, the victory of love over lovelessness, breaking the vicious circle of sin, hell, and death. But is this not mythology? Technically, formally, yes; it is mythological language that was vigorously developed in the ancient church's concepts of redemption. Yet this mythological language and form powerfully illumine the real ground of the Christian faith and its connection to history and to reality—the renewal of the covenant. They show how the human condition with respect to salvation and damnation is radically changed—changed in the direction of hope. This is the fundamental reality to which baptism has reference, on which faith in the remission of sins is based.

There could hardly be a more vivid illustration of this understanding of human life as viewed from the standpoint of forgiveness than that given in Jesus' own parable of the prodigal son (Luke 15:11–32). As has already been pointed out, this parable has been called the "gospel within the gospel"—and justly so insofar as the gospel is the message of the forgiveness of sins. The parable is a story of a misconceived freedom—a way that fails and ends in human distress. The story is told simply and soberly, without a trace of indignant moralizing—and therefore all the more effectively. But besides speaking of the distressing failure, the parable also describes how the lost son "came to himself," clearly acknowledged his own guilt and accepted its consequences. Above all, however, contrary to all the principles of a patriarchal order, the parable tells the incredible story of the father's compassionate kindness. The prodigal son is not abandoned, not even put in his proper place; much to the disgust of his upright elder brother, he is accepted without reservation and, in spite of all that had happened, the rights he had forfeited are restored to him. From the standpoint of the gospel, this is our unconditional human right—to be in good standing not by what we achieve for ourselves but through the gracious acceptance of a merciful Father. According to the gospel, the forgiveness of sins is the magna charta of human life.

Never in the history of the church was this view of human life as based on the forgiveness of sins more forcefully and effectively articulated than by the sixteenth-century Reformation in its doctrine of justification. The central focus of this vision of human life is stated with great clarity by Martin Luther in his Galatians commentary:

> And this is our foundation: The gospel commands us to look, not at our own good deeds or perfection but at God himself as he promises, and at Christ himself, the mediator. . . . And this is the reason why our theology is certain: it snatches us away from ourselves and places us outside ourselves, so that we do not depend on our own strength, conscience, experience, person, or works but depend on that which is outside ourselves, that is, on the promise and truth of God, which cannot deceive.[8]

This anchoring of the Christian life outside ourselves in the forgiveness of sins was seen by Luther and the other reformers as an incomparable deliverance, the source of the Christian's freedom— freedom from self, freedom from every pressure to justify ourselves by our own merits and achievements, freedom from every form of egotism (and endogamy, inbreeding!) on the part of hearts—both religious and irreligious—that are turned in upon themselves. The reformers rediscovered something of the contagious joy and freedom that swirled about the Jesus of the Gospels with his preachments and practice of the forgiveness of sins. To a great extent, this air of freedom and joy was lost in the course of the church's history; the forgiveness of sins was widely replaced by a gloomy and legalistic penitential system—a caricature that almost predictably led critics of Christianity (such as the Marxists mentioned earlier) to understandable misunderstandings and suspicions about the theme. In view of the way the forgiveness of sins has been misinterpreted, both inside and outside the church, it is essential that the gospel framework of this credal clause should be laid bare. Only then will it be possible to see how relevant forgiveness is even in today's world—especially in today's world. The Creed shows the forgiveness of sins to be not a burden but a boon, warmly supportive of human freedom and fulfillment.

A Creative New Beginning

I want to conclude this interpretation of the forgiveness of sins with two suggestions about its relevance for us today. I see it as potentially important for both individual ethics and social ethics.

The anthropological focus of the Creed in its emphasis on the forgiveness of sins suggests in the first place an unusual but ultimately liberating approach to the question of individual human identity. For many of us today this is an important question, and rightly so. In our Western culture we all feel the manipulative pressures of a technological society—in the East the ideological pressures predominate—and these pressures make the question of the authentic and inalienable individuality of each human life a vitally important one for each of us. In a situation of wholesale alienation we all have a need "to come to ourselves"—and the need becomes a quest. The human sciences probe, and the therapeutic disciplines of psychology commend ways of self-discovery.

These efforts are certainly to be taken seriously. Yet many of the people engaged in them regard the forgiveness of sins as a strange and disconcerting approach. "Forgiveness" clearly locates our hope outside ourselves, and "sin" clearly intensifies our sense of individual responsibility for the alienation we see everywhere within and around us. Is not the forgiveness of sins thus a double impediment to self-discovery? I do not believe this to be the case. In his exposition of this credal clause, Wolfhart Pannenberg offers some helpful thoughts on this question:

> Certainly the acknowledgment of one's own sins also entails a certain repudiation of oneself. But that is only one aspect of its meaning. Acknowledgment of one's sins is always self-affirmation as well: the declaration of one's willingness to accept responsibility for oneself. Seen in this way, the Christian sense of sin need not necessarily mean a disavowal of oneself or hostility to life but can, on the contrary, be understood as an affirmation of life even in face of its distortion. The very confession of sin then appears as an act of freedom; for genuine freedom is responsible freedom. Only as we take responsibility for ourselves individually do we achieve real identity.[9]

Affirmations about the forgiveness of sins are truly helpful only if they do not demand too much of tempted and defeated human beings—which happens when they are construed as moralistic demands—but are instead brought within the magnetic field of Jesus' own ministry of forgiveness. When this is done such affirmations prove a stimulus to greater freedom—and Pannenberg properly emphasizes here the social dimensions of the achievement of identity. For him the degree of freedom is measured

> by the degree to which we are ready to recognize our responsibility not only for ourselves individually but also for the society in which we live, for everything which happens or fails to happen within it; for we are not even our individual selves individually but only as members of our society and of the whole human family. We achieve individual identity to the degree that we each assume our own guilt and responsibility for failures and shortcomings in our society, instead of looking for it only in others.[10]

In view of the frequent attempts to smooth the hard road to self-discovery by shifting the burden of guilt onto others—parents, family, society—these remarks of Pannenberg provide a valuable corrective.

Besides having implications for personal identity, the forgiveness of sins has implications also for social ethics. If, as the Creed suggests, human existence must be seen in the context of the forgiveness of sins, then forgiveness must have consequences also for social ethics, for the way we humans behave in our lives together. This is why Christian ethics continues to make a case for the creative potential of forgiveness. Indeed, it goes even further: in light of the clear teaching of Jesus, it regards the willingness to forgive and to be reconciled in *social* life as the real test and measure of every life lived on the basis of forgiveness: "Forgive us our debts as we also have forgiven our debtors" (Matt. 6:12). To refuse to forgive other human beings—both near and far—is really to remove ourselves from the range of Jesus' forgiveness and its renewing power. Hence, by the forgiveness and reconciliation we show and do not withhold, the credibility of our own Christian existence is decided.

This is not to say that we have to construct an *ideology* of forgiveness and reconciliation. In the face of misunderstandings on this point on the part of church people and on the part of the church's critics—I am thinking here of the other Marxist objection to the Christian stress on forgiveness referred to earlier—it has to be made clear that the readiness of Christians to forgive implies no trivialization of guilt, no blurring of differences, no concealment of conflicts, no forgetfulness of history. "We can forgive: we cannot *forget*," I heard a Jewish speaker say on the fortieth anniversary of the infamous "Crystal Night" pogrom in Nazi Germany. The comment was justified—in both its parts. To conquer guilt—whether in the private or the public sphere—does not mean sweeping it under the rug of history, either privately or publicly. Christian forgiveness (and Jewish forgiveness too, of course) is not a virtue based on a defective memory. On the contrary, it is based on an alert memory, the memory of the forgiveness of God that reaches out to us all and saves us all. If the cross of Christ is the seal of this forgiveness, then clearly the guilt is not ignored but endured.

Endured, of course, on the basis of forgiveness and with forgiveness as the goal. "We cannot forget, but we can *forgive*." The Christian ethic champions this opportunity for a new beginning—between individuals but also between nations and peoples. At least it prefers not to see the opportunity squandered because the tensions are sharp and feelings running high. This indicates the contribution Christians can make in situations of conflict in the world. They will not naively trivialize these conflicts or adopt an attitude of false neutrality; they will rather analyze the differences soberly and make serious efforts to resolve them. In doing so, however, they will patiently and persistently champion the standpoint of forgiveness and reconciliation, even with those who at the moment may be on the other side of the barricades. People who confess their faith in the remission of sins must certainly not forget or suspend what for them has been a liberating faith the moment they have opportunity to demonstrate it in practice toward others—for their liberation.

In conclusion I would cite a concrete illustration of the radiant power of this vision in the practical social and political context. It concerns the German theologian Hans-Joachim Iwand, a politically alert contemporary. In the years of the cold war, Iwand strove vigorously to bridge the appalling gulf between the peoples of Eastern and Western Europe. This effort owed its inspiration to a meeting he had had with the Czech theologian J. L. Hromadka, which Iwand describes in moving words:

> It was more than just a run-of-the-mill encounter . . . We both knew that nothing and no one could possibly put right that which had happened. . . . Only one thing can be said: "Our own most grievous fault." In the case of guilt, the primary question is not who is guilty. Many people approach history with the benefit of hindsight, like a state prosecutor bent on establishing who was and who was not to blame. In the case of guilt in the historical sense—guilt that is irreparable—the question lies elsewhere: it is the question of who will assume the guilt. It is through *this* strait and narrow gate that the way to the future lies. In and of itself, guilt is like a huge stone blocking access to the way. No one wants to roll it away. No one wants to lift it up and carry it. Those who are not stirred to act boldly will simply keep their distance. Thus do we run away from our own history, and in so doing flee from God's visitations—and from his promise. . . . Something had happened here that demanded action; people had to deal with it if history, European history, was to move forward and not become trapped in a barren marshland. . . . This was the theme of our first conversation—guilt and how to overcome it, and our friendship, which was offered that evening like a present, a gift that had long been ready even before we met that evening and came to know one another.[11]

I believe in the remission of sins.

18

The Resurrection
of the Flesh

The Spirit of the Future

In its final clauses the Creed turns its attention to certain basic human questions that directly concern the thinking, life, and death of every one of us: What may I hope for? What is our future as human beings? What is to become of our world? It is not the first time the Creed has touched on this theme of the future. Already in the Second Article we met the statement concerning the future: "He will come to judge the living and the dead." There it was a case of confessing faith in the future of Jesus Christ, in the final outcome of his story. Here in the Third Article the focus is on our future, the final outcome of our story. In theological terms: there the future was a christological theme, here it is an anthropological theme.

It must at once be made quite clear that there can be no divorce or rivalry between the two statements and standpoints. Once again, the principle of inclusiveness must be applied in our exposition. The Creed is speaking of something that is an integral whole, the *one* faith of Christians; its three main articles confess this one faith in the Triune God, in the richness of his being and in the richness of his history. The terms used in the present credal clause make this close interrelationship particularly clear—"the resurrection of the flesh." A theme that was central already in the Second Article is picked up again here in the Third—the theme of resurrection. This formal agreement—unique in the text of the Apostles' Creed—must also be respected in substance. In other words, from the standpoint of the Creed, the anthropological question can be answered only on the basis of Christology. The Creed offers no general and abstract answer but a concrete one with a quite definite basis: "For no other foundation can any one lay than that which is laid, which is Jesus Christ"

233

(1 Cor. 3:11). This familiar christological axiom applies also, and above all, to the future prospect of humankind. From the standpoint of the Creed, the Christian hope is a hope based on Christology.

In taking this view, the Creed is simply reflecting the view of the New Testament. Only from the perspective of Christ's history do the disciples and apostles of Jesus see any future. As they see it, this applies to the future generally but also and above all to the question of our future as human beings who face death.

In the Old Testament, the biblical witnesses are very reticent on this point. Unlike most religions, the Old Testament knows nothing of any universal immortality within the realm of created things. Human beings are not only finite and mortal; they are also a race on which sin has left its mark. Faced with the onslaught of death, therefore, we are in and of ourselves without any justifiable hope. There is no such thing as human immortality, either as possibility or as fact. So far as the Old Testament is concerned, in the encounter with death only one hope remains, namely, the promise of the faithfulness and grace of Yahweh, who alone is Lord of life and death.

This promise is picked up again in the New Testament. What appears only incidentally and marginally in the Old Testament now becomes a central testimony—the prospect of the resurrection of the dead. How is this to be explained? Is it simply a further advance in the progressive history of religion? Hardly. When we examine the New Testament writings it is at once clear that the fulfillment of the promise is based on a very concrete event, namely, the Easter destiny of Jesus. It rests on the experience of the apostles that, with his death on the cross at Golgotha, the history of Jesus was not finally ended and written off but, in his resurrection "on the third day," achieved an incomparable new beginning. From what happened to Jesus at Easter, the apostles learned and knew that God's faithfulness abides even in and beyond death. God's faithfulness and commitment to Jesus Christ, even in death, were the basis of the apostolic faith in the resurrection of the dead.

The disciples then sought to understand and live their *own* lives too in this light, in the light of the life of Jesus. They had always surmised that the cause of Jesus was no private matter but one that concerned them all. The Easter events now confirm this with finality. The resurrection of Jesus is not just a singular historical event; it is (see the section on "Risen Indeed" in chapter 12) *the* eschatological event, which in biblical language means the "final" event. In other words, the resurrection of Jesus is an event with universal consequences. The apostles see it as completely changing their own condition, indeed the whole human condition, as the detonator which sets off a chain reaction in human life.

The clearest account of the apostles' experience of the resurrection and its detonating character and universal "follow-through" is found in 1 Corinthians 15, the key New Testament passage on the resurrection. Paul begins very concretely and precisely with the Easter event, then goes on to narrate experiences of the risen Christ and to cite witnesses. The resurrection is not a general notion, a universal idea, but a concrete event with a quite specific beginning. There is no room for any doubt on that score. Yet, precisely as such it is also an eschatological event; no isolated episode in a purely individual destiny, but an incursion into the whole realm of death, a breakthrough for the many. Paul calls the risen Jesus Christ "the first fruits of those who have fallen asleep" (v. 20). In Rom. 8:29 Paul speaks of him even more vividly as "the first-born among many." Biblically, this can only mean that Christ's history becomes human history, Christ's destiny *our* destiny. "For as in Adam all die, so also in Christ shall all be made alive" (1 Cor. 15:22).

This "in Christ" becomes for Paul the decisive sign outside the brackets of our human life. The brackets are still there: we still live and die as mortal and sinful human beings. But outside the brackets there now stands this key signature that qualifies (and changes) everything within the brackets. According to the New Testament this "in Christ" shifts our human life out of the blind necessity and fatalism of fortuitous circumstances and inexorable processes into the wider horizon of eschatological hope, a horizon that immediately, here and now, upholds us and transforms our human condition. Thus at the end of this resurrection chapter the message that had its original setting in the Easter event is now extended to us all: "Death is swallowed up in victory. O death, where is thy victory? O death, where is thy sting? The sting of death is sin, and the power of sin is the law. But thanks be to God, who gives us the victory through our Lord Jesus Christ!" (vv. 54ff.). In the Easter event *our* future has already begun!

235

In its uniqueness, this Easter event certainly is past history. Hence the question quite naturally arises: How is the nasty ditch between that past event and our future bridged? How is what happened then communicated to us now so as to become a present reality? The New Testament is not at a loss for an answer to these questions. Engaged as we now are in an exposition of the Third Article of the Creed, we cannot fail to be impressed by the number of important New Testament passages in which this answer is given in pneumatological terms, in terms of the work of the Holy Spirit. In Paul's letter to the Romans, for example, we read: "If the Spirit of him who raised Jesus from the dead dwells in you, he who raised Christ Jesus from the dead will give life to your mortal bodies also through his Spirit which dwells in you" (Rom. 8:11). There is no room for doubt: the Spirit is the bridge! In the power and presence of the Holy Spirit, Christ's past is firmly connected with our future. The eschatological event of Jesus' resurrection is communicated and made operative in the experience of the Spirit. It is for this reason, this good and valid reason, that the Creed continues its Third-Article affirmation of faith in the Holy Spirit with the words: "I believe in the resurrection of the flesh."

Why Not the "Immortality of the Soul"?

We turn now for a closer look at this credal clause. In choosing the formulation "the resurrection of the flesh," the Creed was taking an independent line; indeed given the religious and philosophical background of that time, it was being extremely headstrong. This is evident from the audible uproar the formula produced in intellectual circles. There were the indignant and often scornful comments of contemporaries outside the church who found in this formula the confirmation of all their worst suspicions that Christianity's appearance in Hellenistic culture represented the resurgence of a peculiarly primitive and even barbaric way of thinking. Within the church itself fellow Christians with Gnostic leanings felt that any notion of the flesh inheriting the eschatological hope was definitely going too far; it ran counter to the spiritualizing of the faith, which was assumed to be both culturally and religiously desirable. Above all, for those church fathers having a special interest in "apologetics"—presenting the Christian faith to the world—the line adopted here by the Creed presented serious problems for the church both internally and externally. Was there not a less repugnant alternative?

There certainly was. The most important and certainly the most profound alternative was the idea of the immortality of the soul. This idea was deeply rooted in the oldest tradition of mystical religious thought and, under the influence of Plato in particular, had become the paramount form of philosophical hope in the face of death. Far from being a real threat for the thinking human being death is, on the contrary, a metaphysical liberator. For what passes away in the onset of death is only the outward physical aspect of our human life—which is an impediment and antagonist anyway to that which is the real essence of human being, the soul. In the last analysis, therefore, death is to be seen as something positive, as a "negation of negation," as that which demolishes the walls of our prison and sets our captive souls free. For the soul cannot die. It is the authentic life principle and as such exempt from the onslaught of death. The soul can no more die than snow can be hot or fire cold, argues Plato. That being so, only children can be afraid of death. The philosopher—unforgettably exemplified in the person of Socrates—faces death calmly and even expectantly.

For those who share the anthropological and metaphysical assumptions underlying this argument, its strength and worth are almost irresistible. And most contemporaries of the first Christians, especially if they had been trained in philosophy, did in fact share these assumptions. Even today it is not difficult to understand why such people were necessarily scandalized by a formulation of the Christian hope in terms of resurrection of the flesh. It is also easy to see how great the pressure must have been on philosophically trained Christians to conform to this very powerful and attractive Platonic idea. In the subsequent course of history, theologians and the church did in fact yield to the pressure by accepting as Christian doctrine the immortality of the soul. But for the Creed such acceptance was out of the question. The basis reason was because the Christian hope has a quite different foundation. For the Creed, Christian hope rests not on general anthropological and metaphysical assumptions (as does the doctrine of the inherent immortality of the soul) but on the faithfulness of God revealed in the history and destiny of Jesus Christ. And Jesus Christ is not the obviously immortal one, but—most unobviously—the crucified one who is also risen. In addition to this basic reason, however, there are other concrete reasons that made the choice of this formula, "the resurrection of the flesh," an apt one. In the section that follows I shall mention three such reasons.

Unrestricted Hope

1. The phrase "resurrection of the flesh" expresses the completeness, the all-encompassing character of the Christian hope of salvation. Justin, a Christian apologist who was trained and interested in philosophy, states this concern with admirable clarity:

> God has called to life and resurrection the whole person, not just a part but the whole being—body and soul.[1]

If any facet of our creaturely existence is allowed to fall by the wayside in our metaphysics or eschatology this is an unwarranted short circuiting of the will of God, which according to the Bible involves a creation and redemption that is all-encompassing. When the horizon of hope is thus restricted, our perspective on life itself is also distorted. Understandably, less significance is attached to what is mortal than to the immortal soul, and hence a dividing line is drawn right through our lives—certain aspects of life are considered a priori as significant and valuable while other aspects are classified a priori as unimportant and worthless.

Biblical thinking runs directly counter to this view, this prejudice. Biblical thinking is clearly oriented toward completeness both in its view of humanity and in its view of the world. Heaven and earth, soul and body together constitute the "theater of God's glory." Not just the soul but soul and body together are the "temple of God" (1 Cor. 3:16ff.; 6:19). In every facet of life we humans are subject to the command of God—and by the same token to the one divine promise.

This fundamental approach became exceedingly relevant in the confrontation with Gnosticism both inside and outside the church. It was in Gnostic thought in particular that the tendency to ontological, soteriological, and ethical dualism was most pronounced. Gnosticism represented a deadly danger to the infant church, above all because of the variety of ways in which it abandoned the distinctively biblical

238

approach for a welter of mystical and mythological modes of thought. Its challenge was especially great as regards the Christian view of salvation and the future.

> St. Irenaeus, in whose theology the doctrine of the resurrection was a theme of prime importance, introduces us to these Gnostic-minded persons who, believing that matter is essentially evil, deny the physical resurrection. Salvation, they plead, belongs to the soul alone, and the body, derived as it is from the earth, is incapable of participating in it. His own rejoinder is to insist that "salvation belongs to the whole human being, that is, soul and body." This is the universal Catholic teaching.[2]

It is for this reason that the Creed speaks of "resurrection of the flesh," not "immortality of the soul."

2. This credal formula emphatically affirms not only that the Christian hope embraces the whole of reality but also that the human being has a physical aspect, indeed that the cosmos has a material aspect. It has already been pointed out in reference to the arguments of the Platonists, and above all of the Gnostics, that the dualism inherent in these arguments took its sharpest and most concrete form in the discrimination against everything physical and material. The physical and material were considered inferior and regarded with suspicion. From the standpoint of theory, ideals and criteria of value were elaborated that clearly gave priority to the spiritual world. And in practice physical activity and human responsibility for external matters were devalued. As far as the future was concerned, and the prospect for humanity, this meant that the physical and material areas of life are fundamentally without hope.

In contrast to this idealistic prejudice, the credal affirmation of the resurrection of the flesh insists on the eschatological claim and the dignity of the physical and the material. Not in such a way, of course, that the body is played off against the soul, or matter against spirit. That would simply be to replace one idealistic prejudice with another—this time a materialistic prejudice—that would hardly be any improvement. Biblical thinking is concerned not to exchange one prejudice for another but to demolish all prejudices against the inclusiveness of created reality. The Bible does not glorify, much less idolize the body; that would be sheer paganism. Confronted with the widespread devaluation of the body, however, the Creed clearly champions the cause of this "marginalized" realm, as Trillhaas points out:

> The physical and earthly dimension of our human existence is indeed mortal dust, but it is not only that. It is also agent and medium of the blessing of God, recipient of grace, an image and vessel of all joys and sorrows. The sacraments of the church are received physically. How then could the body not also be a partner in the hope of our eternal life?[3]

3. But we have also to point here to another emphasis of the Apostles' Creed. The Creed speaks not merely of the resurrection of the body but specifically of the resurrection of the flesh. At first sight this emphasis seems utterly shocking. The term poses a problem not only for people of our day who find the association of "flesh" with eschatological hope rather strange. It also presents a problem so far as the New Testament background is concerned.

The New Testament has two Greek terms for "body"—*soma* which normally stands for the physical condition of our human life in its naturally created form, and *sarx*, or "flesh," which denotes the human situation marked by sin and alienation due to sin: our resistance to God and the consequences of that resistance. In expressing their eschatological hope the New Testament witnesses employ the concept "body" (*soma*). This is particularly true of Paul, for example in his already noted "resurrection chapter" (1 Corinthians 15). The term "flesh" (*sarx*), on the contrary, seems hardly to qualify in this connection; indeed Paul expressly states (in the same chapter) that "flesh and blood cannot inherit the kingdom of God" (1 Cor. 15:50).

Yet it is precisely this term *sarx*, and not the more neutral term *soma*, that the Apostles' Creed chooses to employ. Is this then a deviation from the New Testament? Some scholars, such as Trillhaas, interpret the evidence that way. Their embarrassment is not surprising. And one may be grateful that the Nicene Creed does not use the problematic phrase "resurrection of the flesh," choosing instead the more biblically warranted "resurrection of the dead."

However I would like to make a more favorable interpretation of this surprising emphasis in the Apostles' Creed. Connected with its preferred term may be an important point, one that I consider to be vital not only in the New Testament view of salvation but also for our own understanding of salvation today. First, as regards the New Testament view of salvation: I am thinking of how *sarx* is used in the New Testament, especially in John, to describe the incarnation of the Son of God—the Word "became flesh." In other words, God identifies himself not with something ideal—a "good body," but with something normal—our human "flesh," stained and assailed as it is in so many different ways by sin. Second, as regards our own understanding and hope of salvation today, another point must be mentioned that is connected with the first: It is good news that the echatological hope is a complete and all-encompassing hope that embraces even the physical aspects of our human life and reaches right down into the very depths of all our alienations and afflictions. We do not believe in the resurrection of some elite, whether real or supposed. We believe in the resurrection of the flesh!

What concrete conclusions can be drawn from these preliminary clarifications and reflections? At the beginning of this chapter we posed a couple of questions: What may I hope for? What is our future as human beings in the face of death? I want to present my substantive answer in the form of two closely connected arguments, dealing respectively with the individual and the social dimensions of the resurrection hope.

Everlasting Covenant: Dialogue Beyond Death

What may I hope for? The use of the first-person singular in this question must be treated seriously, just as it must also be treated seriously in the very first word of the Creed—twice repeated—the keyword *credo*, "I believe." The Apostles' Creed is from start to finish a personal document; it is rooted in and related to a personal decision, the baptismal situation. I am asked about my faith and I give an account of my faith; I can even make the answer contained in the Creed my own answer. And when the Creed affirms "the resurrection of the flesh," this affirmation too concerns me. It has to do with me. It is speaking of my future—my death and my resurrection. This clause too, like the Creed as a whole, has its unmistakably personal dimension.

This aspect of the resurrection hope has been questioned, and even roundly rejected, by certain leading theologians. I am thinking here of the young Schleiermacher, for example, who indignantly repudi-

241

ated any notion of a personal resurrection, or "personal immortality," as he preferred to call it. He did so, moreover, not on irreligious grounds but out of a concern for the purity of true religion. What the truly religious person longs for and seeks is that "the sharply delineated outlines of our personality should expand and gradually be lost . . . in the infinite."[4] The idea of personal immortality is said to be a hindrance to this concern of true religion; its champions demonstrate their lack of religious wisdom:

> Death offers them the unique opportunity to surpass their humanity and they refuse to take it; instead they worry about how they are to carry their humanity with them into the beyond, and the most they yearn for is a wider vision and improved faculties.[5]

We shall be wise not to dismiss Schleiermacher's argument too hastily; it is still relevant as a warning against equating the individual hope with a self-centered hope—as the devotees of individualistic piety often tend to do. In the light of the Creed and of the New Testament, however, Schleiermacher's position is to be rejected. Emil Brunner seems to me to come closer to the truth in this regard:

> The resurrection of the individual is clearly meant to be understood in the New Testament as that of the individual person. This is poles apart from Goethe's idea: "To find himself in the Infinite, the individual will gladly disappear; self-surrender is delight." New Testament faith knows no other eternal life than that of the individual person. This is how Jesus sees the matter when he says of "Abraham, Isaac, and Jacob" that they are alive because God is a God of the living and not of the dead (Matt. 22:32). But how could it possibly be otherwise in the personalistic thinking of the Bible, rooted in God's revelation as a Person? "I have called thee by thy name, thou art mine" (Isa. 43:1). This "thou," and not an abstract spiritual "it," is the authentic biblical category.[6]

The most important point in this quotation is its emphasis on the dimension of dialogue. The resurrection hope is not simply "my cause"; it is "my cause *with God.*" But the converse is also true: the resurrection is not simply "God's cause," not some sheer metaphysical and apocalyptic fact, a "fact of salvation" in the sense of a power to dispose of objects; it is "God's cause with me," a personal event, a dialogue. We are to reject, therefore, not only the "subjectivist" error but also the "objectivist" error that interprets the resurrection as some sort of apocalyptic panorama of world events taking place above and beyond us. Transcending all subjectivism and objectivism, we are to understand the resurrection as a dialogical event taking place between persons.

To illustrate and support this interpretation biblically and theologically, we turn to the idea of the covenant. The covenant between God and his people is, of course, the central theme of both the Old Testament and the New. In our present context too this idea is fundamental. Earlier, when I briefly described the Old Testament hope in the face of death, I stressed that Israel's only hope in the face of Sheol—a very open hope—is based on the faithfulness of Yahweh. When death threatens, appeal is made to God—in a preeminently dialogical form, as can be clearly seen in the book of Job and in the Psalms. Israel's hope is the covenant, Yahweh's faithfulness to his covenant in life and in death, come what may. The only hope of the New Testament—now, to be sure, a fulfilled hope—is similar in structure. Here again, it is a question of God's covenant faithfulness, the "new covenant" sealed in the cross of Jesus and finally confirmed in his resurrection. The covenant is a dialogical event between persons. We can therefore state the position as follows: in the context of the covenant the resurrection means that even in the hour of my death it is God who has to do with me, God who approaches me, and at the same time, as the opposite side of the same event, it is I—just as I am—who has to do with God, who turns to God. *This* is the substance of my Christian hope.

It is on this basis that we should approach what is often regarded as the most pressing issue with respect to this whole matter of the resurrection: What about the identity of our human life before and after death? How does the resurrection affect the relation between our former life and our new condition? Is there continuity here or only a breach? To seek an either/or answer to this question is to set up a false alternative. There is no possibility of continuity in the sense of a more or less direct continuation of earthly conditions in the heavenly places, a simple transfer of the here and now into the beyond. Neither is there any possibility of a radical breach in the sense of an entry into something totally other, completely different, with no connection whatever between our historical present and the eschatological future. These are false alternatives.

Biblical thinking resists all such simplistic unilinear assertions. The apostle Paul wrestles with this problem in his resurrection chapter; his argument in 1 Corinthians 15 is an impressive one. He warns the Corinthians not to be in too much of a hurry to produce blueprints: "But some one will ask, 'How are the dead raised? With what kind of body do they come?' You foolish man! What you sow does not come to life unless it dies" (v. 35f.). "It is sown a physical body, it is raised a spiritual body" (v. 44). Clearly as regards continuity there is here no simple prolongation and perpetuation of the earthly form such as we could on our own imagine—or even attain. Equally rejected, however, is the idea of a complete breach, the absence of any connection whatever between time and eternity. It is *we* who are involved in the resurrection—we in our complete humanity, including even our bodily nature, our "flesh," which is the unvarnished reality of our threatened human existence. In the resurrection, there is no creation out of nothing; no wholly unconnected discontinuous "new bodies" come into existence. What happens, rather, in the words of Paul, is that "this perishable nature must put on the imperishable, and this mortal nature must put on immortality" (v. 53). When I arrive at heaven's gate, my "self" is not discarded but transformed. My history is not dissolved into nothingness but is taken up (integrated) into the history of God's covenant. Here is where my life's true continuity and identity lie—in that covenant history. The personal dialogue between God's I and my thou, between my I and God's Thou, does not cease as I approach the threshold of death, or end when I cross it. "The rest is silence"? No, Hamlet was mistaken. The rest is not silence. The rest is our Yes to God and, above all, God's Yes to us: the fulfillment of our human destiny. So we too need not be silent: I believe in the resurrection of the flesh.

Rebellion Against
the "Lord of All Lords"

Here in this next-to-last clause of the Creed our personal question, indeed my most personal question, is answered: What can I hope for? That to which the clause makes reference, however, cannot possibly be restricted to this individual personal question. The equally important and inseparably connected reference is also to the common prospect of the whole human race, the future of the world. In other words, the

244

resurrection hope has not only an individual personal dimension but also a social dimension. When we take our bearings from the Bible, and that means from Christology, it is impossible to separate these two dimensions. We spoke earlier of the importance of the apostolic "in Christ" as the basis of the resurrection faith.

> This "with Christ" immediately lifts the individual personal event out of the sphere of the *purely* individual and gathers it into that of the history of humanity as a whole. My death as a dying in Christ, a sharing in his death, is not only mine, but that of humanity in general. For Christ is the second Adam, hence he in whom human history is recapitulated. I die not only my death but the death of humanity. My self-identification with Christ by faith makes the beginning of the new life in me a participation in the kingdom, thus an event affecting humanity as a whole.[7]

There are biblical passages in which we find a most vivid attestation of this social, humanly universal, and even cosmic dimension of the resurrection of the body. It is enough to recall here once again the testimony of Paul, which in addition to its "mystical" features also has "apocalyptic" dimensions. Paul can speak of his resurrection hope in very personal, even intimate terms—it is the center of his life, the source of his faith, his love, his hope. In his resurrection chapter, however, he also speaks of the all-inclusive horizon of the resurrection: Paul is concerned not only with his own personal destiny but with the common destiny of all God's children; indeed, as comes out particularly clearly in Romans 8, he has in view the hope of the whole afflicted creation. The resurrection message concerns us all.

This inclusive reference of the ultimate hope is clearly articulated also in other biblical passages. I am thinking here, above all, of the next-to-last chapter of the Christian Bible, Revelation 21: "Then I saw a new heaven and a new earth; for the first heaven and the first earth had passed away, and the sea was no more. And I saw the holy city, new Jerusalem . . ." (vv. 1f.). It is difficult to overlook this emphasis: At the end of the New Testament—indeed, the end of the biblical covenant history in its entirety—the new creation and the new city appear. Just as it was legitimate for us to say that "my history" is integrated into God's covenant history, so too we can say, in the light of this message, that not even our common history, not even the history

245

of humanity and the world, is reduced in the end to nought, not even at the end of the world—indeed then least of all, whether this end be near or utterly remote. Even to our heaven and our earth, even to our cities, we are to relate the prospect of the resurrection of the flesh—not in the sense of a prolongation of their present state, not in the conditions of the old world, but in their transformation, their renewal, in God's new world.

This aspect of our credal clause has been neglected in the history of the church—and in the recent history of theology too, as has been pointed out by Helmut Gollwitzer:

> In contemporary theology . . . Christian references to the resurrection have been "demythologized," interpreted as referring to nothing more than personal communion with God in faith—lest we otherwise land ourselves in absurdities and become unintelligible to our contemporaries, who have settled for the irrevocability of death. . . . There is a heavy price to be paid for this . . . an extremely questionable "two-kingdoms doctrine," involving the dualism of an "inner kingdom" of faith and an external kingdom—a doctrine that has dangerous consequences since society too, along with the external kingdom, is inevitably emptied of its meaning. . . . Interpreted in this way the resurrection message no longer provides inspiration for the struggle—the struggle against domination by that death in which people so willingly believe, the struggle against murder and oppression of human beings by other human beings, whether on a large or a small scale. Instead it leads only to impotence and a self-centered religious complacency.[8]

Our credal clause points in quite a different direction. I said earlier that, unlike the idea of the immortality of the soul, the "resurrection of the flesh" includes all human reality within its purview. This point now needs to be emphasized in respect of society. The apostolic faith sees the whole of human life in all its domains and aspects in the light of the resurrection. The promise of victory over death, fulfilled in the resurrection of Jesus Christ, begins already here and now to disrupt the circumstances of death's dominion; it initiates a countermovement to change them. No one who believes in the resurrection of the flesh can acquiesce in the dominion of death—or indeed of any tyranny that regards itself and is deadly serious about establishing itself as irrevocable and unchallengeable.

The element of protest in the resurrection hope and its social and even political implications have sometimes been expressed more clearly by Christian poets than by the doctrinal experts. Consider, for example, the hymn of Ephraim the Syrian (A.D. 306–373):

> In equality he created them,
> In equality makes them rise again.
> In the resurrection, no elite ones,
> None inferior to the rest.[9]

Or, again, we think of many of the Easter hymns of the Reformation. An example from our own day is that of Kurt Marti, whose next-to-last "Funeral Oration" reproduces in an explosive and precise way this basic aspect of the resurrection:

> it might suit many lords fine
> if everything were settled in death
> the dominion of the lords
> the servitude of the slaves
> would be confirmed for ever
>
> it might suit many lords fine
> if in eternity they stayed lords
> in expensive private tombs
> and their slaves stayed slaves
> in rows of common graves
>
> but a resurrection's coming
> quite different from what we thought
> a resurrection's coming which is
> god's rising against the lords
> and against the lord of all lords—death[10]

If we are to have any chance of success in proclaiming the obscure—the radiant!—message of the resurrection credibly and convincingly today, it will largely depend on whether or not we Christians prove willing to join in "God's rising against the lords and against the lord of all lords—death" or whether we become fatalistic in face of death's stubborn resistance, to which we are still exposed in our personal lives and in the life of society, and finally capitulate to the "inscrutabilities" and "dead ends" of existence. The resurrection is God's alternative to all the destructive tendencies in our human life. Those who believe in it will no longer blindly or lazily yield to these destructive tendencies but, amid all their sustained pressure, keep a sharp outlook for alternatives pointing to the new life—in our attitude to ourselves (how often we live in a thoughtlessly self-destructive way!), to other human beings, and indeed to all creatures. We are meant to demonstrate the resurrection in our attitudes and in our relationships.

In 1978 I participated in the Bangalore assembly of the Faith and Order Commission, which engaged in an ecumenical study "Accounting for the Hope that is in Us." One of the things that impressed me most as I was preparing for that occasion was how vividly and realistically the resurrection hope sounded forth from those parts of the world, particularly Latin America and Korea, where Christians are subject to oppression, yet also participate in "God's rising" against the forces of oppression and death. I shall always remember the testimony of one Latin American Christian, written in prison. The prisoner recalls the first Easter morning, the day of Christ's resurrection. He calls it "the day which can no longer be denied us." And he adds that, in that somber situation where human rights are denied, the memory of Easter morning strengthens "the murmur which announces that the triumph of violence is not a final one." Here are Christians living in the shadow of death, yet who refuse to believe in death. They believe in the resurrection of the flesh.

What is involved in our credal clause is this decision of faith. Ernst Lange, an outstanding German servant of the ecumenical movement who died in tragic circumstances, left behind a number of papers now collected together under the significant title *On Not Believing in Death: The Practical Consequences of Easter.* One of his statements points the way:

> What Christians mean by the strange word "resurrection" is this: that death is no argument against life. No argument against faith in the significance of every single human life. No argument against love, which is the creative force that energizes every form of life. No argument against hope in the world's fulfilment. Quite simply, no argument against God. No reason for despairing of God. Death cannot remove us from God. However incomprehensible it may seem—and continue to be—it is through death that we come to God, come into his very presence.[11]

19

And Eternal Life

In the Light of Eternity

The directive of the next-to-last clause of the Apostles' Creed, that we are "not to believe in death," is positively reinforced—in no uncertain terms—in the final clause: "I believe . . . in eternal life." The content of this final clause is in itself instructive: the Creed ends with an affirmation of faith in life. What the Christian faith is concerned with is life. This is no mere statement of the obvious. There are philosophical and religious traditions that hold aloof from life—especially life in the form of vital biological and physical forces. Examples can be found in the main schools of idealism of classic antiquity and in the Eastern religions of redemption with their ascetic tendencies. The biblical witnesses, on the contrary, especially in the Old Testament, greet life—their own and that of other human beings and all other creatures—with confidence and with a bias in its favor. This trust finds expression even in the little everyday things, as when, for example, the Old Testament "Preacher" (he of all people!) remarks: "Better a living dog than a dead lion!" (Eccles. 9:4, au. trans.). But even in the New Testament, the mission of Jesus is interpreted by the statement: "I came that they might have life, and have it abundantly" (John 10:10).

This important biblical note is sounded here in the final words of the Apostles' Creed. We have to say at once, however, that our clause is not speaking of life in general. The Creed is not advocating a vague vitalism or a positivistic view of life. It is speaking of *eternal* life. It is pointing, in other words, in a direction that is even more precisely formulated in the Nicene Creed in the words: "the life of the world to come." As is also clear from the context (immediately following "the resurrection of the flesh"), the clause is concerned with what happens after death, with our destiny beyond the resurrection. If we are faithfully to follow the instruction furnished by the Christian confession of faith, it is to this reality, eschatological in the fullest sense,

249

that we must turn in this concluding chapter. In order to obviate all misunderstandings, however, we shall look by way of introduction at these inevitable questions: Does not this concentration of attention on the heavenly reality inevitably lead to devaluation of our present life and its earthly conditions? Is not our biological life criticized and even dismissed as negligible and meaningless in comparison with eternal life?

Such views are found not just in non-Christian traditions but also in the history of the church and of theology. I am thinking not only of the well-known ascetics but also of certain tendencies in this direction even in Reformation thought. To give just one example: in his Geneva Catechism, Calvin explains the presence in the Creed of "the resurrection of the flesh and eternal life" as follows: they are there "to show that our happiness is not situated on the earth . . ."

> We are to learn to pass through this world as though it were a foreign country, treating lightly all earthly things and declining to set our hearts on them.[1]

Though this may not be Calvin's only answer, it is indeed the characteristic one and points in a questionably one-sided direction. Earthly life and eternal life are set over against one another as antithetical. In the light of eternal life, earthly life seems to be shown up as something foreign and contemptible.

I would not deny that this answer reflects certain notes unmistakably present in the biblical message. But a glib contrast between earthly life and eternal life hardly does justice to the biblical view. To be sure, the Bible does distinguish between the earthly and the eternal. This is clearly seen in its two-dimensional concept of life, as illustrated by the two Greek terms employed. The New Testament uses not only the general term *bios*, denoting life in its earthly conditioned form—what we call biological life—but also the theologically significant term *zoē*, denoting life in its true and spiritual form, a term that is therefore used also to denote eternal life. But this distinction implies no sharp dualism nor any disqualification of our present earthly life.

In the Bible, time and eternity are not antonyms as in Greek thought. There is a fundamental christological reason for this: In Jesus Christ, the eternal entered into time, "in the fullness of time" (Gal. 4:4, au. trans.). From the New Testament standpoint, therefore, "eternal life" is not to be understood solely in future terms, as only something after death. For us—in Christ—it has already begun: "For you have died, and your life is hid with Christ in God. . . . Christ who is our life . . ." (Col. 3:3f.). For the apostle, this is not some dream of the future; it is the basic dimension of the Christian life here and now, with all its temporal limitations. Over against the well-known medieval dictum, "In the midst of life, we are encompassed by death," we must now emphasize—not in contradiction of that dictum but as its governing rubric—the New Testament truth, "In the midst of death, in this world marked by death, we are encompassed by life." This vision too, in fact this vision especially, is part of the Christian understanding of life. Our earthly life also has this dimension, this life-giving dimension, of Christ. However much this dimension may be assailed and even buried by all kinds of difficult experiences, crises, and failures, it can never be completely erased. It is the inherent and ineffaceable character or mark of human life, its abiding dignity. How then could the reference to eternity ever be made a reason for regarding human life as trivial or even contemptible? Ought we not, rather, to take this dimension of eternity seriously, and respond to it by renewing and ordering our human life accordingly? We have learned from Bonhoeffer to recognize the beyond as the power of the here and now.

I am reminded in this connection of one of the favorite maxims of T. G. Masaryk—I have mentioned it before—"in the light of eternity." Throughout his life this Czech philosopher and statesman tried to do all that he did—not just in his philosophy of humanity but also in his political actions—to live his whole life "in the light of eternity." It was his underlying conviction that once purely temporal considerations become life's be-all and end-all, people begin to make a fetish of things as they are and the horizon of eternity disappears from view, human life is in danger of immobility and stagnation. Once human politics, which is the "art of the possible," timorously defines the "possible" exclusively in terms of the status quo—and administers its affairs accordingly—once it cynically or complacently obstructs the vision of the "impossible," the vision of the greater justice of the kingdom of God, then it loses its humanity and degenerates into a dehumanizing technocracy or politocracy. Masaryk is right: "the standpoint of eternity" helps us to maintain a certain objectivity in the heat of battle and to pluck up fresh courage when things are at their lowest ebb; it helps us "to breathe in some fresh air"—a vital need for every human being and for society.

Our "Beyond" Is God

"The beyond is the power of the here and now." It is important not to misunderstand this Bonhoeffer dictum. It does not assert that the beyond is *only* the power of the here and now. The biblical beyond is related to the here and now, but that is not all there is to it! "Eternal life" is not merely an aid for living, not merely a means or instrument enabling us to cope with earthly life. It is in fact the *goal* of life. Eternity is not adjectival to time; time is adjectival to eternity. Human history does not turn into the kingdom of God by its own potentialities and achievements; it is a case of the kingdom of God turning toward human history. This is the biblical order of precedence, the way the Bible connects earthly life and eternal life—of that there can be no doubt. The biblical witnesses are unanimous in emphasizing that the reality of the future life, though already present in Christ and the Holy Spirit, is unimaginably superior to any present experience. In one passage, for example, Paul makes the comparison between temporal and eternal sharp and precise:

> For this slight momentary affliction is preparing for us an eternal weight of glory beyond all comparison, because we look not to the things that are seen, but to the things that are not seen; for the things that are seen are transient, but the things that are unseen are eternal (2 Cor. 4:17).

The apostle speaks of a "goal" he "has not yet attained," a perfection not yet achieved, toward which however, he presses forward (Phil. 3:12f.). What is this goal? In what terms are we to envisage this eternal life? Here the New Testament is very reticent, extremely sparing in the use of images or pictures. And for very good reason—since eternal life surpasses all our expectations, all our capacities to imagine or describe.

> What no eye has seen, nor ear heard, nor human heart conceived, what God has prepared for those who love him (1 Cor. 2:9).

The apostolic witness to eternal life contains not only its pneumatological dimension of the "already," but also its eschatological dimension of the "not yet."

252

It does not yet appear what we shall be (1 John 3:2).
Now we see in a mirror dimly (1 Cor. 13:12).

But, with that proviso, it is not impossible to give some outline of the
New Testament's mirror image of eternal life. Let us try to indicate
some of its features in at least a fragmentary way.

One point must be clearly understood from the very outset unless
we are to go badly astray in our vision of eternal life: biblically, eternal
life is conceivable only before God—only as in the presence of God.
It has to be said of the Creed that its final clause makes no sense
without its first clause: "eternal life" cannot be understood without
the "I believe in God." The Bible knows of no eternal life without
God. This is another reason, indeed the chief reason, why the idea
of an "immortality of the soul" is biblically questionable. For this
idea, in its classic form, ignores this axiom by conceiving of the soul
as inherently indestructible. The Bible displays no great interest in a
general statement of this kind; the basis of its hope is theological, not
anthropological. If the first statement of the Apostles' Creed is not
true, neither is its final statement true; the final word would then be
with death.

> In the Bible, God is centrally and not just incidentally identical with
> a promise of life in the world of death.[2]

This indissoluble bond between God and life applies both pro-
tologically, that is, with respect to the beginnings of life ("For with
thee is the fountain of life; in thy light do we see light"—Ps. 36:9),
and with respect to the ultimate eschatological goal. The goal of
resurrection and eternal life is defined by Paul quite explicitly: "that
God may be everything to everyone" (1 Cor. 15:28). This categorical
affirmation confirms the truth that eternal life is opened up to us
only from the side of God; it is from him and to him. Apart from
God there is no beyond. Indeed, God *is* our beyond, literally and
with no ifs or buts.

> That he, God, as our Creator, covenant Partner, Judge, and Saviour has
> been, is, and will be our faithful "opposite number" in our life already
> here on earth and finally, exclusively and totally in our death—that is
> our human beyond.[3]

In what follows, I shall try to look at some basic aspects of this beyond, some basic aspects of eternal life in its postmortal dimension. Three themes will be given prominence—rest, light, and love.

The "Rest" of the People of God

"Grant them eternal rest, O Lord." There is food for thought in these opening words of the traditional requiem mass. They point to a biblical theme that highlights an important aspect of the biblical view of eternal life. One aspect of the goal of human life is certainly to "find rest" and to be "at rest" in the presence of God. This fundamental aspect of human life before God is memorably described in what is probably the best-known passage in all the writings of Augustine:

> Thou hast made us for Thyself and our hearts are restless until they find their rest in Thee.[4]

These words refer explicitly to the beginnings, to the original source and ground of all being. They refer to the seventh day of creation when after all his labors God, the Supreme Creator, rested (Gen. 2:2). What for God was a day of rest, was for us the day of beginnings. This first day of humanity is where we have our start; here is our launching pad. Our human works and actions follow, but they are not the starting point of human life.

Neither are they our end. The seventh day, the day when God rested from his labors, soon became the symbol of the final eschatological horizon of creation, the image of eternal life. This theme was emphasized, above all, in the Letter to the Hebrews. In all the labors and struggles of history, the Old Testament promise holds good: the ultimate goal is the "sabbath rest for the people of God" (Heb. 4:9). Another oft-quoted saying of Augustine points in the same direction: "On the seventh day we shall be ourselves." The identity of the people of God—the true identity of our human existence with all that we do and all that is done to us—lies beyond our achievements and failures, beyond the debts incurred and the pains endured, beyond the attainable and the attained. Our identity lies in the encompassing rest of God.

This aspect of eternal life must not be mistaken for a "sedating" of human life; it does not mean that the goal of life is a sort of "retirement," neither is it an invitation to quietism or even immobility as a life style. No such misinterpretation is countenanced in the Bible, least of all in the Letter to the Hebrews. The "rest" promised to God's people is not some sweet period of idleness; it is the goal of a pilgrimage, a pilgrimage marked by costly struggle to abide in the promise and to sustain faith. We have only to recall the dynamic concept of faith in the Letter to the Hebrews, to which reference was made already in chapter 3. The more seriously we take the active role of faith and try to live it out, however, the greater the comfort and relief we find in knowing that activity and effort are not the final word but that there is a final rest after the storm, peace after the struggle—even after the final struggle with death—"the peace of God, which passes all understanding" (Phil. 4:7).

It is this promise of ultimate peace that makes human life a hopeful enterprise in spite of everything, that is, in spite of failure, disaster, and abrupt ending. We are not to deny the bitterness of such experiences, much less disguise them in a sentimental (or religious) sugarcoating. Human life has its genuinely tragic and even demonic twists and turns, its ruined possibilities, its thwarted plans, its missed opportunities. In face of all such experiences, the Creed utters the "nevertheless" of faith, its conviction that there is an eternal completion of our always-fragmentary lives, a fulfillment rooted in the forgiveness of sins and promised in the resurrection of the flesh, the healing of our wounds in the rest of the people of God. Dietrich Bonhoeffer was one who meditated deeply on the fragmented character of human life and who himself experienced its pain. He describes this experience of being both shattered *and* comforted, in his well-known lines:

Suffering
Wondrous sea-change. The strong active hands for you are bound. Helpless and alone, you see the end of your act. Yet you breathe in. Calm and comforted you entrust your cause to stronger hand and are content. Blissfully you touch freedom just for a moment, then commit it to God for his glorious completion.[5]

Eyes Enlightened by Grace

"And let light eternal shine upon them." The intimate connection between life and light is an age-old fact of human experience, having its roots in biology. When a Goethe or a Karel Capek cries out long-ingly in the moment of death for "More light!" this is something we can all begin to understand. This connection is also found in the Bible—only here there is no room for misunderstanding as to its course. In the Bible the fundamental thing is not some ambiguous view or metaphor of light and shade, but the connection between life and light is rooted and grounded in the understanding of God and Christ. God himself is light (1 John 1:5, 7; 2:8ff.). His light is the light of "eternal life" ("The Lord is my light"—Ps. 27:1). Christ, too, the incarnate Word of God, is described as both life and light: "In him was life, and the life was the light of men. The light shines in the darkness" (John 1:4). "Light in the darkness"—this is the keynote and promise for our life today, for our dying tomorrow, and for our life after death, the day after tomorrow. The motto of the Geneva Reformation, "After darkness, light," vividly encapsulates the fundamental situation of the Christian life and of human history.

God's light leads to human seeing: "In Thy light we see light" (Ps. 36:9). The biblical theme of eternal life clearly includes the human longing for sight, knowledge, and truth (including insight into the mysteries of existence, as in *alētheia*, the Greek word for "truth"). The basic difference between our present life and the future life is even defined from this standpoint by Paul: "Our knowledge is im-perfect . . . now we see in a mirror dimly"—and, going on to point out the contrast—"but then face to face" (1 Cor. 13:9, 12). This is why eternal life is often referred to in the church tradition as "the beatific vision"—vision not in the sense of a "show" that detached television viewers can sit back and watch but in the sense of a "take" that incorporates us wholly into the truth of God. In the poem just cited Dietrich Bonhoeffer appropriates this theme with matchless profundity. He regards the beatific vision as a final stage in the in-evitably fragmentary history of our human freedom, which is never-theless brought to its ultimate fulfillment in the presence of God. Himself staring death in the face, Bonhoeffer describes this last of his "Stations on the Road to Freedom" in these moving words:

Death
Come then, chief feast on our way to eternal freedom.
Destroy, O death, the chains and walls
of our mortal bodies and purblind souls, that we
at last may see what here is hidden from our sight.

Freedom, you, long-sought in discipline, deed, and pain,
your true self we now in God's presence know.[6]

The beatific vision is the liberating revelation of the face of God and
of his now still hidden ways. At the same time, however, it also has
to do with our often opaque and tortuous human ways in life as they
are revealed in the light of God. As Calvin properly insisted, almost
as a basic principle of his theological work,[7] the knowledge of God
and the knowledge of ourselves are inseparable. Paul articulates this
hope: "Then I shall understand fully, even as I have been fully
understood" (1 Cor. 13:12). Our own life, so often incomprehensible
even to ourselves, is thus set within the light of eternity—not, be it
noted, within the harsh glare of human legal processes (with their
public washing of dirty linen) or within camera range of the mass
media (with their disclosures of intimate secrets to titillate and satisfy
a primitive prurience and curiosity). Far removed from all that, the
point to be emphasized here is one that clearly emerges in the life and
work of Jesus: Not every dark stain is dragged out into the light "at
all costs," remorselessly, mercilessly, for scrutiny by God. Indeed, in
the fire of God's judgment *and* in the merciful judgment of God's
grace, there is much that disappears without a trace. This has been
well expressed by H. J. Iwand:

> So what we ask of God is precisely this . . . that he will really wipe away
> our tears, so that our memory will no longer reach back into the time
> from which we come, into the struggles and distresses, the temptations
> and sins that wearied and exhausted us then. Our prayer is that when
> we awake there, it will be as if with this waking from the sleep of death,
> the first day of our life begins.[8]

Yet what then begins is *our* life—only seen now from God's point
of view, and hence in his true, judging, and uplifting light; *our*
"warped timber" (to borrow a phrase from Gollwitzer[9])—only now
in its true form, by the power of its Maker and Redeemer "walking
upright"; *our* life in the light of the liberating truth of God. Eberhard
Jüngel seems to be pointing in this direction when he writes:

> In a Christian eschatology, eternal life would need to be thought of as
> the revelation of the life that has been lived, with all its constantly
> beckoning possibilities; not only the "eternalizing" of the one
> possibility *out of which* our life was in fact realized, but at the same

257

time the revelation and realization of those possibilities *toward which* our life constantly moves even though they are never realized. Thus it is through the missed possibilities as well as the hidden and determinative possibilities as such that the truth of our life is revealed—revealed to every single one of us as the active subject of the concrete life actually lived.[10]

This is also the significance of the moving words written by Karl Barth in the draft of his final circular letter shortly before his death:

> How do I know whether I shall die easily or with difficulty? I only know that my dying, too, is part of my life . . . And then—and this is the destiny, boundary, and terminus of us all—I shall no longer "exist" but assuredly be revealed in and with my entire "existence" with all the real good and the real evil I have ever thought, said, and done, with all the really hard things I have ever suffered and all the really beautiful things I have ever enjoyed. . . . Then . . . in the light of grace, all that is now dark will become very clear.[11]

But the Greatest of These Is Love

"Love never ends" (1 Cor. 13:8). In our reflections on eternal life we have often referred to 1 Corinthians 13—in reference, for example, to the fragmentary nature of our knowledge, and the promise that then we shall see "face to face." It is well known that 1 Corinthians 13 is a hymn in praise of love as the supreme gift of grace. Is it not appropriate, too, to make this same chapter central for the theme of eternal life? It is in this chapter, at all events, that we find the unambiguous affirmation: "Love" (it is clear from the context this means love *alone*) "never ends" (v. 8). An affirmation of this sort clearly has some connection to eternal life: it is speaking of the reality that never passes away. In other words, the essential "content" of eternal life is inconceivable without love. Love is the basis, the fundamental theme, the definition of eternal life.

This conclusion, however, is not drawn just on the basis of a single New Testament chapter, even as important a chapter as 1 Corinthians 13. It follows from the fundamental thrust of the entire biblical message, especially that of the New Testament. Here too the indissoluble connection between the first and final affirmations of the Creed shows us the way. In view of this intimate connection the most salient biblical affirmations about God are all concerned also with the definition of eternal life. Statements such as "God is light" or "Christ our life," surely culminate in what is the Alpha and Omega of the apostolic confession of faith: "God is love" (1 John 4:8). Hence it is valid to argue that since eternal life means God, it also means love:

> God is love, and whoever abides in love, abides in God, and God abides in him (1 John 4:16).

Here is the bond that connects our life today with our eschatological future—love, the bond of charity. Moreover, love, the Holy Spirit's foremost and paramount gift of grace, is at the same time the firmest of bridges across the historical gulf between the Christ event of yesterday and our Christian life today. Love, therefore, is clearly the beginning, the present reality of eternal life, and its eschatological goal.

Another reason for emphasizing the centrality of love in the context of eternal life is that, by doing so, we rectify a misunderstanding that has unfortunately marred the practice of Christianity so often in the history of the church. It has so often been assumed that faith in eternal life could only be practised and understood in a purely spiritualistic and even individualistic way—as a private matter between the individual and God. In the light of the love of Christ, faith in eternal life is certainly not that. For one thing, the theme of eternal life is closely related in the New Testament to the theme of the kingdom of God (which in the synoptic Gospels, in contrast to John, takes pride of place in the eschatological hope), so that Paul can use the image of our being made citizens of the (heavenly) kingdom to describe the meaning of eternal life (Phil. 3:20). But even John points clearly in this social direction; think for example of the self-evident way in which he points out the indissoluble connection between the eschatological mystery of eternal life and the practical demonstration of brotherly and sisterly love here and now:

> We know that we have passed from death to life because we love our brothers and sisters. Anyone who loves not, abides in death (1 John 3:14).

The message is crystal clear: however ardently we may long for eternal life, if we ignore our brothers and sisters (those whom Jesus would call "the least," cf. Matt. 25:31–46), we ourselves are an obstacle to the fulfillment of that longing. Neither today nor on the last tomorrow is there any eternal life that does not include other human beings. For love alone never ends.

Love alone never ends. That statement can bring to a close this brief exposition of the final clause of the Apostles' Creed. It serves equally well, however, to round off our entire attempt to interpret the Christian faith. For Paul's dictum "the greatest of these is love" (1 Cor. 13:13) is true not only with respect to the hope of Christians, but also with respect to their faith. One does not have to be a specialist in Pauline studies to know that the apostle's comparison of faith, hope, and love—the so-called three cardinal virtues—is in no way intended to minimize the importance of either faith or hope. Here at the end of our exposition, nothing said at the beginning about the Creed's first word, *Credo*, needs to be cancelled. To the legacy bequeathed to us in the Creed by those who have gone before us in the faith, we add our own "Amen," in the hope that even this humble attempt at interpreting the faith has not been in vain. Yet it was no more than a journey, an attempt, an incomplete and fragmentary part of a pilgrimage. The goal of Christian dogmatics is beyond all discursive argument, whether successful or not. It lies rather in the truth and love of the triune God—and in that search for truth which constitutes our loving response:

> If I speak in the tongues of men and of angels but have not love, I am a noisy gong or a clanging cymbal. And if I have prophetic powers and understand all mysteries and all knowledge, and if I have all faith, so as to remove mountains, but have not love, I am nothing.
> If I give away all I have, and if I deliver my body to be burned, but have not love, I am nothing. . . .
> So faith, hope, love abide, these three;
> but the greatest of these is love (1 Cor. 13:1–3, 13).

Notes

Introduction

1. Leonhard Ragaz, *Das Glaubensbekenntnis*, 2d ed. (Zurich, n.d.), 5.
2. Wolfgang Trillhaas, *Das Apostolische Glaubensbekenntnis. Geschichte, Text, Auslegung* (Witten, 1953), 7.
3. Jan Amos Comenius, *Unum necessarium*, 10,9, German trans. J. Seeger (Jena and Leipzig, 1904).

The Apostles Creed: Its Origin and Earliest Context

1. J. N. D. Kelly, *Early Christian Creeds* (New York and London: Longmans, Green, & Co., 1950), 3.
2. Ibid., 4.
3. *Religion in Geschichte und Gegenwart*, 3d ed., I, 513.
4. Ibid., 515.
5. Kelly, *Early Christian Creeds*, 6.
6. Ibid., 7.
7. Oscar Cullmann, *The Earliest Christian Confessions*, trans. J. K. S. Reid (London, 1949).
8. Kelly, *Early Christian Creeds*, 29.
9. Ibid., 35.
10. The Latin and English versions of the Old Roman Creed given here are taken from ibid., 102.
11. Ibid., 434.

The Credal Frame—"I Believe . . . Amen"

1. Leonhard Ragaz, *Das Glaubensbekenntnis*, 2d ed. (Zurich, n.d.), 8.
2. Ibid.
3. Josef Ratzinger, *Einführung in das Christentum. Vorlesungen über das Apostolische Glaubensbekenntnis* (English translation: Introduction to Christianity: Lectures on the Apostles' Creed) (Zurich, 1968), 34.
4. Ibid., 37.
5. Ibid., 39.
6. Ibid., 41.

7. Ibid.

8. Dietrich Bonhoeffer, *Nachfolge*, 6th ed. (Munich: Chr. Kaiser, 1958), 19. Cf. the English translation of *The Cost of Discipleship*, 2d ed., trans. Reginald Fuller (New York: Macmillan Co., 1959), 54.

9. Ratzinger, *Einführung in das Christentum*, 45ff.

10. Heinrich Vogel, *Das Nicaenische Glaubensbekenntnis. Eine Doxologie* (Berlin, 1963), 21.

11. Ibid., 22.

I Believe in God

1. Rudolf Bultmann, in his essay "On the Question of Christology" (1927), in *Faith and Understanding. Collected Essays*, ed. R. W. Funk, trans. L. P. Smith (London: SCM Press, 1969), 119f.

2. Wolfhart Pannenberg, *The Apostles' Creed in the Light of Today's Questions*, English trans. Margaret Kohl (London: SCM Press, 1972), 15.

3. Dietrich Bonhoeffer, *Letters and Papers from Prison*, enl. ed., ed. E. Bethge (London: SCM Press, 1971), 325f.

4. Ibid., 360.

5. H. G. Geyer, "Atheismus und Christentum," *Evang. Theol.* (1968): 266.

6. Helmut Gollwitzer, *Krummes Holz—aufrechter Gang. Zur Frage nach dem Sinn des Lebens* (English translation: Warped Timber—Walking Upright. On the Question of the Meaning of Life) (Munich: Chr. Kaiser, 1970), 284.

The Father Almighty

1. Eberhard Jüngel, *Gott als Geheimnis der Welt. Zur Begründung der Theologie des Gekreuzigten im Streit zwischen Theismus und Atheismus* (English translation: God as Mystery of the World. On Constructing a Theology of the Crucified in the Conflict Between Theism and Atheism), 2d rev. ed. (Tübingen: J. C. B. Mohr [Paul Siebeck], 1977), 30.

2. Joachim Jeremias, "The present position in the discussion of the problem of the historical Jesus." In German in H. Ristow and K. Matthias, *Der Historische Jesus und der Kerygmatische Christus. Beiträge zur Christusverständigung in Forschung und Verkündigung* (English translation: The Historic Jesus and the Kerygmatic Christ. Contributions to Understanding Christ in Research and Proclamation) (Berlin, 1961), 23. See also J. Jeremias, *New Testament Theology*. Part One: *The Proclamation of Jesus* (London: SCM Press, 1971), 61–68.

3. Thomas Aquinas, *Summa Theologica*, I, 25.

4. Heinrich Vogel, *Das Nicaenische Glaubensbekenntnis. Eine Doxologie* (Berlin, 1963), 33.

5. Ibid.

6. A. Cochrane, *The Glory of God and the Glory of Man* (1975), a working paper for the World Alliance of Reformed Churches, p. 5.

7. Karl Barth, *Dogmatics in Outline*, Eng. trans. G. T. Thomson (London: SCM Press, 1949), 48f.

Maker of Heaven and Earth

1. Karl Barth, *Church Dogmatics*, Vol. III, *The Doctrine of Creation*, Part 1, § 41, p. 42: "The history of this covenant is as much the goal of creation as creation itself is the beginning of this history."

2. Jenni-Westermann, *Theol. Wörterbuch zum AT*, I, 337f. Cf. Alan Richardson, *A Theological Word Book of the Bible* (London: SCM Press, 1950), 93, col. 1.

3. Gerhard von Rad, *Ges. Studien zum AT*, 316. Cf. J. M. Lochman, *Signposts to Freedom: The Ten Commandments and Christian Ethics*, trans. David Lewis (Belfast, Dublin, and Ottawa: Christian Journals, 1981), 45ff.

4. G. Glöge, "Schöpfung," *Religion in Geschichte und Gegenwart*[3], vol. V, col. 1488.

5. L. Köhler, *Theologie des AT*, 72.

6. Heinrich Vogel, *Das Nicaenische Glaubensbekenntnis. Eine Doxologie* (Berlin, 1963), 38.

7. Ibid., 39.

8. Martin Luther, The Small Catechism (1529). Cited here from Theodore G. Tappert, ed., *The Book of Concord: The Confessions of the Evangelical Lutheran Church* (Philadephia: Fortress Press, 1959), 345.

And in Jesus Christ

1. Oscar Cullmann, *Die ersten christlichen Glaubensbekenntnisse* (1943), 45. (English translation: *The Earliest Christian Confessions*, Eng. trans. J. K. S. Reid [London: Lutterworth Press, 1949], 63).

2. Karl Barth, *Dogmatics in Outline*, English trans. G. T. Thomson (London: SCM Press, 1949), 65f.

3. Vogel, *Das Nicaenische Glaubensbekenntnis*, 46.

4. Joseph Ratzinger, *Einführung in das Christentum. Vorlesungen über das Apostolische Glaubensbekenntnis* (English translation: Introduction to Christianity: Lectures on the Apostles' Creed) (Zurich, 1968), 220.

5. Cf. Oscar Cullmann, *The Christology of the New Testament*, Eng. trans. Guthrie and Hall (Philadelphia: Westminster Press, 1959), 114f.

6. Ibid., 117ff.

7. W. Grundmann, in *Theological Dictionary of the New Testament*, ed. Kittel and Friedrich, trans. G. W. Bromiley (Grand Rapids: Wm. B. Eerdmans, 1971), vol. 9, pp. 538f.

8. Förster, in *Theological Dictionary of the New Testament*, vol. 3, p. 288.

9. Ibid., 289.

10. J. Schniewind, *Das Neue Testament Deutsch 2: Das Evangelium nach Matthäus*, 8th ed. (Göttingen: Vandenhoeck & Ruprecht, 1956), 14.

His Only Son, Our Lord

1. Karl Barth, *The Faith of the Church. A Commentary on the Apostles' Creed according to Calvin's Cathechism*, ed. Jean-Louis Leuba, trans. (from French) G. Vahanian (London: Collins, Fontana Books, 1960), 62.

2. Karl Barth, *Dogmatics in Outline*, trans. G. T. Thomson (London: SCM Press, 1949), 85.

3. Oscar Cullmann, *The Christology of the New Testament*, Eng. trans. Guthrie and Hall (Philadelphia: Westminster Press, 1959), 277.

4. Ibid., 275.

5. Ibid., 282.

6. Ibid., 217.

7. *Martyrdom of Polycarp.* See *The Martyrdom of St. Polycarp*, in *The Fathers of the Church. A new translation. The Apostolic Fathers.* (Washington, D.C.: Catholic University of America Press, 1969), 155.

8. J. A. Comenius, "Legacy of the Dying Mother, the Unitas Fratrum," trans. (from German) M. Bic, 1958, 99f. Cf. on this whole theme J. M. Lochman, "Herrschaft Christi in der säkularisierten Welt," (Zurich, 1976). On the "Doctrine of Christ's Threefold Office," see Lochman, *Reconciliation and Liberation: Challenging a One-Dimensional View of Salvation*, Eng. trans. David Lewis (Philadelphia: Fortress Press, 1980), 58–76.

9. Cf. W. A. Visser't Hooft, *The Kingship of Christ* (New York and London: Harper & Brothers, 1948).

10. A. Ritschl, *Die christliche Lehre von der Rechtfertigung und Versöhnung* (Bonn, 1970–74), Part III, pp. 383f.

11. Leonhard Ragaz, *Das Glaubensbekenntnis*, 2d ed. (Zurich, n.d.), 16f.

Conceived by the Holy Spirit, Born from the Virgin Mary

1. Walter Kasper, *Jesus the Christ*, Eng. trans. V. Green (London: Burns & Oates; New York: Paulist Press, 1976).

Notes

2. Barth, *Dogmatics in Outline*, 97.

3. For an excellent account of this doctrine and its relevance today, see Hans Stickelberger, *Ipsa assumptione creatur. Karl Barths Rückgriff auf die klassische Christologie und die Frage nach der Selbständigkeit des Menschen* (Berne, Frankfurt am Main, and Las Vegas: Peter Lang, 1979).

4. Kurt Marti, *gedichte am rand* (1974).

5. Cf. Emil Brunner, *The Mediator*, Eng. trans. O. Wyon (London: Lutterworth Press, 1934), 322–27.

6. Cited in Barth, *Church Dogmatics*, Vol. I, *Prologomena*, Part 2, p. 184.

7. J. M. Lochman, "Das Wunder der Weihnacht — Matthäus 1:18–25," in Lochman, *Das Radikale Erbe. Versuche Theologischer Orientierung in Ost und West* (Zurich: Theologischer Verlag, 1972), 263–73.

8. E. Lohmeyer and W. Schmauch, *Das Evangelium des Matthäus* (1956), 17.

9. Barth, *Church Dogmatics*, Vol. I, *Prologomena*, Part 2, p. 182.

10. Bonhoeffer, in *Bonhoeffer Brevier*, ed. O. Duzdus, 501.

11. Josef Ratzinger, *Einführung in das Christentum. Vorlesungen über das Apostolische Glaubensbekenntnis* (Zurich, 1968), 228.

Suffered Under Pontius Pilate

1. Gregory of Nazianzus, *Epistle* ci.

2. Rufinus, *Comm. in symb. apost.* 18 (*PL* 21, 356), as cited in J. N. D. Kelly, *Early Christian Creeds* (New York and London: Longmans, Green, & Co., 1950), 150.

3. Barth, *Dogmatics in Outline*, 111.

4. Ibid.

5. Geneva Catechism, in T. F. Torrance, *The School of Faith: The Catechisms of the Reformed Church* (London: J. Clarke & Co., 1959), 13.

6. Torrance, *School of Faith*, 75.

7. *The Sermons of John Donne*, vol. 7, ed. E. M. Simpson and G. R. Potter (Berkeley: University of California Press, 1953), 279.

8. Kurt Marti, *gedichte am rand* (1974).

9. Barth, *Dogmatics in Outline*, 101ff.

Crucified, Dead and Buried, Descended to Hell

1. *The Common Catechism: A Christian Book of Faith*, ed. J. Feiner and L. Vischer (London: Search Press; New York: Seabury Press, 1975), 154.

2. Ratzinger, *Einführung in das Christentum*, 231.

3. *Common Catechism*, 158.

4. Jürgen Moltmann, *The Crucified God. The Cross of Christ and Criticism as the Foundation of Christian Theology*, Eng. trans. R. A. Wilson and J. Bowden (London: SCM Press, 1974), 150f.

5. Heinrich Vogel, in *Communio Viatorum* II (1959), 299.

6. H. J. Iwand, in B. Klappert, *Diskussion um Kreuz und Auferstehung*, 288.

7. Vogel, in *Communio Viatorum* II (1959), 299.

8. See further J. M. Lochman, *Reconciliation and Liberation: Challenging a One-Dimensional View of Salvation*, Eng. trans. David Lewis (Philadelphia: Fortress Press, 1980), 84ff.

9. J. N. D. Kelly, *Early Christian Creeds* (New York and London: Longmans, Green, & Co., 1950), 379.

10. Johann Sebastian Bach, *The Christmas Oratorio*, Eng. trans. J. Troutbeck (New York: Schirmer, 1909), 193–95.

11. *Geneva Catechism*, Question 65, in T. F. Torrance, *The School of Faith: The Catechisms of the Reformed Church* (London: J. Clarke & Co., 1959), 15.

On the Third Day He Rose Again
from the Dead

1. Rudolf Bultmann, "New Testament and Mythology," in *Kerygma and Myth: A Theological Debate*, ed. H. W. Bartsch, Eng. trans. R. H. Fuller (London: SPCK, 1972), vol. 1, p. 38.

2. Ibid., 41.

3. Barth, *Dogmatics in Outline*, 123.

4. Wolfhart Pannenberg, *The Apostles' Creed in the Light of Today's Questions*, Eng. trans. Margaret Kohl (London: SCM Press, 1972), 97.

5. Ibid., 105.

6. Ibid., 114.

7. Vogel, *Das Nicaenische Glaubensbekenntnis*.

8. Roger Garaudy, in *Marxisten und die Sache Jesu*, ed. I. Fetscher and M. Machovec, 40.

9. Ibid., 42.

10. In *Křeslanská Review* (1957), 129ff.

11. Ratzinger, *Einführung in das Christentum*, 252.

12. Vogel, *Das Nicaenische Glaubensbekenntnis*, 109.

13. Dietrich Bonhoeffer, *Ethics*, ed. E. Bethge, trans. N. H. Smith (London: SCM Press, 1955), 16f.

14. Ragaz, *Das Glaubensbekenntnis*, 26.

Notes

Ascended To Heaven, Sits at the Right Hand
of God the Father Almighty,
Thence He Will Come to Judge
the Living and the Dead

1. Emil Brunner, *The Misunderstanding of the Church*, Eng. trans. H. Knight (Philadelphia: Westminster Press, 1953).

2. W. G. Kümmel, in *Religion in Geschichte und Gegenwart*[3], III, col. 335.

3. Walter Kasper, *Jesus the Christ*, Eng. trans. V. Green (London: Burns & Oates; New York: Paulist Press, 1976), 149.

4. Barth, *Dogmatics in Outline*, 125.

5. Ratzinger, *Einführung in das Christentum*, 260.

6. Ibid.

7. *Hymns Ancient and Modern*, No. 398 (cf. No. 206).

8. I use here some points already set forth in Buri, Lochman, and Ott, *Dogmatik in Dialog*, Vol. I: *Die Kirche und die Letzten Dinge* (Gütersloh: Gerd Mohn, 1973), 280ff.

9. T. F. Torrance, *The School of Faith: The Catechisms of the Reformed Church* (London: J. Clarke & Co., 1959), 78.

10. Ibid., 18f.

11. Emil Brunner, *Eternal Hope*, Eng. trans. H. Knight (Philadelphia: Westminster Press; London: Lutterworth Press, 1954), 180.

12. Wolfhart Pannenberg, *The Apostles' Creed in the Light of Today's Questions*, English trans. Margaret Kohl (London: SCM Press, 1972), 121.

I Believe in the Holy Spirit

1. Otto A. Dilschneider, in *Evang. Kommentare* (1973), 333.

2. See, for example, Heinrich Ott, *Die Antwort des Glaubens. Systematische Theologie in 50 Artikeln* (Stuttgart, 1972); and H. G. Pöhlmann, *Abriss der Dogmatik. Ein Repetorium* (Gütersloh, 1973).

3. Rudolf Bohren, *Predigtlehre*, 75ff.

4. Cf. Karl Barth, *"Evangelical Theology in the 18th Century,"* in *God, Grace and Gospel*, Eng. trans. J. S. McNab, Scottish Journal of Theology Occasional Papers No. 8 (Edinburgh: Oliver & Boyd, 1959), 67. Cf. also Barth, *From Rousseau to Ritschl* (London: SCM Press, 1952), 341.

5. Karl Barth, *The Faith of the Church. A Commentary on the Apostles' Creed according to Calvin's Catechism*, ed. Jean-Louis Leuba, Eng. trans. (from French) G. Vahanian (London: Collins, Fontana Books, 1960), 108f.

6. Barth, *Dogmatics in Outline*, 137.

7. Barth, *Church Dogmatics*, Vol. IV, *The Doctrine of Reconciliation*, Part 3, pp. 941f.

8. Eberhard Jüngel, *Gott als Geheimnis der Welt. Zur Begründung der Theologie des Gekreuzigten im Streit zwischen Theismus und Atheismus*, 2d rev. ed. (Tübingen: J. C. B. Mohr [Paul Siebeck], 1977), 244.

9. Pannenberg, *Apostles' Creed*, 135.

10. Eduard Schweizer, *The Holy Spirit*, trans. R. H. Fuller and I. Fuller (Philadelphia: Fortress Press, 1980), 109f.

11. Joachim of Fiore (1135–1202), *Concordia novi et veteris Testamenti*, V, 84. German text in *Joachim von Fiore. Das Reich des Heiligen Geistes*, ed. A. Rosenberg (Munich: Planegg, 1955), 82. The Latin text and a French translation of this famous passage are given in Henri Mottu, *La Manifestation de l'Esprit selon Joachim de Fiore* (Paris: Neuchâtel, 1977), pp. 232f. and n. 2 on p. 233. See also Marjorie Reeves, *Joachim of Fiore and the Prophetic Future* (London, 1976).

The Holy Catholic Church

1. Barth, *Dogmatics in Outline*, 141f.
2. Ratzinger, *Einführung in das Christentum*, 276f.
3. Ignatius, *Ad Smyrn.* 8.
4. Irenaeus, *Adv. haer.* 3:24.
5. Cyprian, *De cath. eccl. unitate* 5.
6. *The Mystical Body of Jesus Christ*, Encyclical of Pope Pius XII, 29 June 1943, § 65.
7. "An athlete was always being called a weakling by his compatriots. So he went abroad for a time; and on his return he boasted . . . of a jump he had made at Rhodes. . . . 'I can prove it by the testimony of eye-witnesses,' he said, 'if any of the people who were present ever come here.' At this one of the bystanders said: 'If what you say is true . . . you don't need witnesses. The place where you stand will do as well as Rhodes. Let us see the jump.'" (*Fables of Aesop*, tr. S. A. Handford [Harmondsworth, England: Penguin Books, 1954], 185).
8. Karl Barth, *The Knowledge of God and the Service of God According to the Teaching of the Reformation: Recalling the Scottish Confession of 1560*, the Gifford Lectures 1937 and 1938, Eng. trans. J. L. M. Haire and I. Henderson (London: Hodder & Stoughton, 1938), 198.
9. Theodore G. Tappert, ed., *The Book of Concord: The Confessions of the Evangelical Lutheran Church* (Philadelphia: Fortress Press, 1959), 32.
10. *Confessio Bohemica* (1575) XI, 6.
11. Barth, *Dogmatics in Outline*, 148.

Notes

The Communion of Saints

1. Niceta of Remesians (d. ca. 420), *De symb.* 10. Cited from Kelly, *Early Christian Creeds*, 391.
2. On the St. Laurence legend, see Ambrose, *De officiis* (I,41)—the earliest documentary reference. See J. Lebreton and J. Zeiller, *The History of the Primitive Church*, Eng. trans. (from French) E. C. Messenger, vol. III, *The Church in the Third Century—Part I* (London: Burns, Oates & Washbourne, 1946), 656f. and n. 1. Also vol. IV, *The Church in the Third Century—Part II*, 1039.
3. D. Wiederkehr, in *Reformatio* (1977), 151.

The Remission of Sins

1. Kelly, *Early Christian Creeds*, 161.
2. Cited from Karl Barth, *Credo*, Eng. trans. (from 1935 German original) with a Foreword by Robert McAfee Brown (New York: Charles Scribner's Sons, 1962), 154.
3. Barth, *Credo*, 153.
4. Karl Barth, *The Faith of the Church. A Commentary on the Apostles' Creed according to Calvin's Catechism*, ed. Jean-Louis Louba, Eng. trans. (from French) G. Vahanian (London: Collins, Fontana Books, 1960), 133.
5. Ibid., 134.
6. Cf. *Letters and Papers from Prison*, enl. ed., ed. E. Bethge, (London: SCM Press, 1971), 303. Letter to Bethge 20.5.1944.
7. Ernst Käsemann, "Die Heilung des Besessenen," *Reformatio* (1979), 12.
8. The American edition of *Luther's Works*, ed. Jaroslav Pelikan (St. Louis: Concordia Publishing House, 1963), 26:387.
9. Pannenberg, *Apostles' Creed*, 168f.
10. Ibid., 169.
11. Hans-Joachim Iwand, "Der Brief zum 70. Geburtstag von J. L. Hromadka," in *Communio viatorum* (1959), 126f.

The Resurrection of the Flesh

1. Justin, *De resurrectione*, 8.
2. Irenaeus, *Adv. haer*, I, 10,1; 5,20,1 (cited from Kelly, *Early Christian Creeds*, 164).
3. W. Trillhaas, *Das Apostolische Glaubensbekenntnis. Geschichte, Text, Auslegung* (Witten, 1953), 100.

Notes

4. Friedrich D. E. Schleiermacher (1768–1834), *Reden über die Religion* (1799) (English translation: *On Religion. Speeches to its Cultured Despisers*) (London, 1893; Reprint: New York: Harper Torch Books, 1958, with introduction by Rudolph Otto).

5. Ibid.

6. Emil Brunner, *Eternal Hope*, Eng. trans. H. Knight (Philadelphia: Westminster Press; London: Lutterworth Press, 1954), 148.

7. Ibid., 150.

8. Helmut Gollwitzer, *Krummes Holz—aufrechter Gang. Zur Frage nach dem Sinn des Lebens* (Munich: Chr. Kaiser, 1970), 288f.

9. Ephraim the Syrian (d. 373). Cited in Felix Flückiger, *Geschichte des Naturrechts*, I, 327.

10. Kurt Marti, *Leichenrede* (Funeral Orations).

11. Ernst Lange, *Nichte an den Tod glauben. Praktische Konsequenzen aus Ostern*, ed. Rüdiger Schloz (Bielefeld, 1975).

And Eternal Life

1. *Geneva Catechism*, Question 107, in Torrance, *School of Faith*, 21f.

2. Helmut Gollwitzer, *Krummes Holz—aufrechter Gang. Zur Frage nach dem Sinn des Lebens* (Munich: Chr. Kaiser, 1970), 284.

3. Karl Barth, *Church Dogmatics*, Vol. III, *The Doctrine of Creation*, Part 2, p. 632.

4. Augustine, *Confessions* I, 1.

5. Dietrich Bonhoeffer, *Letters and Papers from Prison*, enl. ed., ed. E. Bethge (London: SCM Press, 1971), 371.

6. Ibid.

7. See Calvin, *Institutes* I, 1.

8. H. J. Iwand, *Nachgelassene Werke 4, Gesetz und Evangelium*, 221.

9. See above, notes 5 and 6.

10. Eberhard Jüngel, *Gott als Geheimnis der Welt. Zur Begründung der Theologie des Gekreuzigten im Streit zwischen Theismus und Atheismus*, 2d ed. (Tübingen: J. C. B. Mohr [Paul Siebeck], 1977), 292f.

11. Cited from Eberhard Busch, *Karl Barth: His Life from Letters and Autobiographical Texts*, Eng. trans. J. Bowden (Philadelphia: Fortress Press, 1976), 499.

Index of Names

Index of Names

Index of Biblical Passages

OLD TESTAMENT

NEW TESTAMENT

273